DISCLAIMER AND TERMS OF USE AGREEMENT

ISBN-13: 978-1-942006-03-9

Table of Contents

Description of the Battle Game 3
Rules of the Battle Game 4
Weapons Instructions 5
Sword 6
Celtic Sword 9
Spear 11
Battle Axe 13
Throwing Axe 15
Blowgun 17
Darts 18
Blowgun Dagger 20
Shield 22
Buckler 24
Barbarian Helmet 25
Frankish Helmet 29
Costumes 31
Money Pouch and Money 33
Patterns 35

"Had I sons I should train them as your husband intends to train your son. It may be that he will never be called upon to draw a sword, but the time he has spent in acquiring its use will not be wasted. These exercises give firmness and suppleness to the figure, quickness to the eye, and briskness of decision to the mind. A man who knows that he can at need defend his life if attacked, whether against soldiers in the field or robbers in the street, has a sense of power and self-reliance that a man untrained in the use of the strength God has given him can never feel. I was instructed in arms when a boy, and I am none the worse for it."
- G. A. Henty
St. Bartholomew's Eve

✺Description of the Battle Game

Battling is at least two teams fighting each other using weapons. We suggest using our foam weapons to minimize injuries.

Divide your players into two teams of about the same strength and even numbers. Say there are four big guys and four little guys. There should be two big guys and two little guys on each team.

Weather is no deterrent to battling. We have had battles in rain and heat.

Object of the game: divide and conquer your enemy!

More than one battle can be played. It is important to keep score of who wins each battle. The one who wins the most battles is the victor!

You can use fortifications. Tree houses work well. Piles of logs or even swing sets can be used.

Naval battles can be fought using non-motor boats such as canoes and row boats. To fight a naval battle, simply row up to them and fight them. Do not use throwing axes, they are not waterproof.

With fortifications, it is often wise to use your spear instead of your axe or sword. The spear has greater length which is helpful in forts. It is very wise to use missiles (water balloons, throwing axes, etc.) so you can bombard the enemy without having to storm the gate.

It is crucial to use shields. People who do not use shields are usually slain early in the battle and are vulnerable to throwing axes and heavy weapons such as battle axes.

Terrible war cries intimidate the enemy.

It is important to have one main leader (general). This keeps the army unified and reduces squabbles.

Rules of the Battle Game

Rule 1
Chivalry and honor must be exhibited at all times.

Rule 2
If any weapon hits your limb (for ex. arm, leg, hand), you are no longer able to use it.
If you are holding a weapon in the hand or arm that is hit, you can't keep using the weapon with **that** arm but could switch it to the other arm and keep fighting. If both arms are hit, you must surrender or run away.
If your leg is hit, you must limp. If both legs are hit, you must kneel or squat.
If you lose all your limbs, you are doomed!

Rule 3
If you get hit in the head, neck or torso, you are officially dead and can't play until the end of the battle.

Rule 4
The only way to win a battle is when all of the enemy (other team) is dead, has surrendered or has run away (escaped).
If a team holding prisoners is defeated, the prisoners are automatically freed.

Rule 5
If someone surrenders, you can either keep them captive, (they are not allowed to escape) or release them and they are free to return to their army (team).

Rule 6
Parley~ A parley is when one or possibly two people from each team talk to each other. To start a parley, one team member must say, "I request an audience." If the other team agrees, they send a person forward to talk to the other.
It is usually used for discussing the release of prisoners by ransom or switching of players. You can be chivalrous and release prisoners. It is important to not carry weapons but must leave them behind during a parley to avoid treachery.

Rule 7
We believe that only boys should battle with other boys. Young men should practice protecting young ladies so it is not appropriate to fight them.

Rule 8
Ransom~A ransom is when a soldier who is captured is released by a payment of money. You can make your own money by folding tin foil into circles, the shape of coins. To ransom a prisoner, first call a parley and then negotiate the price. A general usually costs more than the average soldier. (This rule is optional.)

Weapon Instructions

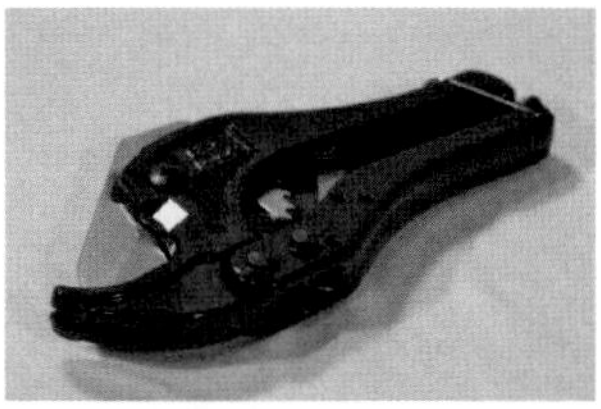

PVC pipe tips: You can find PVC pipe at your local hardware store like Lowe's and Home Depot. You will need a pipe cutter or a saw to cut the PVC pipe to the correct length. If you do not have a saw, the large hardware stores will usually cut it for you.

PVC pipe insulation~the black foam stuff. We usually buy this at the same stores as the PVC pipe. We like the kind that comes in a 4 pack of 3 foot pieces. It says on the package that it is for copper pipe but it works just fine for these weapons.

Foam~the 2 inch thick green stuff. You can find this foam at Wal-Mart and fabric stores like JoAnn.com and Hobby Lobby. It comes in small packages or in large pieces by the yard.

Cardboard: It can be difficult to cut cardboard so younger kids might need some help or supervision. In most of the pieces that use cardboard, it is important to cut the cardboard so the "ridges" (inner corrugated sections) **run across** the narrow width of the piece. This way the piece can bend properly. Check instructions before tracing the pattern onto the cardboard.

½ Width Piece of Duct Tape: Before we begin the weapon instructions, we need to define a term we will use in the book: "½ width". To make a ½ width piece of duct tape, take a piece of duct tape and tear it lengthwise (the long way). Now you have two ½ width pieces of duct tape. Sometimes, even a ¼ width piece of duct tape is used. Just tear the ½ width piece again to make the ¼ width.

Now, on to the fun!

Sword~

Materials:
3 foot piece of ¾ inch PVC pipe
3 foot piece of PVC pipe insulation
(We use 3/8" thick polyethylene foam, fits ¾" pipe)
Duct tape
Scissors
(You may need a saw to cut the PVC to size)
       Please Note: This project may require adult help to use the sharp tools.

Directions:
Cut 8 inches off of your 3 foot piece of insulation.

Next, take the larger piece of insulation and slide it
down the 3-foot PVC pipe.

Leave about 1 inch
extending off of the PVC at
the point of the sword.

Take the **8 inch** piece of insulation foam.

There is a seam down the length of it. Cut a slit 2 inches long on the seam in the middle (center) of the piece.
On the opposite side from the seam cut another slit.

Slide the piece of foam onto the PVC pipe to form the hilt of the sword.

Crisscross the duct tape around the hilt to strengthen it.

Tape across the end of the hilt, turn and do it again. Then tape around the end to make it smooth.
Do this on both ends of the hilt.

Cover the entire hilt with duct tape.
Be sure to wrap around the pipe/ handle.

Tape the point (end) of the sword blade the same way. Wrap the duct tape around a few times to strengthen it so it won't tear during battle.

Now tape the blade. It is helpful to have another person. Start at the hilt and wrap on a slightly diagonal angle towards the tip of the blade.

Cover the handle. Cap the end just as you did with the end of the blade.

Decorate as desired. Often wealthy Greeks and Romans would put a jewel in the center of the hilt.

Celtic Sword~

Materials:
4 foot piece of ¾ inch PVC pipe
3 foot piece of PVC pipe insulation
(We use 3/8" thick polyethylene foam, fits ¾" pipe)
Duct tape
(You may need a saw to cut the PVC to size)

     Please Note: This project may require adult help to use the sharp tools.

Directions:
Slide the piece of insulation down the PVC pipe.

Leave about 1 inch extending off of the PVC at the point of the sword.

That will leave about 14" of PVC pipe for the handle.

Duct tape around the insulation where the blade meets the handle and pinch to the PVC.

Take a half of the width piece of duct tape and tape around the pinched area to secure it to the PVC pipe.

9

Cap the end of the handle. Take a square piece of duct tape, put it on the end and smooth down the edges. Wrap the other half width of duct tape around the end to make it smooth.

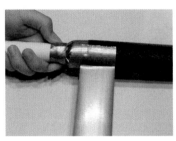

Wrap some duct tape above the handle. It makes it easier to wrap the blade if this is done first.

Wrap a piece of duct tape over the end of the blade. Press down the edges. Turn and repeat, making sure the edges are neatly pressed down.

Wrap a piece of duct tape around the end for a smooth finish.

Now tape the blade. It is helpful to have another person. Start at the handle and wrap on a slightly diagonal angle towards the tip of the blade.

Cover the handle and you're done!

The Celtic sword is longer than the regular sword.

Spear~

Materials:
4 foot piece of ¾ inch PVC pipe
1 foot piece of PVC pipe insulation
(We use 3/8" thick polyethylene foam, fits ¾" pipe)
Duct tape
Scissors
(You may need a saw to cut the PVC to size)

      Please Note: This project may require adult help to use the sharp tools.

Directions:
Slide the 1 foot piece of pipe insulation onto the PVC pipe. Leave at least 2 inches extending past the end of the PVC pipe.

Tape across the end of the insulation at the tip of the spear, turn and repeat. Then tape around the end to make it smooth.

Starting at the tip, wrap the duct tape on a slightly diagonal angle until the insulation is covered and just onto the PVC pipe.

Tape around the base of the blade over the PVC pipe to reinforce it.

Then, taking the color of your choice, tape a long strip down the length of the pipe. Smooth edges of tape.

Tuck end of the tape into the open end of the PVC pipe.

Repeat on the reverse side of the PVC pipe so that the handle is covered. It usually takes 2 strips of duct tape to cover the handle of the spear.

Decorate as desired.

Battle Axe~

Materials:

1 piece of foam 9" by 11" by 2" thick
3 foot piece of ¾ inch PVC pipe
Cardboard 4" x 12"
Duct tape
Scissors
Marker
Pattern
Saw (You may need a saw to cut the PVC to size)

Please Note: This project may require adult help to use the sharp tools.

Directions:

Print and cut out the pattern. Lay the pattern on the foam, trace the blade of the battle axe on the foam using a permanent marker and then cut it out.

 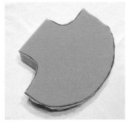

Bend the piece of cardboard in half. Place the blade next to the PVC pipe about 1" down from the end. Fold cardboard over both of them and tape down the cardboard very well. Make sure to go all the way around the base of the blade.

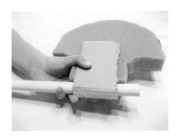 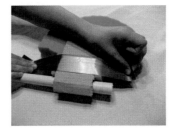

Tape diagonally to keep the pipe from sliding.

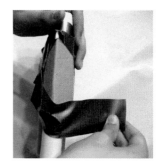

Tape over the place where it crosses the PVC pipe.

Cover the tip of PVC pipe with duct tape.
Cover cardboard with duct tape.

Use a long piece of duct tape to tape over the edge of the blade.

Wrap duct tape around to hold down the ends of that long piece.

Cover the blade with duct tape piecing diagonally in a fan shape from the cardboard around the edge to the other side and up to the cardboard.

Cover handle with duct tape.

Decorate to your liking.

Throwing Axe~

Materials:
1 piece of foam 5 ½" by 11" by 2" thick
Duct tape
Scissors
Marker
Pattern

Directions:
Print and cut out the pattern. Lay the pattern on the foam, trace the throwing axe on the foam using a permanent marker and then cut it out.

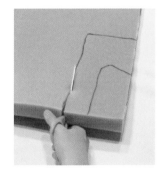

Cover the handle with duct tape the color of your choice.

Carefully tape the end so that the corners stay square.

It is important to put a piece of duct tape on the side of the axe as shown in the picture to reinforce the axe. This prevents the throwing axe from tearing when you throw it.

Do this on both sides.

Press duct tape firmly to foam

Pinch the edges so they don't get dirty.

Cover the inside of the blade.

Starting on the sides, cover the blade, being careful to keep the edges square.

 Using the same technique, you can make throwing knives.

Make up your own shapes and designs.

DO NOT USE IN WATER!! They might get moldy. They are not waterproof.

16

Blowgun~

Materials:
1 foot and 8 inches of ¾ inch PVC pipe (20 inches)
Duct tape
Saw (You may need a saw to cut the PVC to size)
   Please Note: This project may require adult help to use the sharp tools.

Directions:
Wrap a piece of duct tape around the end that will be the mouthpiece, overlapping the ends.

Tuck the edge into the interior of the PVC pipe.

Cover with duct tape and decorate pipe to your liking.

Hint: A longer pipe is more accurate but it is harder to blow.

Darts~

Materials:
Scraps of 2" thick foam 2" x 2" x 1" for each dart
Duct Tape
Scissors

Directions:
Take a 4" piece of duct tape, place foam in the middle of
the length with ½ inch sticking out.

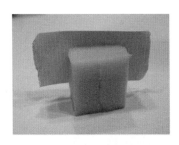

Press thumb in the middle of foam.

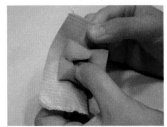

Roll together and tape into a tube so that the diameter of the
finished tube is ½ inch. Use the blowgun as a guide.

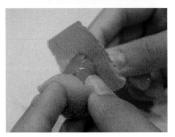

Pinch the end of the tape.
Trim off the pinched end.

Cut a 1 ½" x 1 ½" square of duct tape. Place on the cut
end of the dart.

Press down the points. Press
down all the other edges.

Take a strip of duct tape about 4" x ½" and tightly tape
around the base of the dart.

18

It may be necessary to trim off the points of the foam but be careful not to cut too much.
If there is too much foam on the dart, it will be too hard to blow it out.

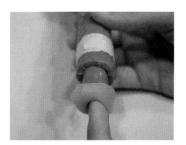

Place the dart into the blowgun (blowgun dagger) with the duct tape going in first near the end where you put your mouth. Push it in a ways.

Try it out!

Blowgun Dagger~

Materials:
1 foot piece of ¾ inch PVC pipe
10 ½ inch piece of PVC pipe
insulation
(We use 3/8" thick polyethylene foam, fits
¾" pipe)
Duct tape
Scraps of 2" thick foam (left over
from the darts)
Scissors
(You may need a saw to cut the PVC to size)

       Please Note: This project may require adult help to use the sharp tools.

Directions:
Slide the piece of pipe insulation
onto the PVC pipe. Leave about 1
inch extending past the end of the
PVC pipe.

Tape across the edges of the end of the insulation leaving the
hole open. Wrap the duct tape around the tip of the dagger.

Starting at the tip, wrap the duct tape on a slightly diagonal
angle until the insulation is covered and just onto the PVC
pipe.

Cover the handle with duct tape.
Tuck in the ends of the tape into the open end of the PVC pipe.

Optional:
To make the hilt, cut two (2) pieces
of foam sized to your liking. Tape
them thoroughly to either side of
the dagger as shown in the picture.

Decorate to your liking.

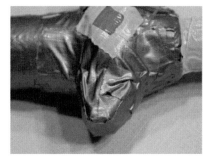

Now for the tricky part. Take a 4" piece of duct tape and trim
about 1/3 of it off lengthwise. This becomes the secret door that
covers the end of the blowgun, like a little flap which allows the
dart to escape from the blowgun.

Put a small piece of duct tape on the
door piece so that the sticky sides meet
each other. That will make the door
smooth on the inside so that the dart will
not stick to it when it is blown out.

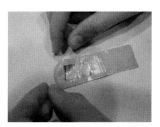

Attach the door piece to the point of the dagger as
shown in the picture. Keep flap closed until you are
ready to surprise your opponent with your secret
blowgun.

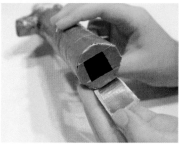

Test the door/flap piece to make sure that it works
well.

Shield~

Materials:
Plywood, size and shape of your choice
Four (4) small blocks of wood 3 ½" x 1 ½" x ½"
Cardboard
Duct Tape
Four (4) Screws 1 ½" long (or long enough to go through
the blocks of wood, cardboard and plywood)
Saw (to cut plywood if needed)
Screwdriver
Sandpaper
Scissors

      Please Note: This project may require adult help to use the sharp tools.

Directions:
Before you begin cutting the wood, plan how big you want your shield to be. We
recommend you measure your arm from the elbow to the knuckles on your hand when
you make a fist. The shield should be at least this wide.

Take a piece of plywood and cut to the shape (square, circle, oval, or rectangle) you want
for the shield. Either sand the wood or cover the front with duct tape. You may want to
add details with duct tape. Usually, we cover the front of the shield with duct tape and
sand the back well so that we don't get splinters.

Cut a strip of cardboard 18" long by 4" wide. Cover with duct tape so as to strengthen it.
Cut another strip of cardboard 12" long by 2" wide. Also cover with duct tape.

Bend up 1 inch on the ends and curve the rest of the piece of
cardboard. Do this to both pieces.

Measure where the large piece of cardboard should go using your arm. Place it near your elbow. (You may need a friend to help you with this.)

Tape down the ends.

Place a block of wood on the end and screw down on each end of the block. Do this on both ends of the piece.
If you have a power screw driver you may want to pre-drill the holes. You can use a regular screwdriver also.

Measure where the smaller piece should go by placing your arm in the large piece. You will grip the smaller piece so place accordingly.

Tape ends to hold in place. Place a block of wood on the end and screw down on each end of the block. Do this on both ends of the piece.

It should look something like this when it is finished.

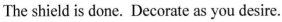
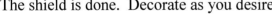

The shield is done. Decorate as you desire.

Here are some examples:

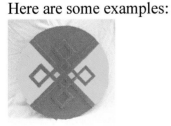

Buckler~

Materials:

Duct tape
Lid from a wheat bucket or ice cream tub
   or a piece of plywood cut into a circle 13" in diameter or size of
your choice

Directions:
Cover the lid with tape. Start with strips across the middle. Cover the entire front.

To make the straps on the back, lay a piece of duct tape sticky side up.

Then cover with a longer strip that goes over the edges. Put 3 more strips over the top of the strap to strengthen it.

Cover the edge with duct tape and decorate as desired.

⚔ Helmet Instructions ⚔

Barbarian Helmet~

Materials:
Patterns
Cardstock
Cardboard
Duct Tape
Scissors
Clear "scotch" tape

Elastic~about ¾" wide by about 8 inches long (If you choose this option, see instructions)
Stapler/Staples

Directions:
Print the helmet pieces on cardstock and cut them out. (If you want the helmet in a smaller size, try minimizing the patterns on a copy machine.) Tape together the upper helmet pieces at the center front with the "scotch" tape.

Tape together the other edges at the top of the helmet pieces.

Cut a piece of cardboard 7" x 1 ½". Bend into a curve. Put a 9" piece of duct tape on it with 1" extending from each end.

Place the cardboard on the front of the helmet right above the eye holes.

Tape over the band and around and through the eye holes.

Cut a piece of cardboard 3 ¼" x 1 ½". Tear a piece of duct tape about 5' long in half lengthwise. Put one piece of that tape on the cardboard (with tape extending past the ends of the cardboard) and tape it to the nose guard. Press the tape under the tip of the nose guard.

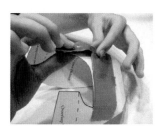

25

Tape on either side of the eye hole.

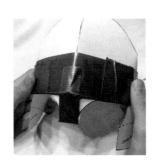

Cover the helmet upper with duct tape.

Tape lower helmet pieces to the upper helmet pieces, making sure they are even.

Cut two (2) pieces of cardboard 5" x 3". Taking a longer piece of duct tape, tape the cardboard to the sides. Line up next to the eye holes. Tape on the inside as well.

Optional: You can trim the edge of the lower helmet to line up smoothly with the upper, but it is not necessary.

Carefully tape around the eye hole, covering the cardboard. This is what you have now.

Cover the sides with duct tape.

To tape the bottom of the lower helmet together, first try it on to see how it fits. If you need to overlap the edges you can or you can just have them meet. Tape. If necessary, trim the edges. Cover with duct tape.

Cover the inside with duct tape. This helps the helmet last longer.

Cut a piece of cardboard 6" x 2 ½" and bend it into a curve. Attach to the lower helmet with tape. Cover with tape.

This is what you have so far.

 For the back of the helmet: Cut two (2) separate pieces of cardboard the size of the back of the helmet piece. Bend into a curve. Tape onto back helmet piece.

Tape the back helmet piece to the top of the helmet. You can pinch the duct tape in the front and then trim it off. Tape the back helmet piece firmly on the sides of the top as well. Cover back helmet piece with duct tape.

Cut the elastic in half so that you have two (2) pieces about 4 inches long. Staple the pieces to the back helmet piece. Be sure to staple so the "pointy" part of the staple is facing outward.

Then try on the helmet. Adjust the elastic to fit and staple it to the helmet.

The Spike: This is optional but it makes the helmet look really awesome. Fold the spike pattern pieces on the dotted lines. Tape. Bend the tabs outward. Place on the helmet in the front and tape down. Cover with duct tape.

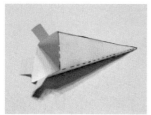  

Decorate with colors as you desire.

You're done! Great job!

Frankish Helmet~

Materials:
Patterns
Cardstock
Cardboard
Duct Tape
Scissors
Clear "scotch" tape
Elastic~about ¾" wide by about 8 inches long (If you choose this option, see instructions)
Stapler/Staples

Directions:
Print the helmet pieces on cardstock and cut them out. (If you want the helmet in a smaller size, try minimizing the patterns on a copy machine.) Tape together the upper helmet pieces at the center front with the "scotch" tape.

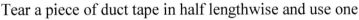

Tape together the other edges at the top of the helmet pieces.

Tape the lower sides on to the upper at the dotted lines.

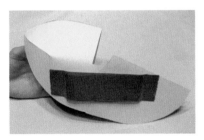

Cut two (2) pieces of cardboard 5" x 2". Tape to sides of helmet to strengthen it.

Cover the lower sides with duct tape.

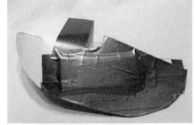

Tear a piece of duct tape in half lengthwise and use one piece of it to cover near the curve of the eye hole.

Cover top of helmet with duct tape. You can crease the duct tape and then trim it off for a more pointed look.

Cut four (4) helmet decorations out of cardboard. Bend the cardboard to give it a slight curve.

Tape on to the top of the helmet, lining up closely to the eye hole. Hint: Use a half width piece of duct tape to tape the edges of the decoration. Press the duct tape down firmly along the edges so the decoration stands out.

Repeat the process on each segment of the helmet.

Cover the inside with duct tape. This helps the helmet last longer.

Back of Helmet: For the back of the helmet: Cut two (2) separate pieces of cardboard the size of the back of the helmet piece. Bend into a curve. Tape on to back helmet piece.

Tape the back helmet piece to the top of the helmet. You can pinch the duct tape in the front and then trim it off. Tape the back helmet piece firmly on the sides of the top as well. Cover back helmet piece with duct tape.

Cut the elastic in half so that you have two (2) pieces about 4 inches long.
Staple the pieces to the back helmet piece. Be sure to staple so the "pointy" part of the staple is facing outward.
Then try on the helmet. Adjust the elastic to fit and staple it to the helmet.

You're done! Good job!

✖Costumes✖

Tunic~

Materials:
Some sort of fabric-knit, sheets, curtains, or whatever you have
Belt or material for a sash
Scissors
Sewing machine or needle and thread

Directions:
First determine the size you will need. Some tunics in the Barbarian time went down to the knees and had no sleeves. They draped over the shoulders a little bit. The size of your fabric may determine the width or measure across the shoulders. Make it wide enough so that you can slip it over your head and shoulders and get the arms out of the arm holes. If you have enough fabric, double the length so you won't need to sew a seam across the shoulders.

Cut a hole for the head to go through. The No-Sew Option is to just pull the tunic over the head and use a belt to keep it around the waist.

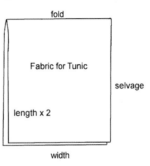

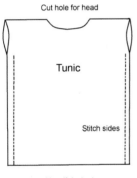

The sewing option is to sew up the sides but leave an arm hole. Hem the bottom if desired. Knit fabric is nice because it doesn't fray and you won't have to hem the edges.

If you want sleeves in your tunic, make a "T" shape of fabric and then sew up the sides. Be sure the main body of the tunic is wide enough so that you can get it on and get the arms through the sleeves.

Maybe almost double the width across the front of the person.

Some children are small and the hole in the neck will gap too much. Just add a button and loop at the back of the neck to close it a little. See Cloak instructions.

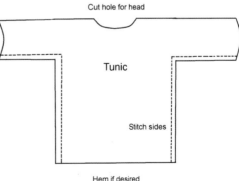

Use a belt or cut a strip of fabric to wrap around the waist.

cCloak~

Materials:
Some sort of fabric-knit, sheets, curtains, or whatever you have
Button
Thin piece of elastic, ribbon, or string
Couple of pins
Scissors
Needle and thread

Directions:
Determine the size of cape that you need. Do you want a cloak that goes down to the knees or almost to the floor? That is your length measurement plus an inch to turn over at the neck. The width of your fabric may determine your width of the cloak, otherwise decide how wide you want it.

Cut your fabric to size. If you are using a fabric that will fray, you may want to hem the sides first. Fold over an inch the top edge which will go by the neck. Try it on. Clasp the cape closed a few inches down from the front of the neck. This where you will attach the button and elastic (ribbon). Mark it on both sides with a pin. Sew on the button on one side. Measure a small piece of elastic (ribbon) around the button so you can still get it on and off. Stitch elastic (ribbon) on both ends to the cape at the mark.

Throw over the shoulders and button at the neck.

The Barbarians wore pants so if you wear pants (jeans, trousers) you will be authentic.

Money Pouch~

Materials:
Fabric: see instructions
String, rope, ribbon, shoe lace or whatever you have
Safety pin
Scissors
Sewing machine or needle and thread
Option: Leg from a pair of cut off pants

Directions:

You can make a money pouch out of almost anything. If you want a money pouch that is a bit fancier, you can use fabric. We just happened to have a scrap of velour that we used for a pouch. Knit fabric won't fray and is easier but any durable fabric will work.

Determine the size of pouch that you want. For example, if you want a pouch that is 5" x 7", allowing for seam allowances and the casing for the drawstring, cut two (2) squares of 6" x 8 ½". You can also cut a long rectangle and just fold over so that you eliminate one seam. The rectangle would be 6" x 16".

Put the right sides together and sew up the seams leaving one 6" side open (use ½" seam). Turn over 1" at the opening. Stitch around using a small seam of about ¼". On the side or center front, make a small cut in

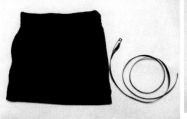 

the casing only on the front piece big enough for the drawstring to go through.

Cut your drawstring to at least twice the length of your opening. In this example, the opening is 10" after sewing, so the drawstring should be 20" long. Put the safety pin in the end of the drawstring and push it through the casing.

A leg from a pair of pants that was cut off into shorts can be made into a pouch. Cut to the size you want. Sew one end. Cut small slits about an inch apart and weave your drawstring in and out through the slits. If you don't have any, thrift stores and yard sales often have pants for cheap.

Coin Money for Ransom~

Materials:
Aluminum foil
Something heavy like a hammer or shoe

Directions:
Take a small piece of aluminum foil about twice the size you want the coin to be and fold in the edges to make a circle. It's all right if it is not perfectly round, ancient money wasn't perfect either. Press down firmly against a hard surface and then hammer flat with the heel of a shoe or a hammer.

Mark the coins with designs or figures so you know which coins belong to you. You can also make a money pouch to keep your money in while you are battling. See instructions for money pouch.

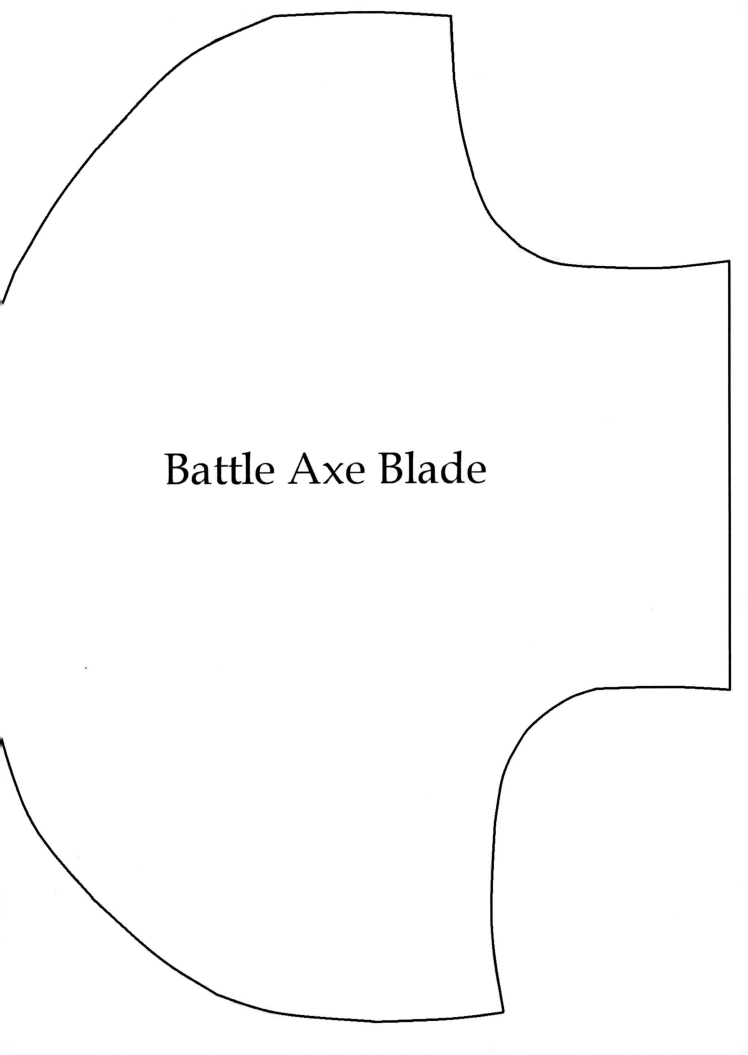

Battle Axe Blade

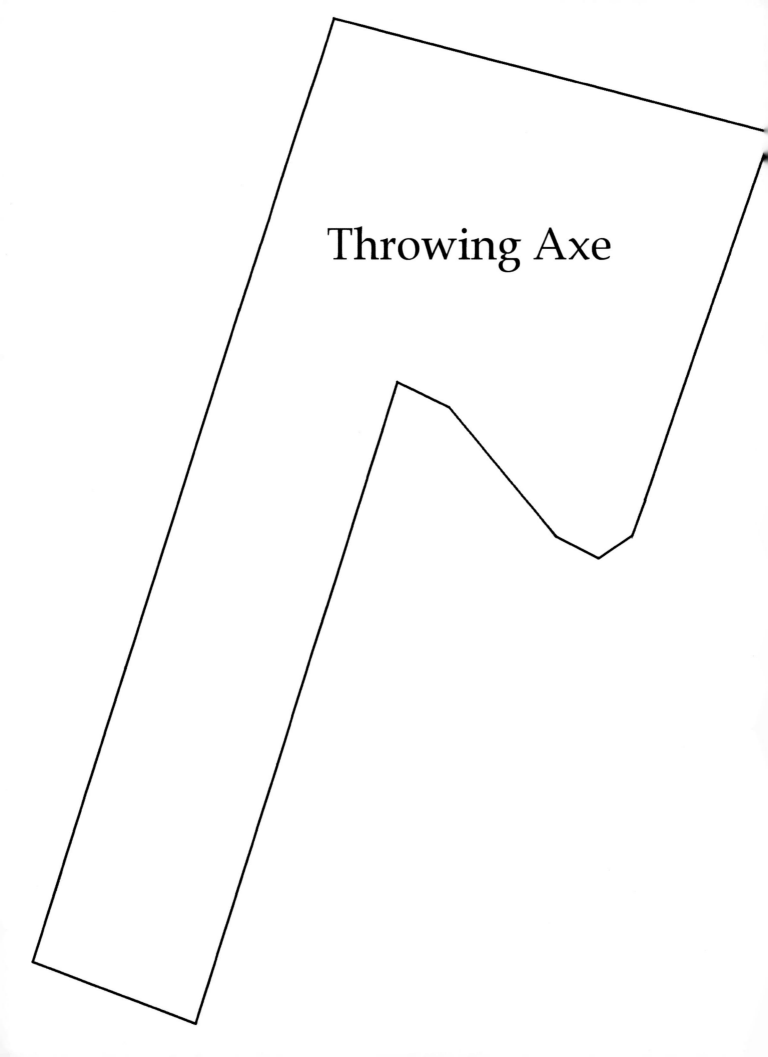

Throwing Axe

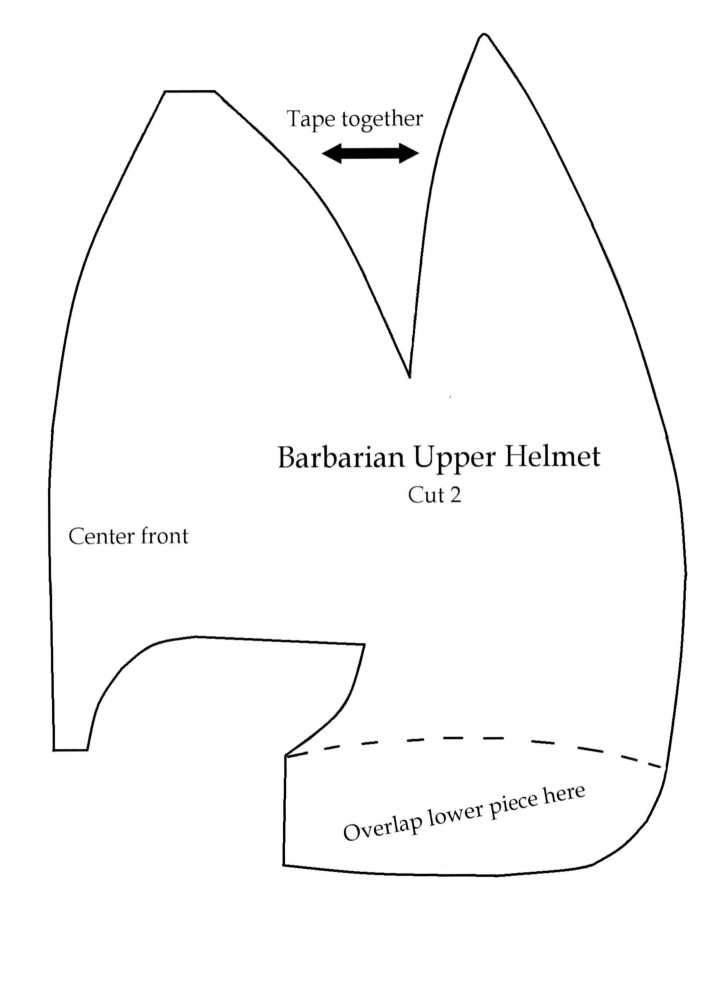

Tape together

Barbarian Upper Helmet

Cut 2

Center front

Overlap lower piece here

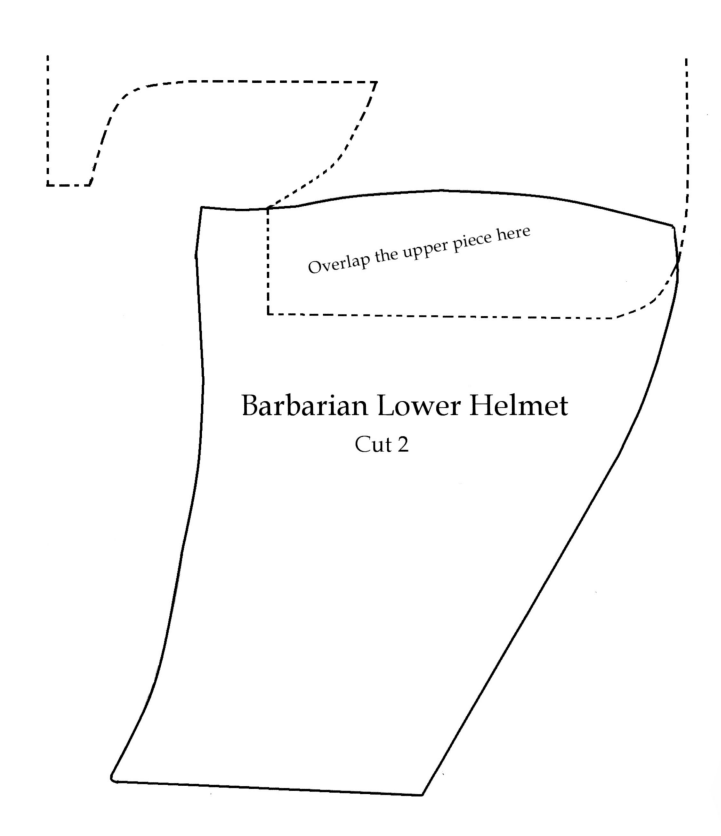

Overlap the upper piece here

Barbarian Lower Helmet

Cut 2

Barbarian Helmet Spike

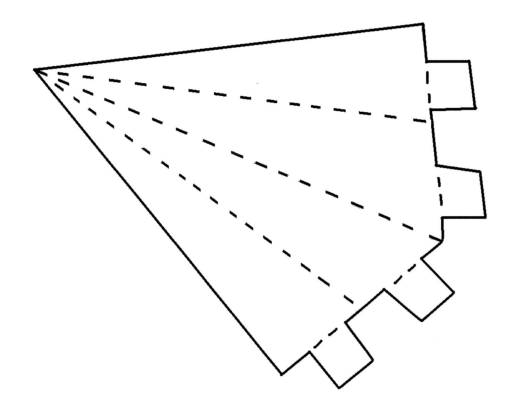

Cut 1

Fold on dotted lines

Cut 1

Back of Helmet

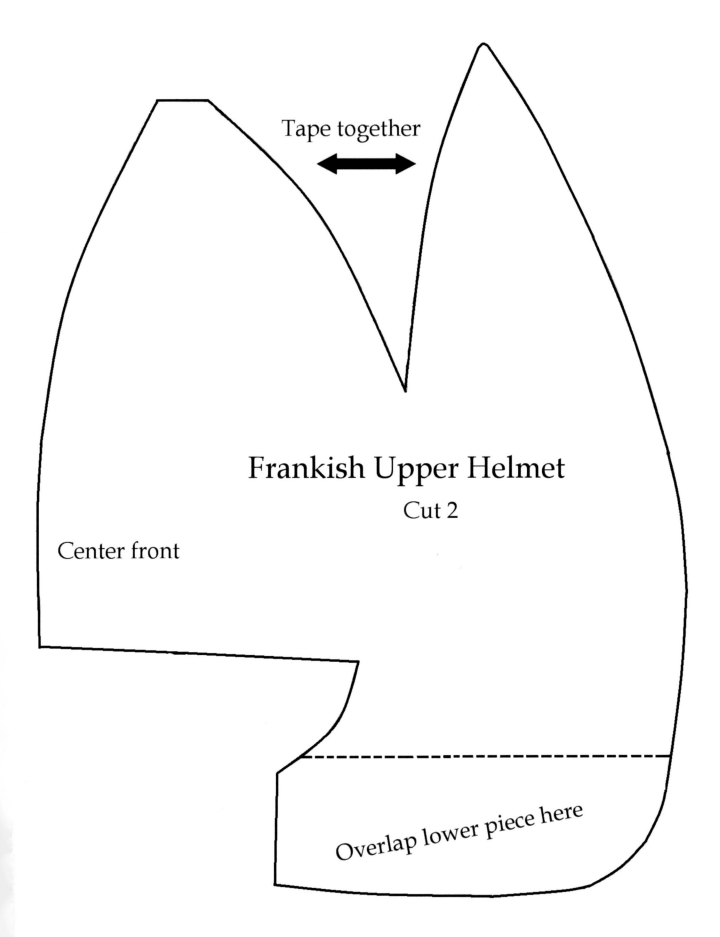

Tape together

Frankish Upper Helmet

Cut 2

Center front

Overlap lower piece here

Overlap the upper piece here

Frankish Lower Helmet

Cut 2

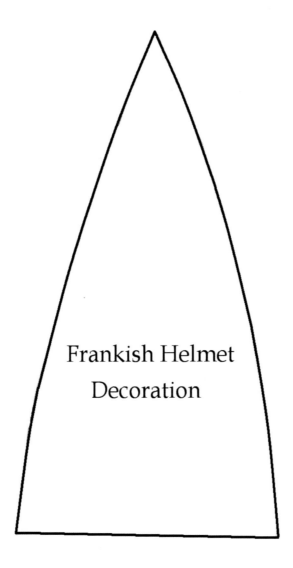

Frankish Helmet Decoration

Cut 1

Back of Helmet

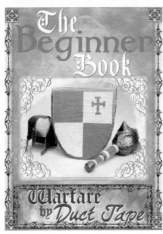 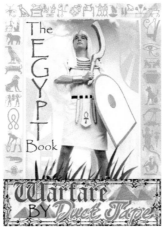 
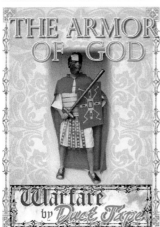

Made in the
USA
Monee, IL

HIDDEN BEAUTY

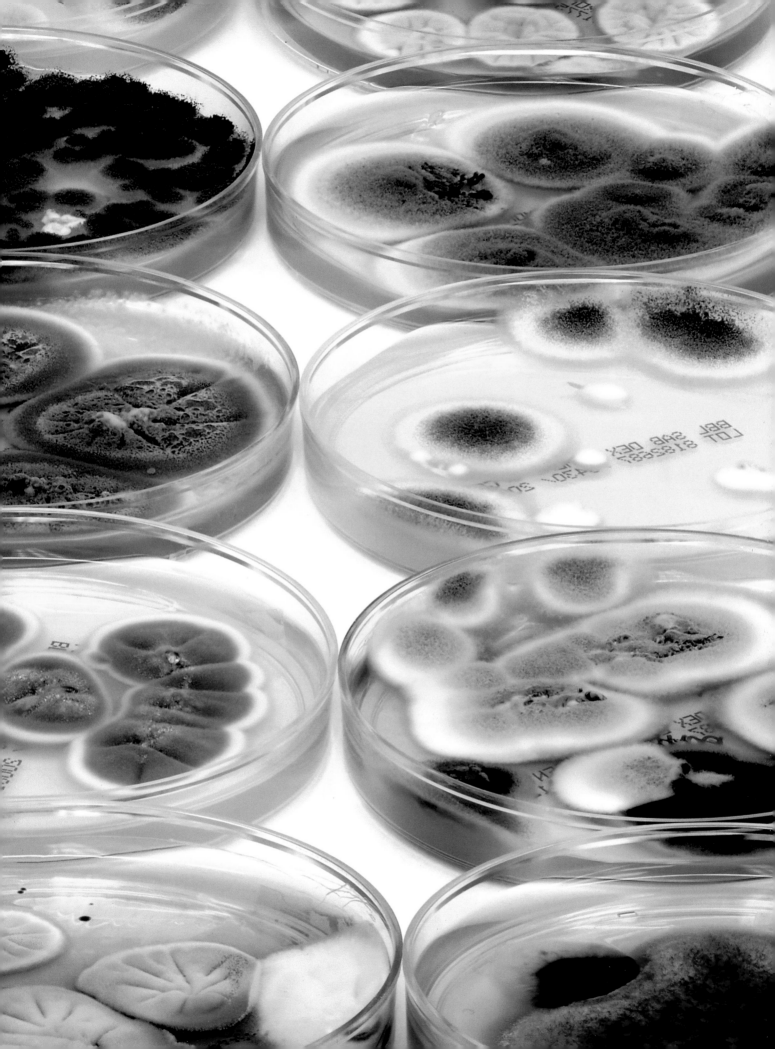

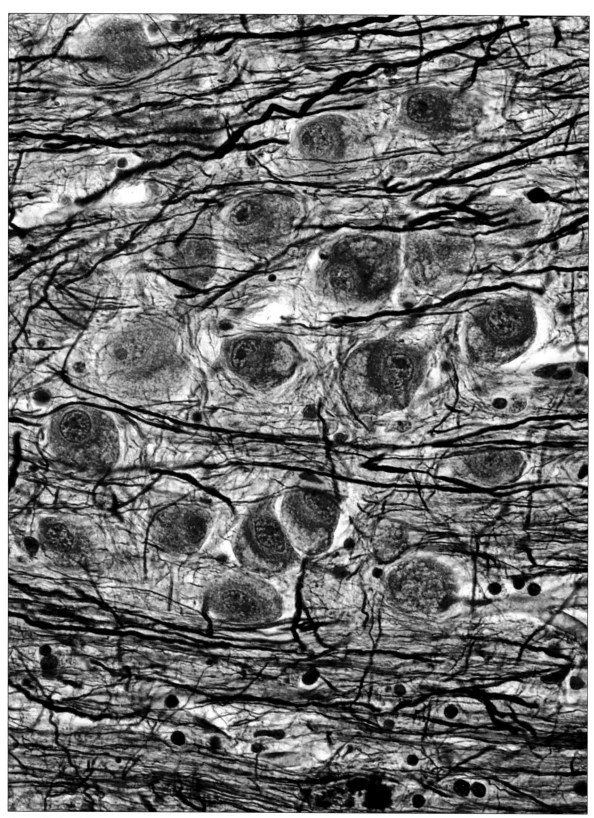

Human Brain x600

HIDDEN BEAUTY

EXPLORING THE AESTHETICS OF MEDICAL SCIENCE

EDITORS

NORMAN BARKER

CHRISTINE IACOBUZIO-DONAHUE

FOREWORD BY
BERT VOGELSTEIN

Schiffer Publishing Ltd

4880 Lower Valley Road • Atglen, PA 19310

Front Cover: Gallstones, which are solid crystalline deposits that develop within the gallbladder.
Photograph by Norman Barker

Back Cover: Illustration depicting the complex cellular landscape and cytoarchitecture
of part of the human brain, the subventricular zone, where a niche of stem cells are found.
Illustration by Ian Suk

End Sheets: DNA sequencing

Pages 2–3: Culture plates

Published by Schiffer Publishing, Ltd.
4880 Lower Valley Road
Atglen, PA 19310
Phone: (610) 593-1777; Fax: (610) 593-2002
E-mail: Info@schifferbooks.com

For our complete selection of fine books on this and related subjects,
please visit our website at www.schifferbooks.com. You may also write for a free catalog.

This book may be purchased from the publisher.
Please try your bookstore first.

We are always looking for people to write books on new and related subjects.
If you have an idea for a book, please contact us at proposals@schifferbooks.com

Schiffer Publishing's titles are available at special discounts for bulk purchases for sales
promotions or premiums. Special editions, including personalized covers, corporate imprints,
and excerpts can be created in large quantities for special needs. For more information,
contact the publisher.

In Europe, Schiffer books are distributed by
Bushwood Books
6 Marksbury Ave.
Kew Gardens
Surrey TW9 4JF England
Phone: 44 (0) 20 8392 8585; Fax: 44 (0) 20 8392 9876
E-mail: info@bushwoodbooks.co.uk
Website: www.bushwoodbooks.co.uk

Copyright © 2013 Christine Iacobuzio-Donahue and Norman Barker
Foreword Copyright © 2013 Bert Vogelstein
Cover Concept: Carisa Swenson
Book Design: Norman Barker

Library of Congress Control Number: 2012953347

Type set in Goudy Old Style/ Minion/ Optima (TT)

ISBN: 978-0-7643-4412-1
Printed in China

Contents

List of Contributors 8

Foreword 11

Introduction 12

The Plates, Head & Neck 17

Chest 53

Abdomen 89

Pelvis 113

Connective Tissue 135

Infection & Inflammation 167

Research 195

Suggested Reading 230

LIST OF CONTRIBUTORS

Robert Anders, MD
Associate Professor of Gastrointestinal Liver Pathology
The Johns Hopkins Hospital, Baltimore MD

Frederic Askin, MD
Professor of Pathology
The Johns Hopkins Hospital, Baltimore MD

Pedram Argani, MD
Professor of Pathology
The Johns Hopkins Hospital, Baltimore MD

Norm Barker, MS, MA, RBP
Associate Professor of Pathology and
Art as Applied to Medicine
The Johns Hopkins Hospital, Baltimore MD

Stephen Bova, MD
Assistant Professor of Urologic Pathology
The Johns Hopkins Hospital, Baltimore MD

Thomas Brushart, MD
Professor of Orthopedic Surgery, Neurosurgery
and Plastic Surgery, Director of Hand Surgery
The Johns Hopkins Hospital, Baltimore MD

Peter Burger, MD
Professor of Pathology, Neurosurgery and Oncology
The Johns Hopkins Hospital, Baltimore MD

Dennis Cain, CRA
Director of Ophthalmic Photography
The Johns Hopkins Hospital, Baltimore MD

Brooks Cash, MD
Professor of Medicine, Gastroenterology Service
Walter Reed National Military Medical Center
Uniformed Services University of the Health Sciences,
Bethesda MD

Muhammad Chaudhry, MD
PET/CT Fellow, Division of Nuclear Medicine
Radiation & Radiological Health Sciences
The Johns Hopkins Hospital, Baltimore MD

Ahley Cimino-Matthews, MD
Assistant Professor of Pathology
The Johns Hopkins Hospital, Baltimore MD

Douglas Clark, MD
Professor of Pathology
The Johns Hopkins Hospital, Baltimore MD

Angelo Demarzo, MD, PhD
Professor of Pathology, Urology and Oncology
The Johns Hopkins Hospital, Baltimore MD

Barbara Detrick PhD
Professor of Pathology
The Johns Hopkins Hospital, Baltimore MD

Timothy Donahue, MD
Assistant Professor, Division of Urology
Walter Reed National Military Medical Center
Uniformed Services University of the Health Sciences,
Bethesda MD

Dennis Dressman, PhD
Research Fellow
Johns Hopkins Medical Institute
Howard Hughs Medical Institute

Stephen Dumler, MD
Professor of Pathology, Medical Microbiology
The Johns Hopkins Hospital, Baltimore MD

Gigi Ebenezer, MBBS, MD
Assistant Professor of Neurology
The Johns Hopkins Hospital, Baltimore MD

Jonathan Epstein, MD
Rose-Lee and Keith Reinhard Professor
of Urologic Pathology
The Johns Hopkins Hospital, Baltimore MD

David Ginty, PhD and Nikhil Sharma
Professor of Neuroscience
The Johns Hopkins Hospital, Baltimore MD

Michael Goggins, MD
Professor of Pathology, Medicine and Oncology
The Johns Hopkins Hospital, Baltimore MD

Marc Halushka, MD
Assistant Professor of Cardiac Pathology
The Johns Hopkins Hospital, Baltimore MD

Alexandra Histrov, MD
Fellow in Hematological Pathology
The Johns Hopkins Hospital, Baltimore MD

Ralph Hruban, MD
Professor of Pathology and Oncology
The Johns Hopkins Hospital, Baltimore MD

Peter Huer, BS
Clinical Lab Manager
The Johns Hopkins Hospital, Baltimore MD

Christine Iacobuzio-Donahue, MD, PhD
Professor of Pathology, Oncology and Surgery
The Johns Hopkins Hospital, Baltimore MD

Rafael Irizarry, PhD
Professor of Biostatistics
The Johns Hopkins Hospital, Baltimore MD

J. Brooks Jackson, MD, MBA
Baxley Professor of Pathology
Pathologist-in Chief
The Johns Hopkins Hospital, Baltimore MD

Sanjay Jain, MD
Associate Professor of Pediatrics and International Health
The Johns Hopkins Hospital, Baltimore MD

Matthew Karafin, MD
Fellow/Assistant Resident of Pathology
The Johns Hopkins Hospital, Baltimore MD

Dennis Kunkel, PhD
Dennis Kunkel Microscopy, Inc.
Kailua HI

LIST OF CONTRIBUTORS

Aneela Mahmud, MD
Clinical Microbiology Fellow
The Johns Hopkins Hospital, Baltimore MD

Gary Lees, MA
Associate Professor and Director
of Art as Applied to Medicine
The Johns Hopkins Hospital, Baltimore MD

Steven Leach, MD
Professor of Surgery and Oncology
The Paul K. Neumann Professor of
Pancreatic Cancer
The Johns Hopkins Hospital, Baltimore MD

Doris Lin, MD, PhD
Assistant Professor of Radiology
The Johns Hopkins Hospital, Baltimore MD

David Loch, PhD
Postdoctoral Fellow, Institute of Genetic Medicine
The Johns Hopkins Hospital, Baltimore MD

Edward McCarthy, MD
Professor of Pathology and Orthopedic Surgery
The Johns Hopkins Hospital, Baltimore MD

Alan Meeker, PhD
Assistant Professor of Urology and Pathology
The Johns Hopkins Hospital, Baltimore MD

Saumil Merchant, MD
Eliasen Professor of Otology and Laryngology
Massachusetts Eye and Ear Infirmary
Harvard Medical School, Boston MA

Paula Mister, MS, MT (ASCP)
Educational Coordinator, Bacteriology Lab
The Johns Hopkins Hospital, Baltimore MD

Susumu Mori, PhD
Professor of Radiology and Magnetic
Resonance Research
The Johns Hopkins Hospital, Baltimore MD

Laura Morsberger
Cytogenetics Technologist for Pathology
The Johns Hopkins Hospital, Baltimore MD

Jacek Mostwin, MD, DPhil
Professor of Urology
The Johns Hopkins Hospital, Baltimore MD

Jeremy Nathans, MD, PhD
Professor of Microbiology and Genetics
The Johns Hopkins Hospital, Baltimore MD

Robert Noonan, BFA
Noonan Photography, Inc.
Shrewsbury PA

Alan Opsahl, BS
Senior Scientist
Pfizer, Global Research & Development
Groton CT

Harshan Pisharath, DVM
Graduate Program in Cellular and Molecular Medicine
The Johns Hopkins University, Baltimore MD

Alfredo Quioñes Hinojosa, MD
Professor of Neurosurgery and Oncology
The Johns Hopkins Hospital, Baltimore MD

Brigitte Ronnett, MD
Professor of Gynecologic Pathology
The Johns Hopkins Hospital, Baltimore MD

Edward Roberts, RT
Clinical Laboratory Specialist
The Johns Hopkins Hospital, Baltimore MD

Karl Schuleri, MD
Research Fellow in Cardiovascular Medicine
The Johns Hopkins Hospital, Baltimore MD

Jennifer Scudiere, MD
Miraca Life Sciences
Phoenix AZ

Peter Searson, PhD
Professor, Whiting School of Engineering
The Johns Hopkins Hospital, Baltimore MD

Jerry Shay, PhD
Professor of Cell Biology
UT Southwestern Medical Center, Dallas TX

Lori Sokoll, PhD
Associate Professor of Pathology
The Johns Hopkins Hospital, Baltimore MD

Ty Subhawong, MD
Fellow in Musculoskeletal Radiology
The Johns Hopkins Hospital, Baltimore MD

Ian Suk, BSc, BMC
Associate Professor of Neurosurgery and
Art as Applied to Medicine
The Johns Hopkins Hospital, Baltimore MD

Hoabing Wang, PhD
Eaton Peabody Laboratory, Harvard Medical School
Massachusetts Eye and Ear Infirmary, Boston MA

William Willner, MA, RBP
Wake Forest University Health Sciences
Winston-Salem NC

Phillip Wong, PhD
Professor of Pathology
The Johns Hopkins Hospital, Baltimore MD

Laura Wood, MD, PhD
Resident in Anatomic Pathology
The Johns Hopkins Hospital, Baltimore MD

Mary Zink, DVM, PhD
Professor of Comparative Medicine
Retrovitus Labratory
The Johns Hopkins Hospital, Baltimore MD

For Barbara, my best friend and beloved companion.
NB

For my mother Eleanor who raised me to believe I could do anything.
CID

FOREWORD

Many have heard the phrase *"A picture is worth a thousand words."* This is no less true for images in medicine that are routinely used to diagnose disease. Images viewed by a radiologist relay critical information, such as the anatomy of internal organs or the presence of a lesion signifying disease. Those viewed by a pathologist indicate whether a tissue is normal or abnormal at the microscopic level, and if a tumor, whether it is benign or malignant.

Scientific images are equally informative and arguably are the most important component of a research study. These images allow simple visual representations of complex scientific datasets or illustrate how variations of an experimental condition can impact cellular behavior.

What is often not verbalized, or perhaps even realized, is how often medical and scientific images are pleasing to look at for their own inherent qualities. For example, colors are often used to highlight differences between normal and diseased tissues or to direct the reader's attention to features of an image or experiment that are most important. However, the colors and the patterns and shapes the colors form can themselves be fascinating, even in the absence of knowledge of the underlying biology or pathology. Normal tissues are organized in extremely specific and reproducible ways, and in diseased tissues this organization is lost, leading to random and unique patterns that can be visually appealing.

Hidden Beauty has amassed an impressive collection of such images. They can be appreciated by scientists and clinicians for the stories that they tell. But they can be equally appreciated by anyone for the sheer beauty they convey and the wonders of nature that they illustrate.

Bert Vogelstein, MD
Director, Ludwig Center at Johns Hopkins
Investigator, Howard Hughes Medical Institute

INTRODUCTION

"Dispel from your mind the thought that an understanding of the human body in every aspect of its structure can be given in words; for the more thoroughly you describe, the more you will confuse: it is therefore necessary to draw as well as to describe."

Leonardo da Vinci (1452–1519)

As (*Christine Iacobuzio-Donahue*) caretakers, researchers and photographers working in a busy academic setting, every day we are faced with images that are awe inspiring for their beauty and for the terror they may represent to our patients suffering from disease. Beauty in this context is a relative term. To us, beauty may be seen as the delicate lacework of cells within the normal human brain reminiscent of a Jackson Pollack masterpiece, the vibrant colored chromosomes generated by spectral karyotyping that reminded one of our colleagues of the childhood game LITE-BRITE, or the multitude of colors and textures formed by fungal organisms in a microbiology lab. Herein lies the juxtaposition we seek to represent. When contemplated in isolation, each represents a visually interesting image. However, when viewed with an awareness of the context in which the image was obtained, each image takes on the ability to evoke an alternative human emotion. For example, the colored chromosomes produced by spectral karyotyping (*page 229*) were obtained from a pancreatic carcinoma, the most lethal solid tumor in humans. This image was created to demonstrate for pancreatic cancer researchers the complexity of chromosomal alterations that occur during the development of this devastating disease.

My concept for this project was born during a casual dinner conversation between myself (CID) and my husband Tim when I recounted to him an interesting clinical specimen I had reviewed during the previous week. You see, I am a pathologist and thus spend many a day looking through a microscope at tissue biopsies taken from patients with a variety of different gastrointestinal diseases that I diagnose. While each biopsy is equally important for the clinical ramifications it carries for a given patient, sometimes a sample will catch my eye for its remarkable beauty due to the patterns the cells create or perhaps the colors that the cellular constituents reflect after histologic processing. A particularly noteworthy example of this is what I encountered during my clinical duties. A patient presented with a large gastric polyp that was removed, processed in the histology lab at Johns Hopkins and slides cut from this polyp for microscopic diagnosis. Fortunately for the patient, the polyp was benign and no further medical management was required. However, what most impressed me about this particular polyp were the intricate and recurrent patterns the cells made that were enhanced by the variety of different colored stains (*page 94*). The idea that disease with all its negative ramifications can still have aspects of beauty intrigued me. After all, the human body truly is a thing of beauty and wonder.

To undertake a project such as this it was necessary to enlist the expertise and experience of a medical photographer, thus I contacted Norman Barker, Director of Photography and Graphics for advice. To my pleasant surprise, Norm revealed he had been contemplating a similar type of project for several years. Thus began our mutual collaboration to bring together a series of images that exemplify the aesthetic side of medicine.

What makes this book different from others on this subject? First and foremost, our goal is to provide a forum for educating those not typically privy to the world of medicine. Second, we have attempted to provide images related to diseases of not only Westernized countries but also developing countries as well. Third, we have included images from medical research.

Finally, and related to our original goal, we hope to show the reader that within the most serious, life threatening and deadly diseases are aspects that, when taken out of their context, have inherently aesthetic qualities. In no way do we propose that disease itself, or the suffering it creates, is aesthetically pleasing.

(Norman Barker) In medicine, nothing exists in a vacuum. Collaboration is the key to the advancement of knowledge. Once research findings are published, they can be tested by others, and knowledge grows. The scientific method, which relies on starting with a question or idea, has been used for thousands of years. Observation is such an important part of the scientific method that as far back as the Ancient Egyptians more than 5000 years ago, documents have been unearthed describing empirical methods in medicine, astronomy and mathematics. By keen observations, scrutiny and research, a hypothesis is developed and tested through experimentation. Once all the data is collected and analyzed, conclusions can be made and the results published, and other medical researchers can test those results. This keen sense of observation, watching, examining and inspecting are one of the many characteristics that scientists and artists have in common. It's through that critical analysis and deep thought process that a significant experiment can be realized or a beautiful work of art can be produced.

Technology is advancing so quickly that the traditional printed page, in many cases, is taking a back seat to the computer screen. Most medical journals and references can be accessed from the online database called Pub Med, which is maintained by the National Library of Medicine at The National Institute for Health. The need for high quality visuals to explain or document complicated medical processes is more important than ever. Whether it is a computer graphic, video segment, photograph or illustration, all types of media are used to visualize science.

Over the last thirty years it has been my job to help physicians and researchers with visualizing their research and creating high quality images for the printed page and electronic screen. As a medical photographer I have always felt privileged to have a behind-the-scenes look at the human body. On any given day I might find myself taking photographs of a complicated procedure in the operating room and that afternoon photographing mice in a research lab and then back to capture some images with the compound microscope. It's always a challenge, and with such a wide variety of specimens and situations you need to be prepared for anything.

As a young medical photographer just out of art school I was asked by a pathologist to photograph a bloody kidney specimen in the autopsy room. The physician told me to make sure that it's "beautiful" because it was being used for publication in a prestigious medical journal. I can remember thinking to myself; this doctor is crazy, how am I going to make this sickly red specimen look beautiful? Of course I did the best I could and the image was published, but I learned a lot from that experience. There truly is beauty in everything, although sometimes it might be in the eye of the beholder. But the importance of a high quality image that documents and explains a process to the viewer in a clear and unambiguous way is essential. In this particular case the image was part of an article about the diagnosis of a polycystic kidney, and probably viewed by thousands of nephrologists (*kidney specialist*). Attributed to Confucius, the old proverb stating that "a picture is worth a thousand words" certainly applies.

The sciences and arts share a common creative aesthetic. There is beauty in a well-designed experiment. Leading scientists are active in the creative process, whether it is an elegant solution to a scientific problem or writing, painting, sculpture or music, the so-called creative arts. The arts and sciences share a common aesthetic of discovery through observation. Aesthetic elements can be observed in a scientific discovery as well as in a piece of poetry, good novel, fine symphony or beautiful painting. The artist and scientist both study the natural world, although for different aims and reasons. The artist tries to represent the world in some way and the scientist tries to discover the basis of how it works. Modern philosophy gives validity to the idea that science and art are not essentially different activities but share many common attributes. The idea of using a well-defined image to explain a complicated scientific problem has a long tradition in Western society. The perceptive artist and scientist share common training in observation and pattern recognition, and they both share a love for creative problem solving.

Medicine along with other disciplines of science depends on the dissemination of new information that can be tested and verified by others. Traditionally this has been accomplished by text and visual images on the printed page. The most important function of a scientific photograph is to document, record and measure, but most importantly that image can be distributed thru publication. Photography has become an essential tool in scientific research and plays a direct role in patient care and discovery. Medicine, botany, geology, anthropology, archeology, astronomy, just to name a few branches of the sciences, are dependent on images, whether they be illustrations drawn by the hand of a skilled illustrator or accurate digital photographs. It's impossible to imagine a book explaining complicated processes without the aid of illustrations or photographs.

Ever since January 7, 1839, when the Secretary of the French Chamber of Deputies, Francois Arago made the announcement of the new invention from the Parisian stage painter Louis Jacques Madé Daguerre, photography has played an essential role in the sciences. The "new art" of photography was seen to be able to give much greater accuracy than was to be provided by painting or drawings.

Arago, an astronomer of note, saw the importance of this new process in the aid of advancement of science. In the twenty-first century it's hard for us to appreciate the idea of an object delineating itself on a sensitized plate without the aid of an artist's hand. The Daguerreotype process had its limitations because it was a one of a kind object on a metal plate; multiple copies were difficult to make. If the image was to be reproduced by the technology of the time, it had to be engraved by an artist and that was extremely time consuming work. With our modern bias it's difficult to imagine seeing a photograph for the first time. In Victorian culture, before the name "Photography" (*literally translated from the Greek, "writing with light"*) was coined by Sir John Hershel, phrases such as fairy pictures, natural magic, natures marvel, and the black art were among the early phrases to describe this new art.

It was thought at the time that an artist's way of describing detail was exaggerated and had what was considered to be the bias of the artist's eye. The logic was that a camera could make an exact copy of what was placed in front of the lens. Now we accept this logic to be incorrect, because in many ways an illustration can show and clarify processes that a photograph could never do.

The photograph being superior when surface detail is needed in a recording. The illustration and photograph are two different tools that can be used to describe a complicated process. Many times a modern computer graphic best communicates complicated scientific data in a simple more elegant way, as a carpenter would select the correct hammer for the job.

While Daguerre was making his announcements in Paris, in England the polymath Sir William Henry Fox Talbot was working on his own process unaware of Daguerre's new invention. The Talbotype or Calotype was the basis for the modern "positive/negative process" that we use today. But more importantly, the difference was that multiple copies could be made from a single negative, which was essential for the distribution of the scientific image. Fox Talbot was one of the true intellectuals of the day. He was a member of the Royal Society, the top scientific body, and could speak five different languages, as well as translate Egyptian hieroglyphics and was well published in mathematics, chemistry, physics, optics and botany. On his 1833 honeymoon trip to Lake Como, Italy, he was sketching the landscape with the aid of the camera lucida, a small device with a prism used as drawing aid. He lamented about his inability to draw, calling his drawings, "traces on paper, melancholy to be held." Talbot was also familiar with the camera obscura, another device with a lens attached to a box and a mirror to project the image on a piece of frosted glass that was used to trace the image projected onto paper.

The camera obscura was used for hundreds of years and very familiar to artists like Johannes Vermeer and Albrecht Dürer who used the device to make sketches in perspective for their final paintings. It was Fox Talbot who solved the problem of being able to fix the projected image to a piece of sensitized paper. Talbot proclaimed that "this led me to reflect on the absolute beauty of the pictures of nature's printing which the glass lens of the camera throws upon the paper in its focus…fairy pictures, creations of a movement and destined to fade away. It was during these thoughts that the idea occurred to me…how charming it would be if it were possible to cause these natural images to imprint themselves durably and remained fixed upon the paper, and why should it not be possible." Being a scientist he recognized the importance of being able to document scientific phenomena. He was one of the first to capture images through the microscope and publish his results.

In many ways scientists created the discipline of photography and were the first to realize the tremendous potential of the new media. Photography is not only a system for illustrating science; in many ways it's also a method for doing science. The context in which a photograph is viewed can have an effect on how the image is interpreted. We ask the viewer to sit back and enjoy a view of medicine and to see that beauty, or the lack thereof, is in the eye of the beholder.

Christine Iacobuzio-Donahue
Norman Barker

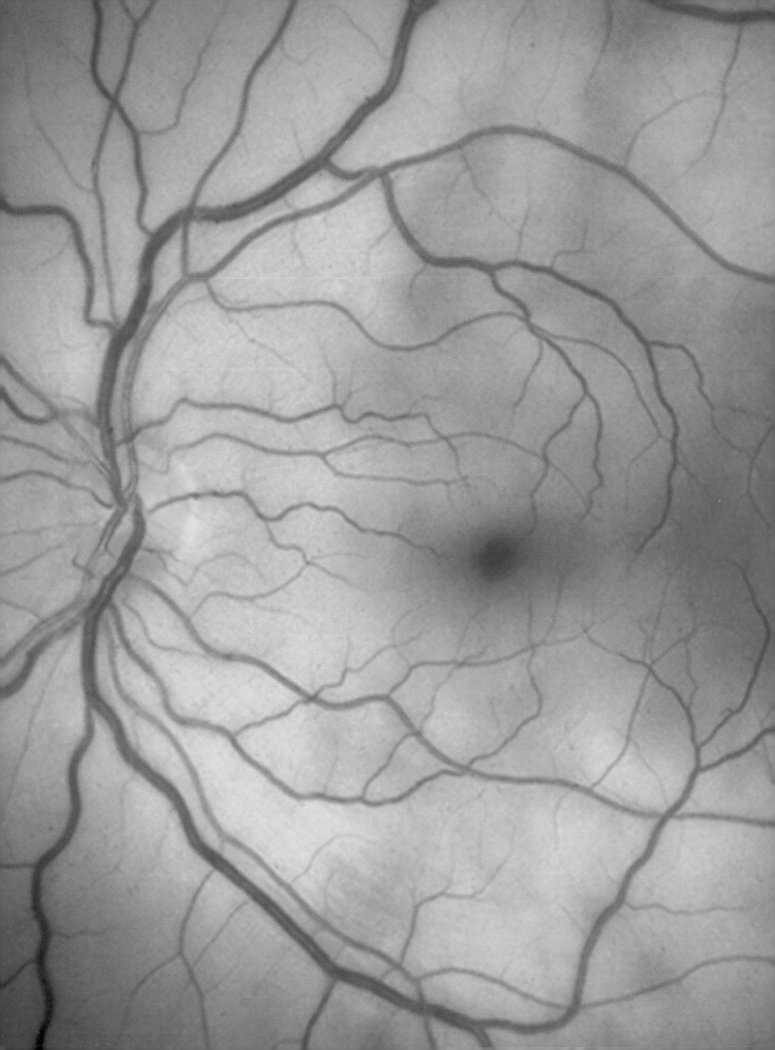

The Plates,
Head & Neck

Blood vessels on the surface of the mouse retina

The retina is a thin sheet of nerve cells that lines the back wall of the eye and functions much like the film in a camera. This image shows the blood vessels that supply the inner layers of the mouse retina. The blood vessels emerge like spokes on a wheel from a central structure called the optic disc, at the top of the image. The main arteries (*colored green*) are arranged in an alternating pattern with the veins (*colored red*). Oxygen-rich blood arrives in the arteries and oxygen-depleted blood leaves in the veins. Although it cannot be seen in this image, the vascular branches that emerge from the sides of the arteries and veins are connected together by a large number of extremely narrow blood vessels, called capillaries, which reside deep within the retina. Many retinal diseases, such as diabetic retinopathy and age-related macular degeneration, involve defects in retinal vascular structure and growth. *x200*

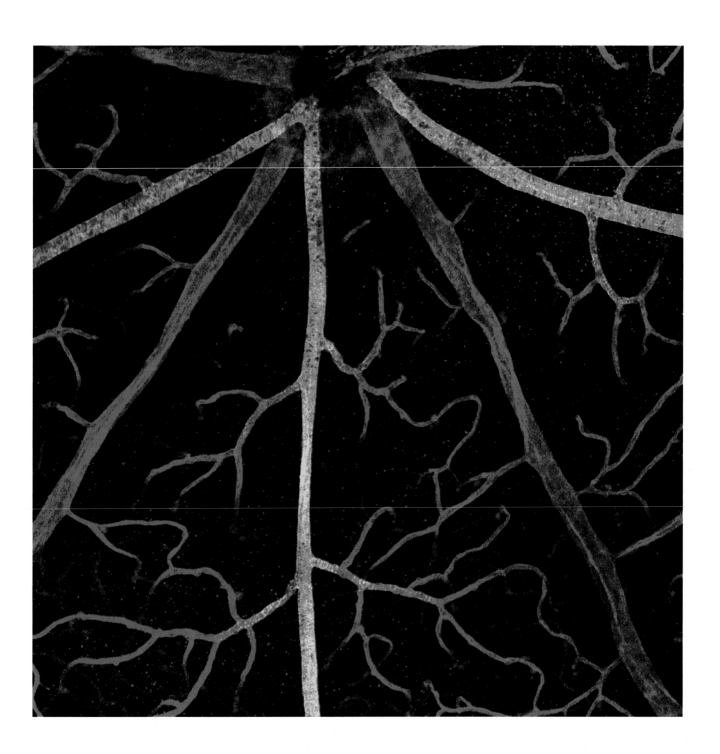

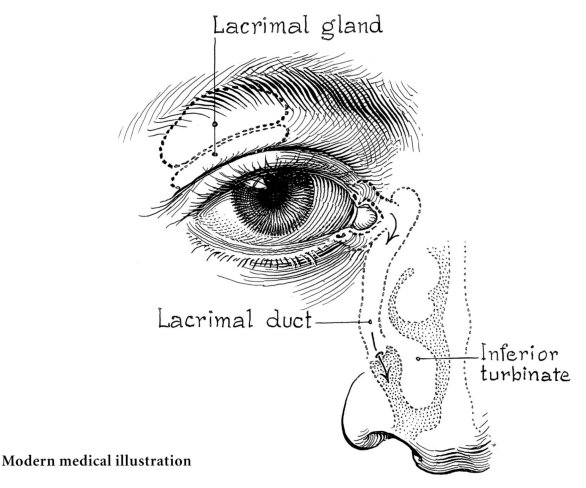

Lacrimal gland

Lacrimal duct

Inferior turbinate

Modern medical illustration

Max Brödel is considered the father of modern medical illustration. A German immigrant, he came to the United States in the late 1890s where he began his career at The Johns Hopkins School of Medicine in Baltimore, Maryland. Here, he illustrated books for many of the great clinicians of the time, including Howard Kelly, William Stewart Halsted, and Harvey Cushing. Besides being an incredible artist he also created many novel techniques for illustration. Dr. Thomas Cullen, realizing the importance of passing along this knowledge and skill to others, contacted Henry Walters, the Baltimore art collector and philanthropist, who provided an anonymous endowment to establish the first art department in the world dedicated to teaching medical illustration. Brödel presided over this first program at Johns Hopkins for more than 30 years until his death in 1941. This training program, *Art as Applied to Medicine and Biological Illustration*, recently celebrated its centennial anniversary of training medical illustrators that have since brought their art and craft all over the world.

Shown above and at right is a pen and ink illustration created for Kenneth F. Macy, M.D. and published in *The Journal of the American Medical Association* in 1919. The title of the illustration is *Transmission of Infection Through The Eye*. Airborne organisms may follow several pathways to cause respiratory infection as this simple yet elegant illustration indicates.

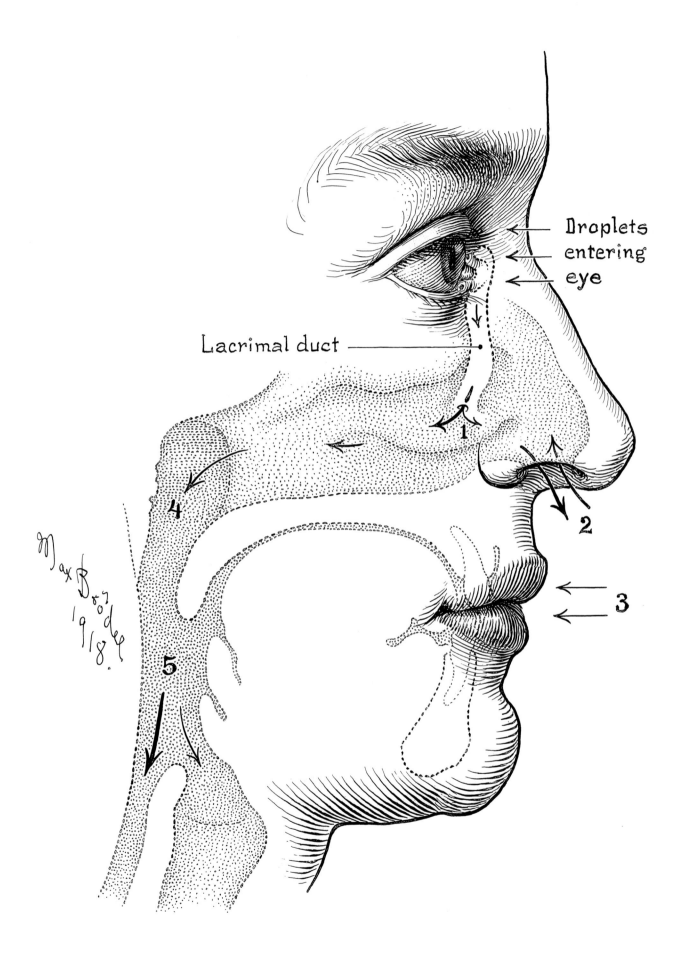

Droplets
entering
eye

Lacrimal duct

Max Broodee
1918.

1

2

3

4

5

Illustration of the inner ear

This, the second of the *Three Unpublished Drawings of the Anatomy of the Human Ear*, was Max Brödel's last illustration utilizing the carbon dust technique he developed to depict human tissue realistically in halftone reproductions. Completed in 1941, only months before he died, it accurately depicts an overview of the intrinsic anatomy of the ear in a majestic frontal plane allowing the viewer to see the essential relations of the component parts of this complicated sense organ in a single image. Sketches for this drawing were made from direct observation of both dry and wet specimens at all stages of exposure of parts, and numerous series of serial sections from the collection of the Ontological Research Laboratory of the Johns Hopkins University School of Medicine. Explaining his approach to an illustration Brödel wrote, "Photography has its limitations and it is not hard to see where and why it falls short. I knew it would be useless for me to compete with the camera in the realistic or imitative field. It was necessary to originate a different type of picture, one that would show far more than any photograph could ever do. To make such a picture is much more difficult. The artist must first fully comprehend the subject matter from every standpoint: anatomical, topographical, histological, pathological, medical and surgical. From this accumulated knowledge grows a mental picture, from which crystallizes the plan of the future drawing. A clear and vivid mental picture always must precede the actual picture on paper. The planning of the picture therefore is the all important thing, not the execution."

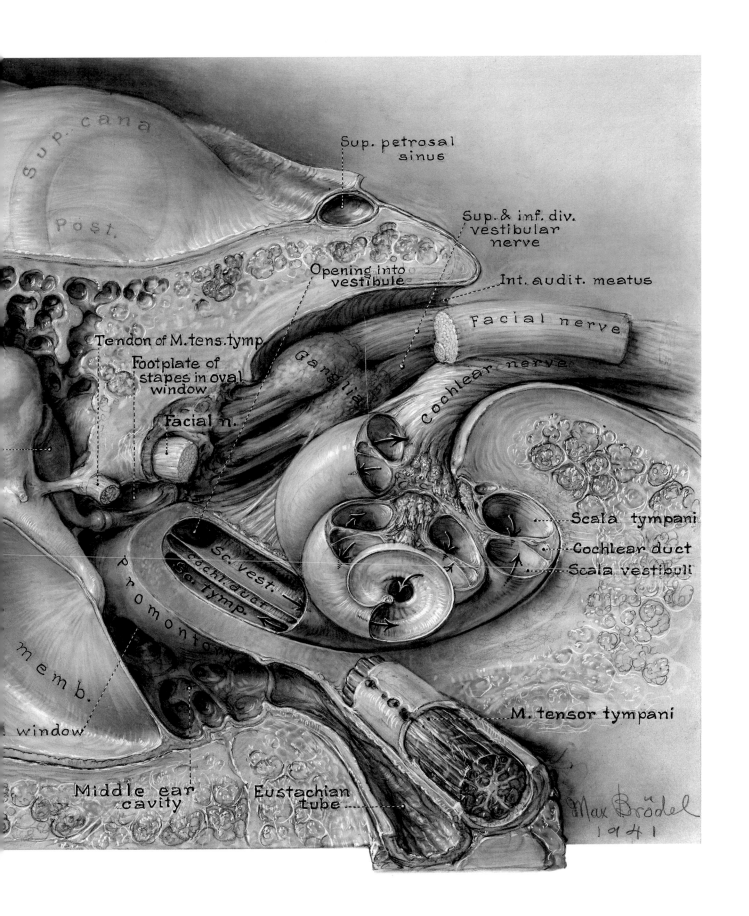

Sup. cana

Post.

Sup. petrosal
sinus

Sup. & inf. div.
vestibular
nerve

Opening into
vestibule

Int. audit. meatus

Facial nerve

Tendon of M. tens. tymp.

Footplate of
stapes in oval
window

Ganglia

Cochlear nerve

Facial n.

Sc. vest.

Cochl. duct

Sc. tymp.

Promontor

Scala tympani

Cochlear duct

Scala vestibuli

memb.

window

M. tensor tympani

Middle ear
cavity

Eustachian
tube

Max Brödel
1941

Temporal bone

The ear, which is responsible for hearing and balance, contains a large number of structures including the eardrum, middle ear bones, the organ of hearing (*cochlea*), the organs of balance (*semicircular canals*), nerves and blood vessels. All these tiny, myriad parts are contained within an incredibly small volume of space within the bony confines of a part of the skull called the temporal bone. In this example, modern-day researchers have used histological sections of the temporal bone to create three-dimensional models such as the one shown here. Such models enable students and trainees to learn the complicated anatomy of the ear. Individual structures are color-coded (*e.g., eardrum in green, middle ear bones in blue, inner ear structures in pink, nerves in yellow, blood vessels in red*). The model allows the operator to control the degree of transparency of individual structures, thus allowing one to "see" through the temporal bone. For example, the bony air cells (*shown in white*) that surround the structures of the ear were rendered semitransparent in this image. See additional three-dimensional models at:

http://research.meei.harvard.edu/otopathology/3dmodels/

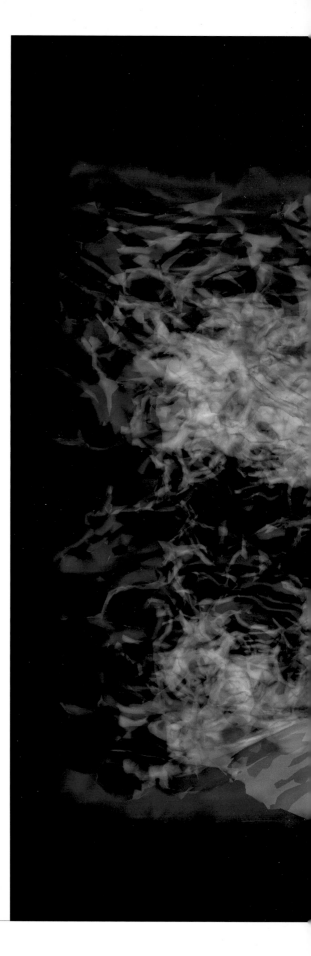

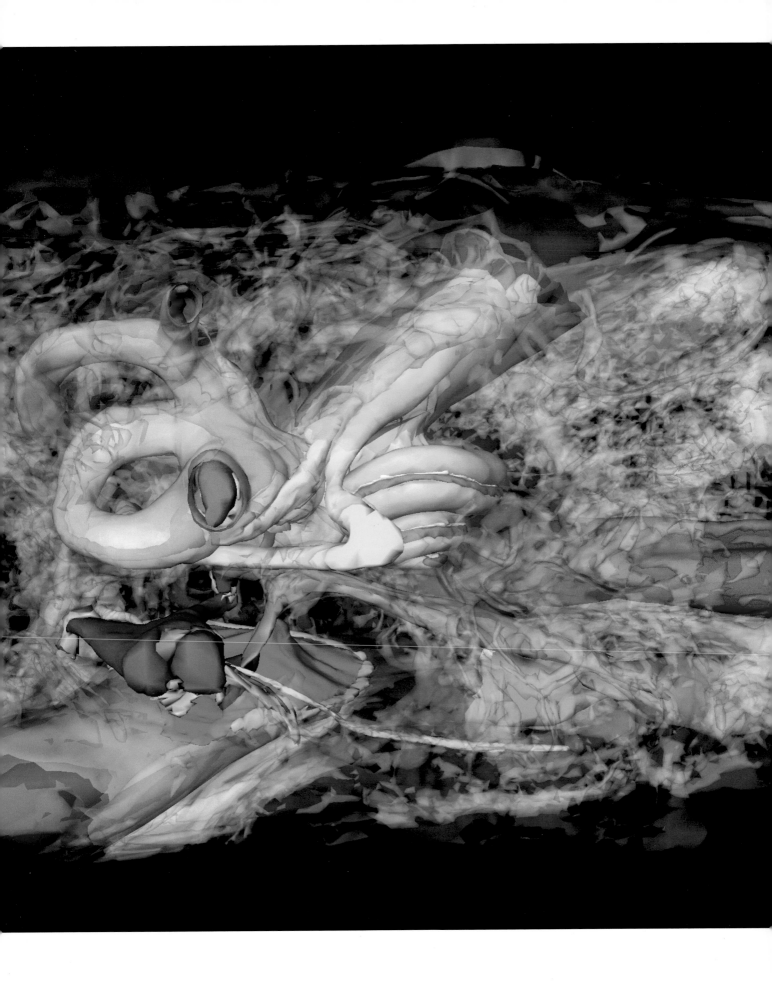

Coronal section through the head

Through the ages, art and anatomy have always had a close relationship. For example, during the Renaissance artists and anatomists were often the same person. From their own dissections and drawings came huge contributions to our understanding of medical science and the human body. One of the most famous drawings illustrating this point is that of the great anatomist/physician Andreas Vesalius on the title page of his classic book, *De Humani Corporis Fabrica*, published in 1543. One of the most influential books on human anatomy for several hundred years, the book plate shows Vesalius performing a dissection with a crowd of interested spectators observing the great anatomist as he points out the salient features from the open belly of a female corpse.

There has always been a fascination in looking to see what's inside the human body. The first Dutch anatomy theatre was at the University at Lieden. For a nominal charge the public could view the dissection of a human corpse. The Latin text *Nosce te Ipsum* ("Know Thyself") established and legitimized the religious context for dissection of the human body and the advancement of anatomical knowledge. In modern times, people are fascinated to watch a live operation in high-definition on The Discovery Channel from the comfort of their couch.

The controversial modern German anatomist Gunther Von Hagens patented the process of plastination that enables museum visitors to view the human body in unprecedented detail. His exhibition entitled "Body Worlds" has been exhibited at science and natural history museums around the world. Literally millions of museum patrons have been awestruck to get close-up views of the inner workings of the human body. The Visible Human Project® by The National Library of Medicine is another marvel of modern anatomy. The initial aim of the project was to create a complete digital image dataset of male and female cadavers using high-resolution photography as well as MRI and CT. The whole catalog of data is available on the Internet. Regardless of these hi-tech approaches to anatomy, the requirement for a medical degree remains the one-on-one dissection of a cadaver to learn human anatomy. The image at right illustrates the anatomy of the human head in nine equally thick serial sections.

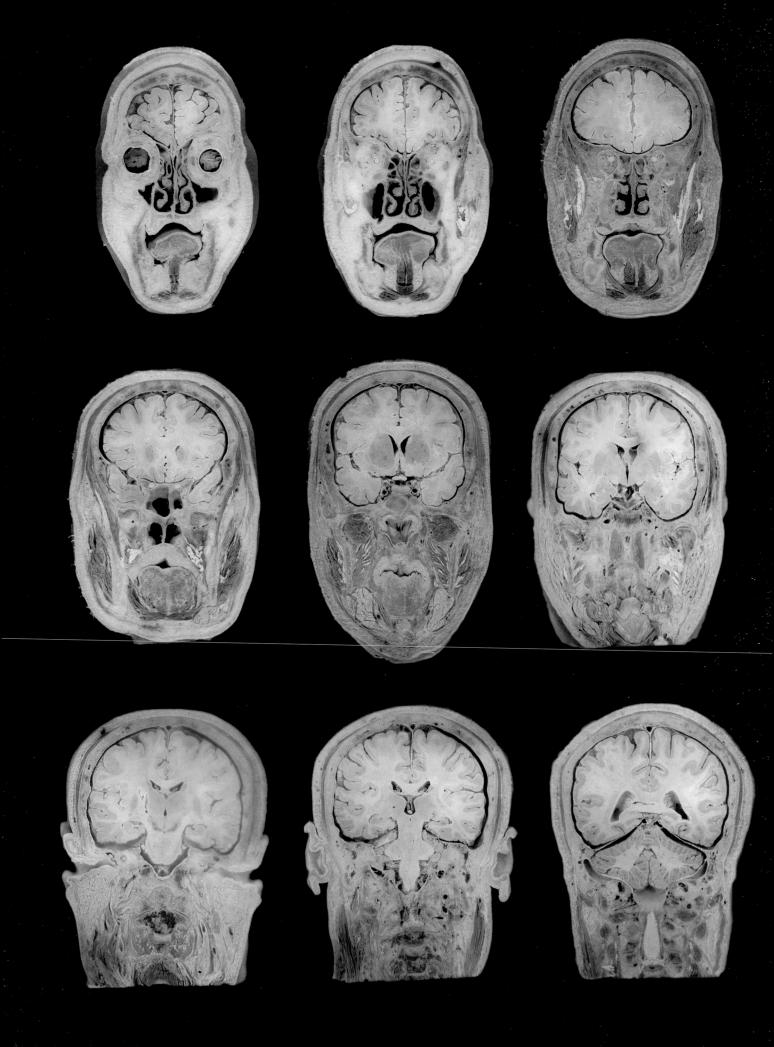

The modern microscope

In 1683, Dutchman Antoni van Leeuwenhoek made a startling discovery that changed the world. His observations through his simple microscope started the discipline of microbiology. Despite all the changes in more than three hundred years of microscopy, the pleasure is still being able to view and show others the invisible world beyond the human eye. The universe beyond what can be comprehended by the unaided eye is unbelievably rich and complex. Early microscopes were used more for entertainment than as a tool for scientific discovery. The beauty and subtlety of nature's work fascinated early microscopists, just as it does the curious viewer in the twenty-first century.

The microscope plays a central role in so many disciplines of science, especially medicine and biology. In the majority of biomedical research there are three types of microscopes in use today. The light microscope, the transmission electron microscope (TEM) and the scanning electron microscope (SEM), all help to extend our inspection inside the human body. The two units of measurement shown at the right, the inch and the millimeter, are shown at actual or life size. Unfortunately, these measurements are of little use in microscopy; for practical applications two smaller units are used. The micrometer is one-thousandth of a millimeter, or one-millionth of a meter. The other unit of measure is even smaller and that is the nanometer. It measures one-millionth of a millimeter or one-thousandth of a micrometer. Just to give an idea of size, twenty atoms side by side would cover the distance of one nanometer, which is about the resolution maximum for a high quality TEM scope. In the modern light microscope, magnification is the result of light passing through a very thin specimen and then up to the objective lens and then the eyepiece, where the virtual image is examined. Magnification occurs in two stages, hence the name: compound microscope. The light that passes through that thin specimen is referred to as transmitted light, or bright field illumination.

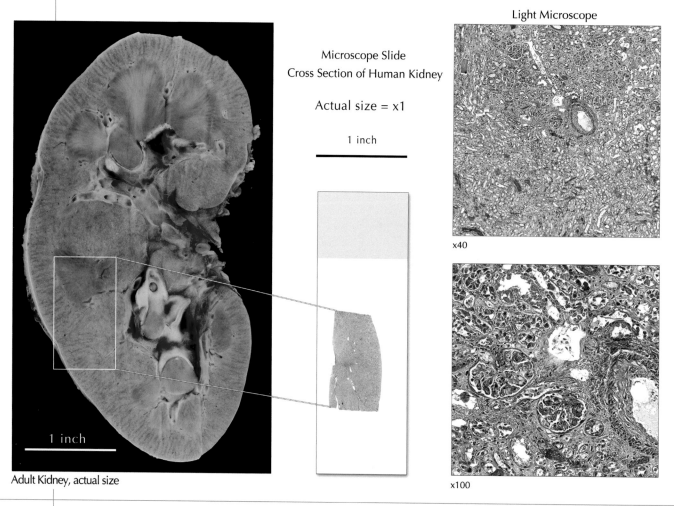

Light Microscope

Microscope Slide
Cross Section of Human Kidney

Actual size = x1

1 inch

x40

Adult Kidney, actual size

x100

Incident light (*reflected off the surface*) is used to view opaque subjects like computer chips or fragments of metal. But, the light microscope has its limitations for the very simple reason of the aberrations of light. In practice, the light microscope has a resolution limitation of approximately one-thousandth of a millimeter (0.001mm). At the highest of magnifications around x1000 we can see structures such as bacteria but they are so small their structure cannot be seen in any detail.

The transmission electron microscope has a resolution limit of (0.000001 mm). This is more than one hundred thousand times smaller than the human eye can see. This instrument can be used to look at the DNA strands inside bacterium with great clarity. This very complicated microscope does not use light to form an image but electrons in a vacuum chamber that bombard the specimen that is usually coated with a very fine layer of platinum or gold to make the specimen electron conductive. Much higher magnifications can be achieved so that we can actually study the basic way in which life functions down to the molecular level.

The scanning electron microscope doesn't have the high resolving power of the TEM. Instead of looking into cells and atomic structures, the SEM is used to see surfaces, such as a kidney glomeruli (*right*) or metal fatigue. A fine beam of electrons projected in a vacuum scans the surface of the subject. As these secondary electrons radiate off the specimen, a detector collects them and they can be viewed on a television screen. Since no light is used to form the image, great depth of focus can be achieved that can resolve a parasite on top of a flea's head. Images produced with the electron microscope are always monochromatic or black-and-white, but they are usually artificially colored by a computer. Known as "false color," the color added has no relation to the real color of a particular specimen but the color is added generally for aesthetic effect and can help distinguish regions of interest in the specimen.

Scanning Electron Microscope

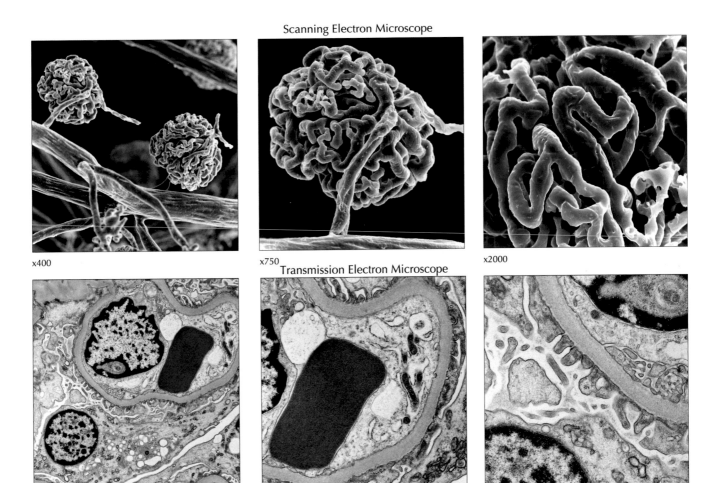

x400

x750

Transmission Electron Microscope

x2000

x3000

x6000

x10000

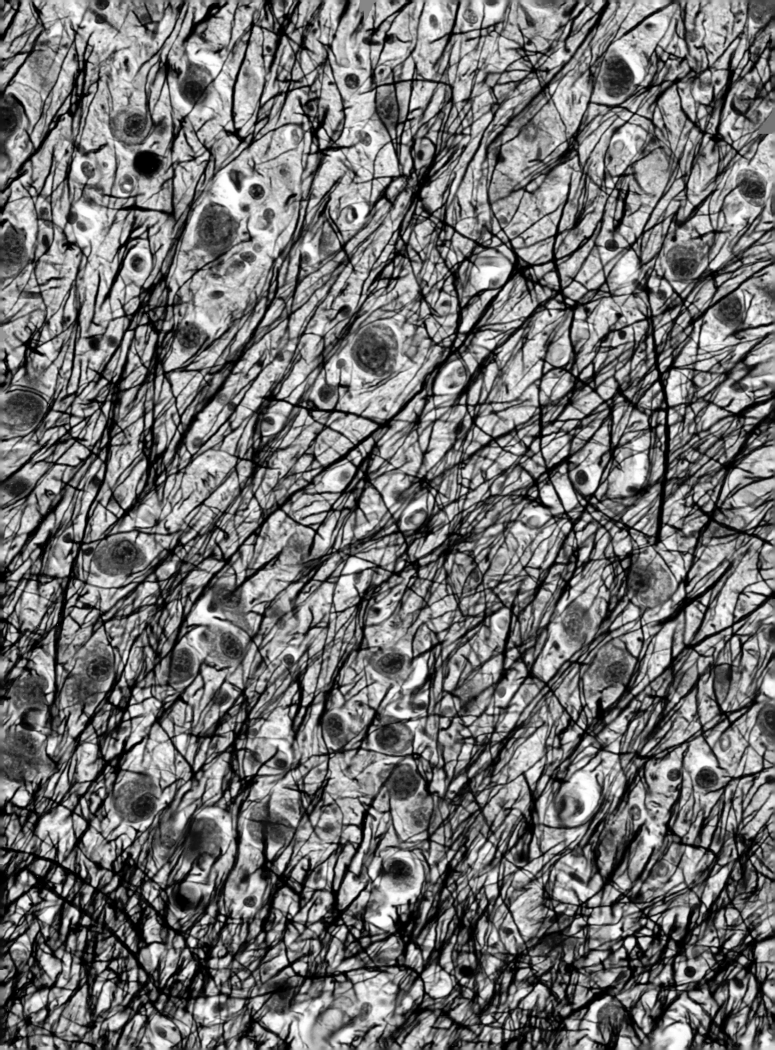

Human brain

The brain is the center of the nervous system in many species, including humans. Some primitive animals such as jellyfishes and starfishes have a nervous system without a brain, and sea sponges lack any nervous system at all. In humans, the brain is located in the head where it is protected by the skull and close to our sensory organs for vision, hearing, balance, taste and smell.

The brain is exceedingly complex. It contains roughly 100 billion neurons that are connected to each other in an elaborate matrix with up to 10,000 connections for each neuron. Neurons communicate with one another by means of long fibers called dendrites and axons, which carry electrical signals to and from other regions of the brain or nervous system. In fact, methods of observation such as an electro-encephalogram (EEG) record these electrical signals and tell us that the communications among neurons is highly organized. However, these methods do not have the resolution to reveal the activity of individual neurons. Despite rapid scientific progress, much about how the human brain works remains a mystery. The operations of individual neurons are now understood in considerable detail, but the way they cooperate in well-orchestrated ensembles of thousands or millions of cells has been very difficult to decipher.

This image is an example of a normal human brain when seen under a microscope. The large round rust colored cells are the neurons, and the tangles of black fibers are the dendrites and axons that connect each neuron to each other and to other neurons in different parts of the brain or body. The image *Motor neurons* (*page 41*) illustrates two individual neurons isolated from brain tissue. In this instance, the axons and dendrites that extend from a single cell are better appreciated. *x400*

Diffusion color map

The brain is made of two major components: an outer cortical layer
of gray matter, and an inner part of white matter. White matter is
composed mostly of myelinated axons which connect different brain
regions by transmitting signals. Although on visual inspection (as in a
brain slice) white matter appears nearly homogeneously white, in reality
it is comprised of packets of nerve fiber bundles that connect different
regions of the brain. These bundles can be depicted with color-coding
using a method called *diffusion tensor magnetic resonance imaging*.
Fiber bundles running left to right are coded in red, front to back in
green and top to bottom in blue. Imaging of brain fiber bundles by
clinicians is useful in diagnosing or monitoring certain neurological
diseases and is used as a tool by neurosurgeons who are planning brain
surgery. Color-encoded, three-dimensional reconstructions of the entire
brain and spinal cord are also possible using diffusion tensor imaging.
See how this method is also used in brain research in the image *Mouse
brain, MRI (page 213)*.

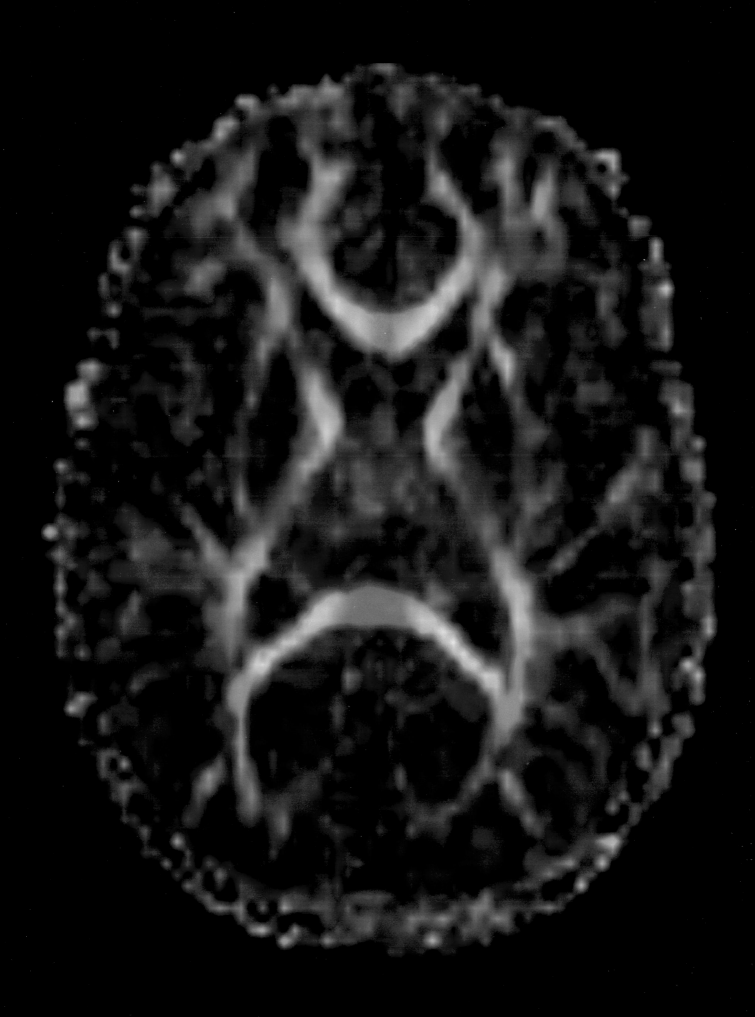

Human eye, fundus

The eyes are said to be the windows of the soul, but in many of these images that window is blurred by disease. These diagnostic images of the eyes were taken by an ophthalmologist in order to diagnose diseases of the eye. The palette of autumn hues is naturally occurring; blood imparts the red and red-orange colors, while ocular pigments provide the blue-black. Rounded bright yellow-white spots in each photo represent the optic nerve where the blood vessels (*the delicate tortuous red lines*) enter the retina to feed the tissues of the eye. A single photo in this series represents a normal eye, the image in the center, and the remainder examples of eye disease.

Top L-R: Lymphoma
                Retinitis Pigmentosa
                Proliferative Diabetic Retinopathy

Middle L-R: Central Retinal Artery Occlusion
                Normal
                AIDS Retinopathy

Bottom L-R: Choroidal Rupture BB Trauma
                Leukemia
                Retinal inflammation with
                para foveal hemorrhage

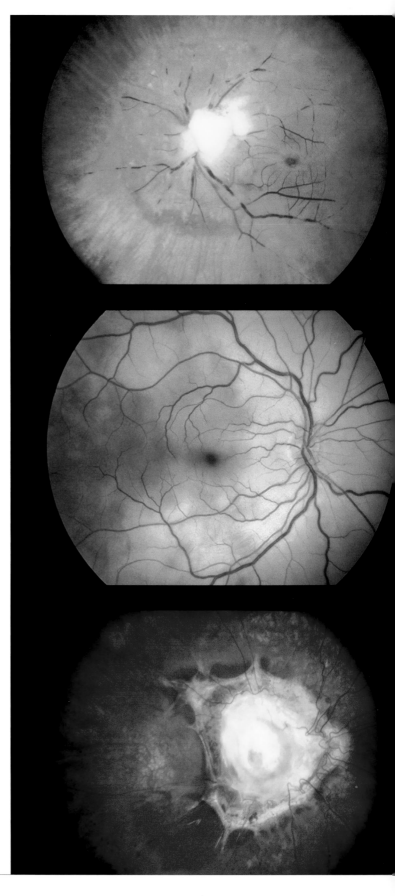

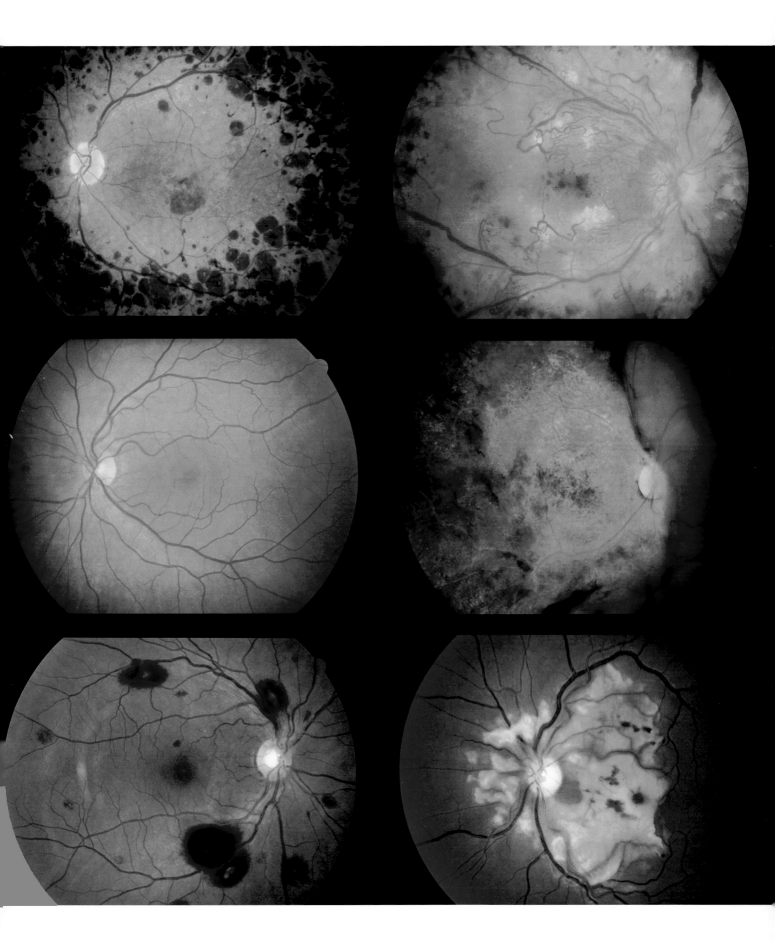

Meningioma, brain tumor

At the time of surgery for brain tumors, neurosurgeons typically
remove minute specimens for intraoperative evaluation. However,
neural tissue is very delicate and frozen section analysis may
be suboptimal in some cases. A way to maximize the tissue and
preserve cellular detail is to stain a smear produced by squeezing
a small piece of the brain tumor between two glass slides. This
smear shows numerous whorled lamellar psammoma bodies,
some of which are calcified, diagnostic of a meningioma. Calcified
psammoma bodies grossly resemble grains of sand, hence its
derivation from the Greek word *psammos* meaning "sand." *x400*

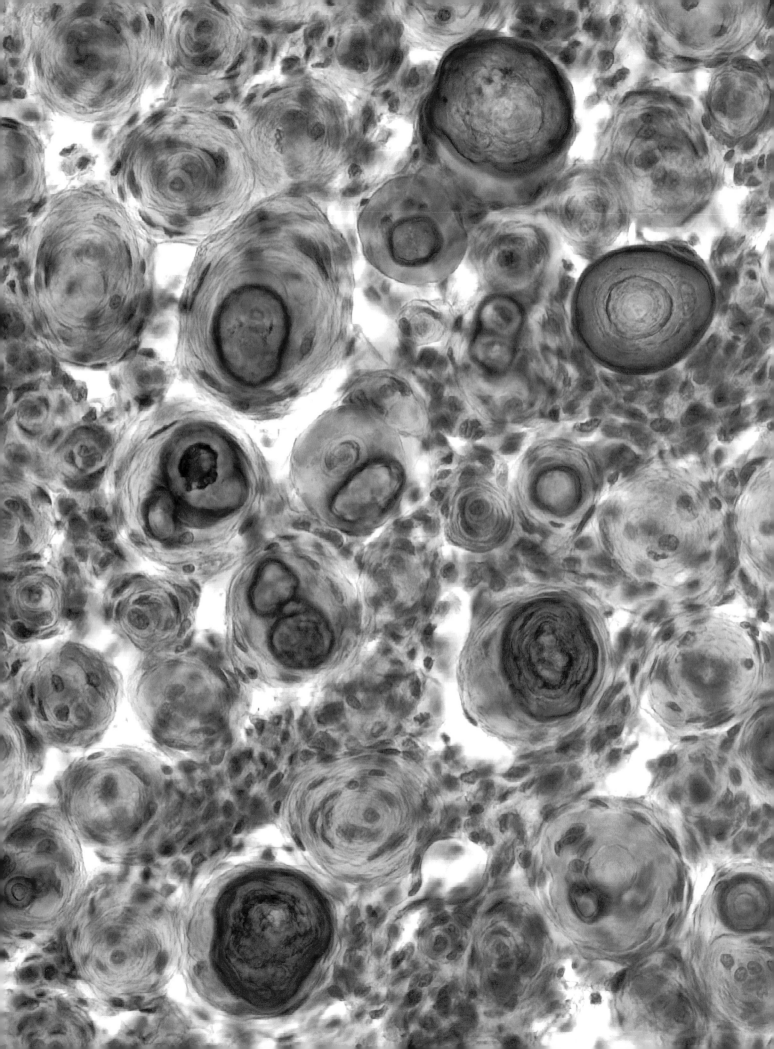

Fluorescein angiography

When blood leaks from the tiny vessels in the innermost portion of the eye (*the retina*), it may cause blurred or even complete loss of vision. These vessels are thinner than a human hair. When leaking vessels are suspected, the ophthalmologist may order a fluorescein angiogram. The fluorescein angiogram is a series of timed photographs performed by a professional photographer that specializes in photographing the many structures of the eye. A fluorescein solution is injected into a blood vessel and the dye is captured as it travels through the circulatory channels of the eye. If the angiogram shows actively leaking vessels, the physician may attempt to control the bleeding by performing laser photocoagulation. The adjacent photograph is an early transit image of a patient that has received prior laser therapy. The laser spots are visible in the upper quadrant of the photograph. *x6*

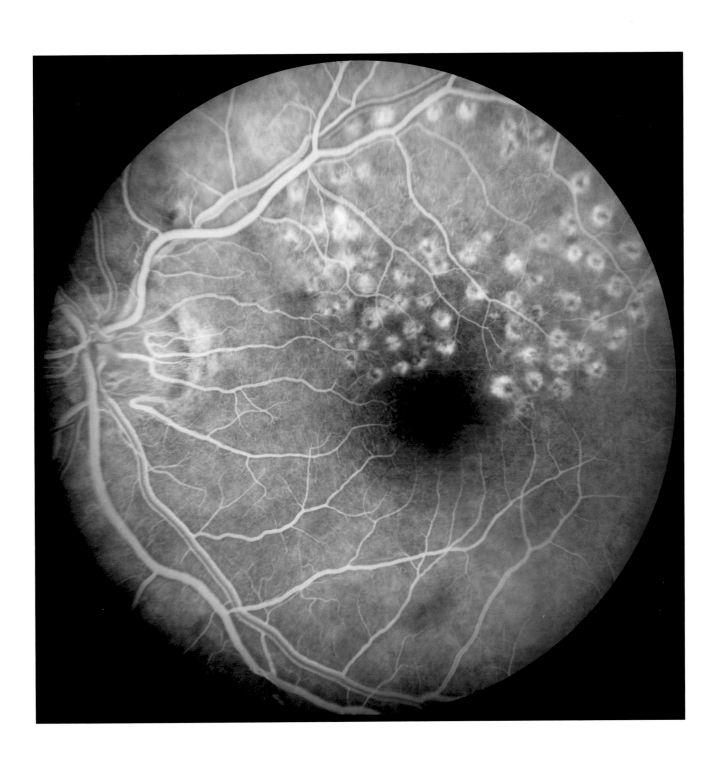

Motor neurons

Motor neurons are nerve cells within the spinal cord that connect through wire-like axons to the muscles they control. When a motor neuron "fires" it sends an electrical impulse down the axon to stimulate muscle contraction. Axons also serve as bidirectional conduits that carry structural components from motor neurons to muscles and carry signaling molecules from muscles to motor neurons. This transport capacity can be harnessed to identify the specific motor neurons that connect to a given muscle. The motor neurons in this image are labeled by horseradish peroxidase that has been injected into the muscle they serve, transported through their axons to the spinal cord and localized using a histochemical reaction that can only take place where horseradish peroxidase is present. The branch-like structures emanating from the two labeled motor neurons are dendrites, specialized "antennae" that receive signals from other nerve cells. *x500*

Cerebellum *(overleaf)*

Charged with coordinating body movements, among other functions, and endowed with more neurons than the rest of the brain, the cerebellum is an enormous data processing center whose layered anatomic infrastructure has fascinated anatomists for centuries. The lighter, pink superficial band is the molecular layer and the adjacent pale blue zone is the molecular layer packed with innumerable small neurons. The most internal, or deepest, zone is the white matter, so designated for its glistening white sheen to the naked eye. Here its fatty layers of insulation around individual neuronal processes are seen in aggregate as the dark blue layer when stained with a lipid-soluble blue dye, in addition to the classic hematoxylin and eosin method widely used in pathology. This static image, complex as it is, does not do justice to the tissue's dynamic flux of impulses through inputs, outputs and feedback loops. *x10*

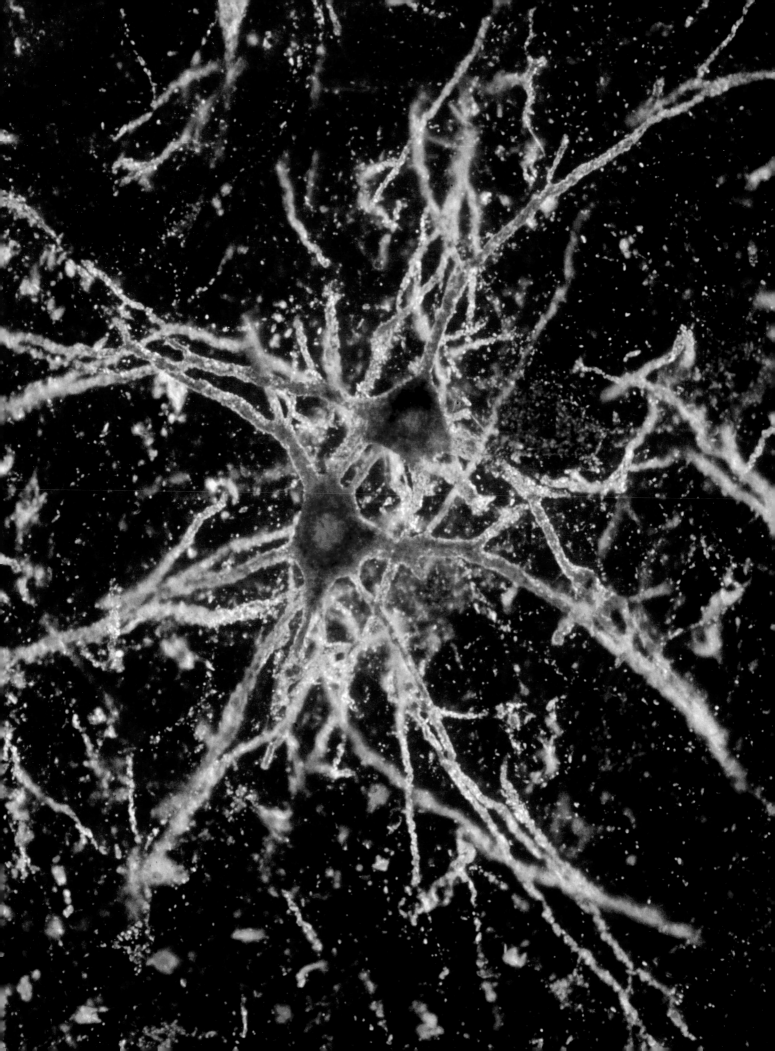

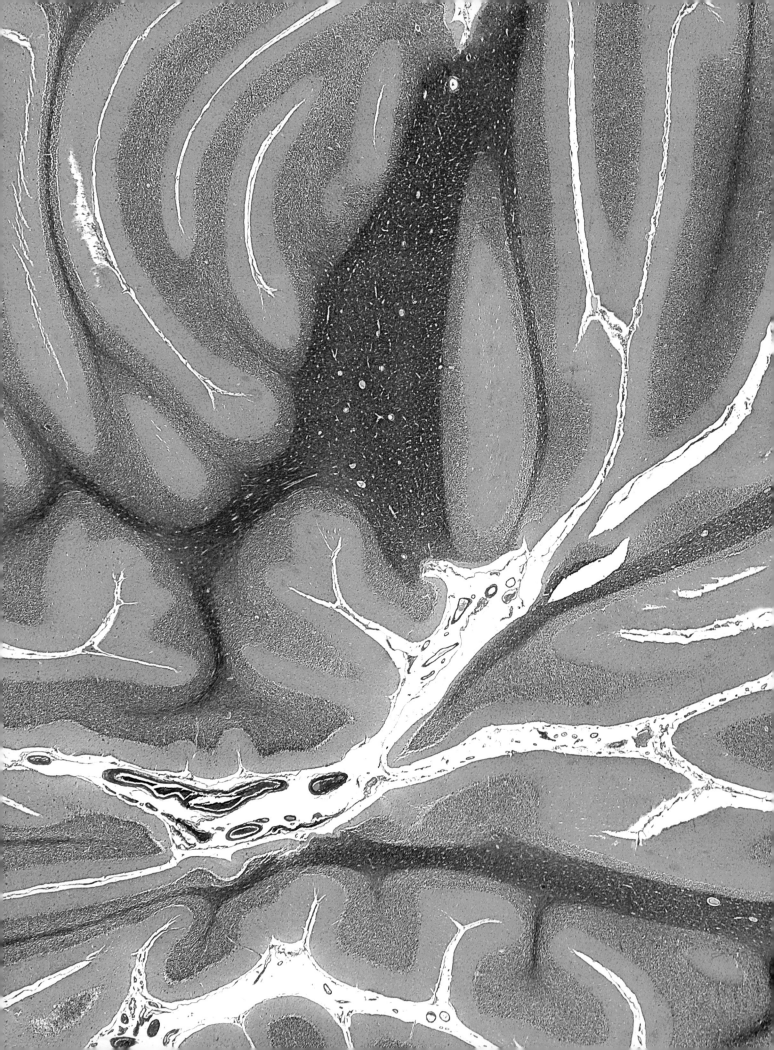

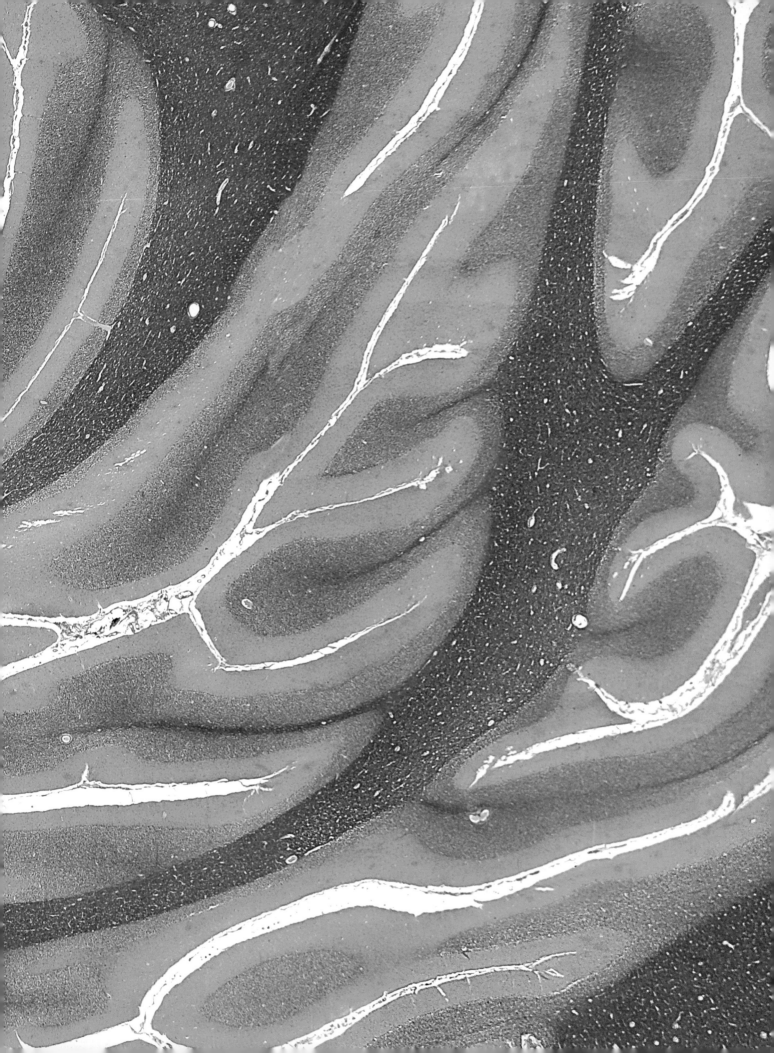

Magnetic resonace imaging, brain tumor

Introduction of magnetic resonance imaging (MRI), and before that computerized tomography (CT), provided a previously unimagined ability to peer into the human body and image internal structures. In this case, MRI shows a deep-seated mass in the region of the brain that includes the visual system and hypothalamus. While the imaging features are not specific for a particular type of tumor, the location and imaging features of the mass in this case are consistent with neoplasm known as craniopharyngioma. Armed with this knowledge, the surgeon can plan the best surgical approach to a lesion that, while very slowly-growing, is densely adherent to vital structures. Total surgical excision, with preservation of neurological function, may be difficult.

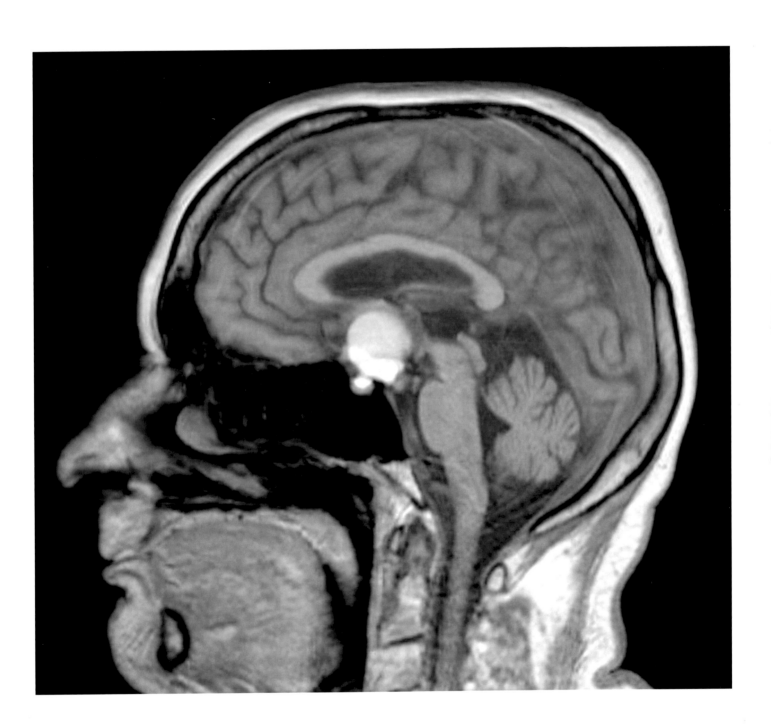

Tools of the trade

Throughout the historical record, man has always attempted to reshape the appearance of the human body. The ideal body aesthetic has changed over the centuries but in the recent decades we have seen exponential growth in plastic surgery. Everything from a rhinoplasty (*nose job*) to breast augmentation has become common place. This photograph shows fine surgical micro burs. These tools are used in many procedures, from dentistry to neurosurgery. Even though they might resemble a tool from the garage, make no mistake: these are very specialized. They are made of the highest quality stainless steel or titanium and many are diamond encrusted for more precise cutting capability. The micro bur tips are used for cleaning, cutting, reshaping, smoothing and carving even the hardest bone. This macro view reveals the organic symmetry and craftsmanship that is commonplace in the surgeon's armamentaria.

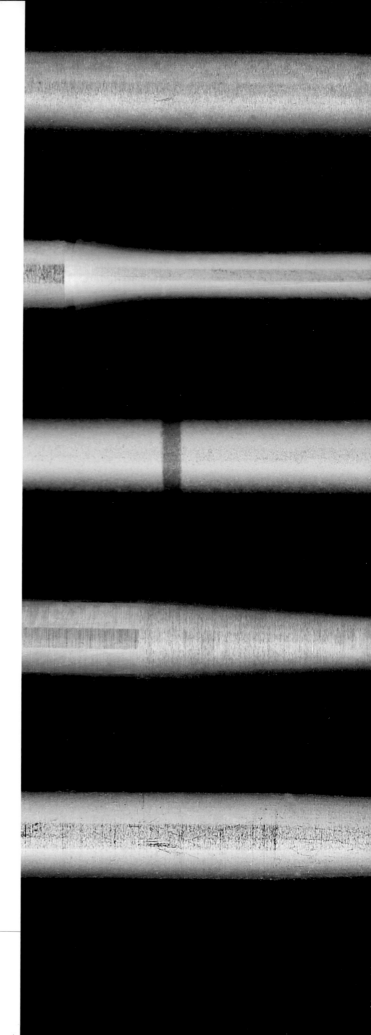

Alzheimer's disease

It is estimated that the adult brain carries more than 100 billion nerve cells (neurons) with branches that connect at more than 100 trillion points. Each nerve cell communicates by way of tiny electrical charges that are transmitted along its axons and dendrites. Where these nerve cells connect, called a synapse, secreted molecules called neurotransmitters are produced that signal to other nerve cells to further propagate the electrical signal. Scientists refer to this branching, dense network of cells as a neural forest. The signals that travel through these neurons form the basis of our feelings, thoughts and memories.

Alzheimer's disease, the most common cause of dementia in the elderly, is characterized by a steady decline in memory and normal everyday mental ability. As our nation grows older and the baby boomer generation ages, studies show that nearly half of people over the age of 85 have Alzheimer's. It is a progressive and fatal brain disease for which there is no cure, but in recent years new treatments have been developed that improve the quality of life for some patients. Alzheimer's disease is caused by the accumulation of abnormal proteins in nerve cells (*Tau proteins, leading to neurofibrillary tangles*) and in neurites (*ß-amyloid proteins, leading to plaques*). These accumulated proteins interfere with the way electrical charges travel within the brain, thus interrupting normal cell-to-cell signaling at synapses. Doctors are able to diagnose most cases of Alzheimer's disease through extensive testing. However, the disease can only be definitively diagnosed after death by performing an autopsy. Microscopic examination of the brain tissue, when stained with specific chemicals, typically reveals the plaques and tangles characteristic of Alzheimer's disease. An example of diseased brain tissue is shown at right. The small dark dots are neurons and the large fuzzy brown patches are amyloid plaques. A blood vessel is present in the upper right corner. *x200*

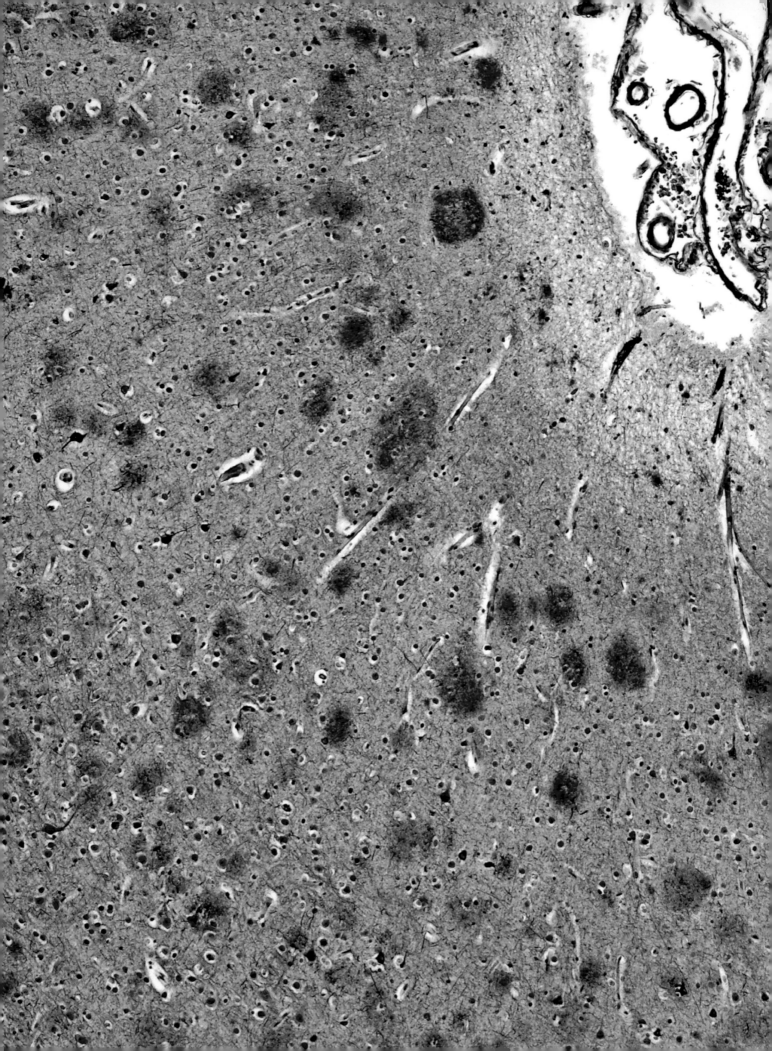

Angiography

Indocyanine green (ICG) is a fluorescent dye that is used
for the imaging of retinal and choroidal vasculatures
in a process called fluorescein angiography. A contrast
medium called sodium fluorescein is injected into a
vein in the patient's arm. The dye travels into the body's
circulatory system and is photographed as it travels
through the eye. Two filters called a barrier and an exciter
are used to limit the image to the color of light being
emitted by the fluorescent dye. Fourteen seconds after the
injection, the dye shows up in the arteries of the retina.
Over a two- to five-second period, the dye travels through
the tiny vessels, or capillaries, and fills the veins. Ten
minutes after the injection, the dye has almost emptied
from the eye, having stained the optic nerve head. This
normal progression of the flourescein dye is interrupted
by many diseases of the choroid, retina and retinal
vasculature. Fluorescein angiography is a test that helps in
the diagnosis of retinal disease and is used to determine if
laser treatment of the retina is warranted. *x60*

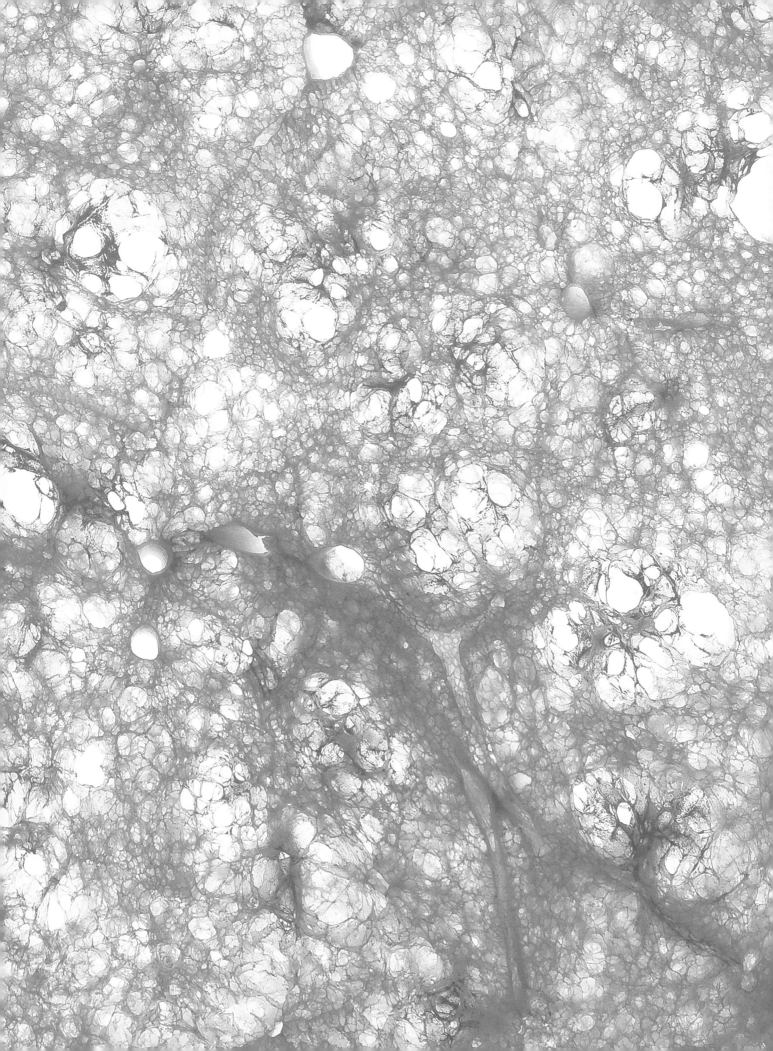

Chest

Paraffin blocks

"Let's see what the pathology shows!"

Many a patient has heard this phrase after a biopsy or surgical procedure, but what exactly does it mean? Anatomic Pathology is a specialty within the medical field that deals with the study of disease in tissues, cells or fluids. Pathologists are medical doctors and are often referred to as the "doctor's doctor" because they play a consultant role by interpreting the findings in biopsies, tissue specimens or body fluids that help a clinician understand his/her patient's disease and how to treat it. But how does an anatomic pathologist do this exactly? When a piece of tissue is taken from a patient, the pathologist fixes the specimen using a chemical called formalin and then dehydrates the tissue by incubating it in solvents and alcohol. Once this occurs, the dehydrated tissue can be permeated with hot wax creating a paraffinized version of the tissue. This is important to do because the paraffin acts as a support that allows histotechnologists to cut very thin sections of the tissue. These thin sections (*the width of a human hair*) are mounted on glass slides and then stained so that the pathologist can examine the tissue sections under a microscope (*for example, see Histological Stains in the chapter "Abdomen"*). The image at right is an example of several different paraffin blocks created from different tissue specimens from different patients. Depending on the pathologist working in the lab that day, this particularly busy histology lab has used different colored plastic holders (*known as "cassettes"*) to keep track of each pathologist's specimens while they are being fixed and paraffin embedded.

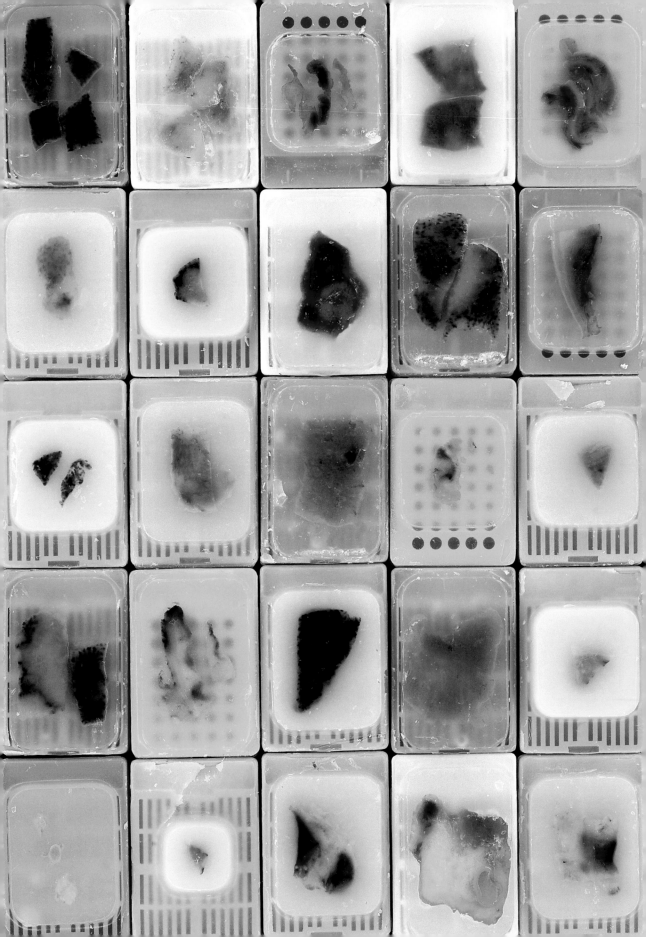

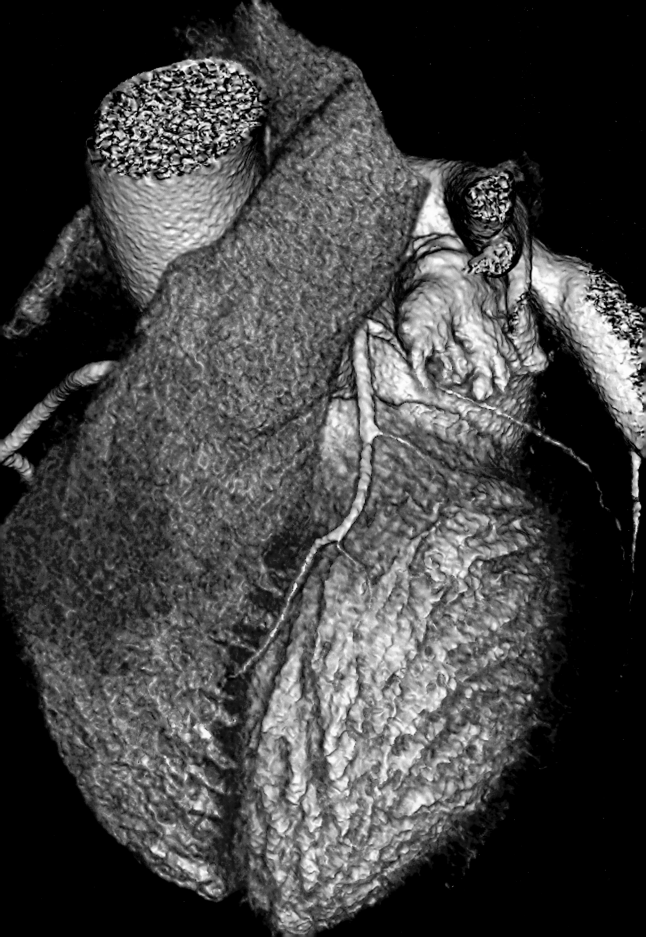

Human heart, multi-detector row computed tomography (MDCT)

The introduction of multi-detector row computed tomography (MDCT) in 1999 provided the technical requirements to perform cardiac imaging with CT systems that followed the traditional design of a rotating X-ray tube and detectors. Rapidly moving anatomic structures, like the heart, could be visualized with good image quality. Early experience with the initial four-row detector scanners demonstrated the potential of MDCT to assess the coronary arteries for the presence of coronary artery disease. Currently, 64-detector row CT scanners are commonly used, and deliver relatively robust morphological and functional imaging of the heart and its blood vessels. The most recent generations of MDCT have the ability to acquire 320-detector rows simultaneously, which provide whole-heart coverage and allow for generating a cardiac image within one heart beat. These state-of-the-art MDCT scanners make coronary CT imaging less susceptible to artifacts from heart rhythm disorders. Three-dimensional (3D) MDCT reconstruction allows viewing the heart from any warranted view, facilitating diagnostic assessment.

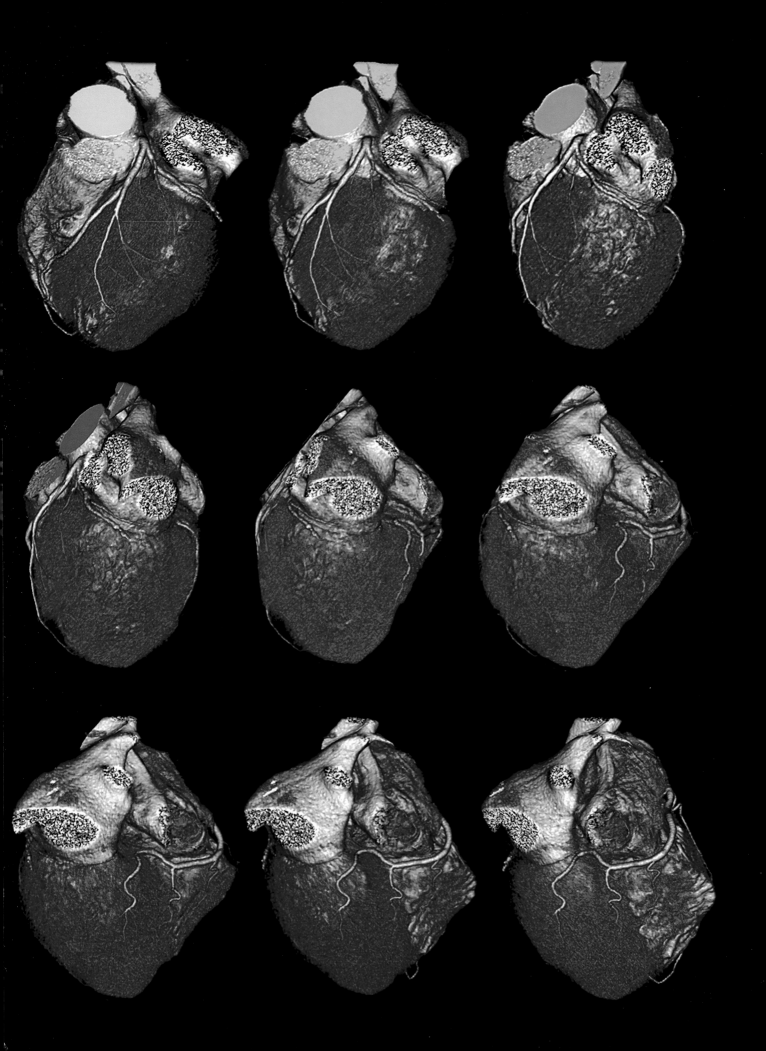

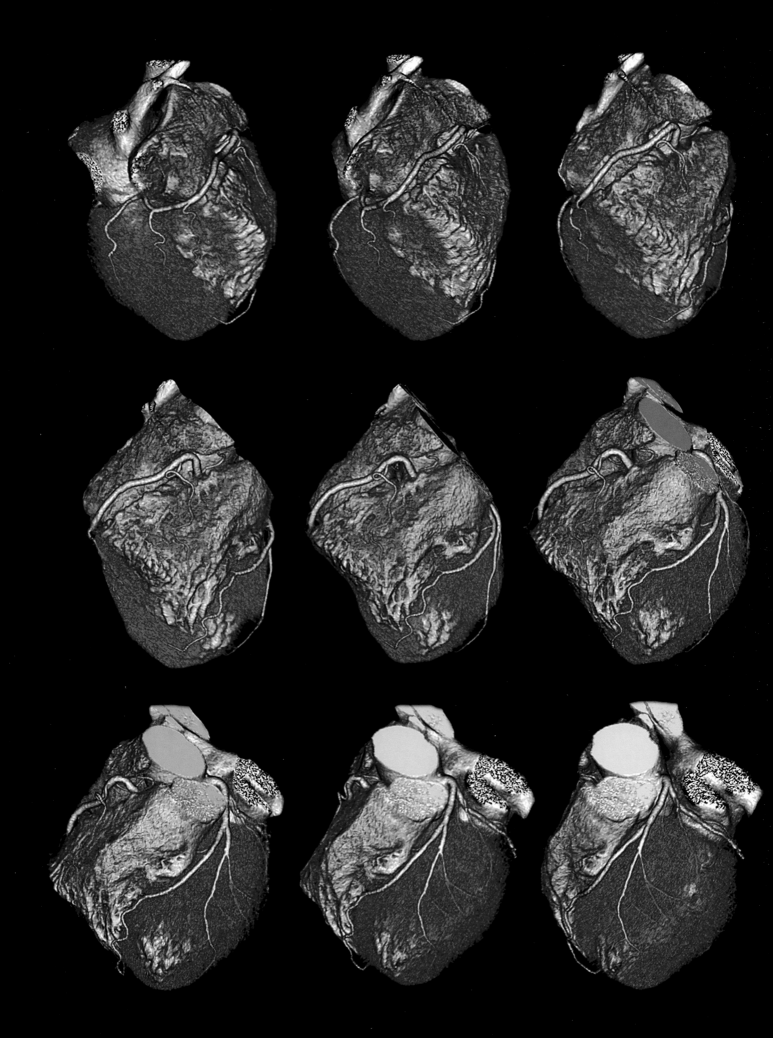

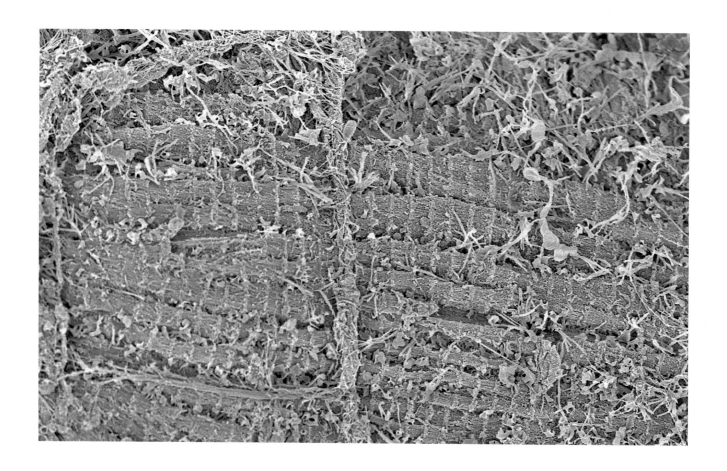

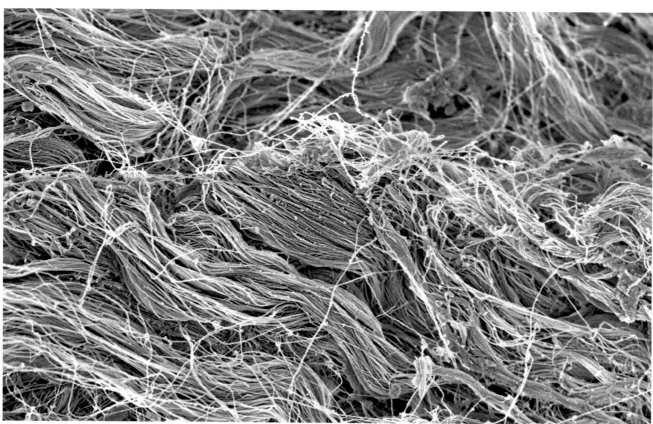

Myocardial infarction and heart failure

Heart failure after a myocardial infarction remains the leading cause of death and hospitalization in industrialized countries and is an emerging public health concern in the developing world. In the US alone, over 5 million people are living with symptomatic heart failure. Therefore, any new treatment modality that benefits heart failure patients has the potential to result in dramatic improvement in health outcomes as well as substantial cost saving for the community.

Major scientific strides in the past few years have challenged the dogma that the heart is a post-mitotic organ and accumulated evidence indicates that cardiac muscle cells have the potential to divide and renew themselves. This has led to the concept that cardiac regeneration can be therapeutically achieved. The utilization of cell therapy for cardiac repair follows this paradigm, and there is hope that stem cells may realize this potential. However, as shown here, it is the ambitious goal of regenerative cell-based therapies to transform a chronic collagen-dense infarct scar (*bottom image*), which is commonly found in heart failure patients, back into viable functional myocardium (*top image*). The different characteristics of both tissue types can be clearly appreciated in these three-dimensional scanning electron microscope images. *x7000*

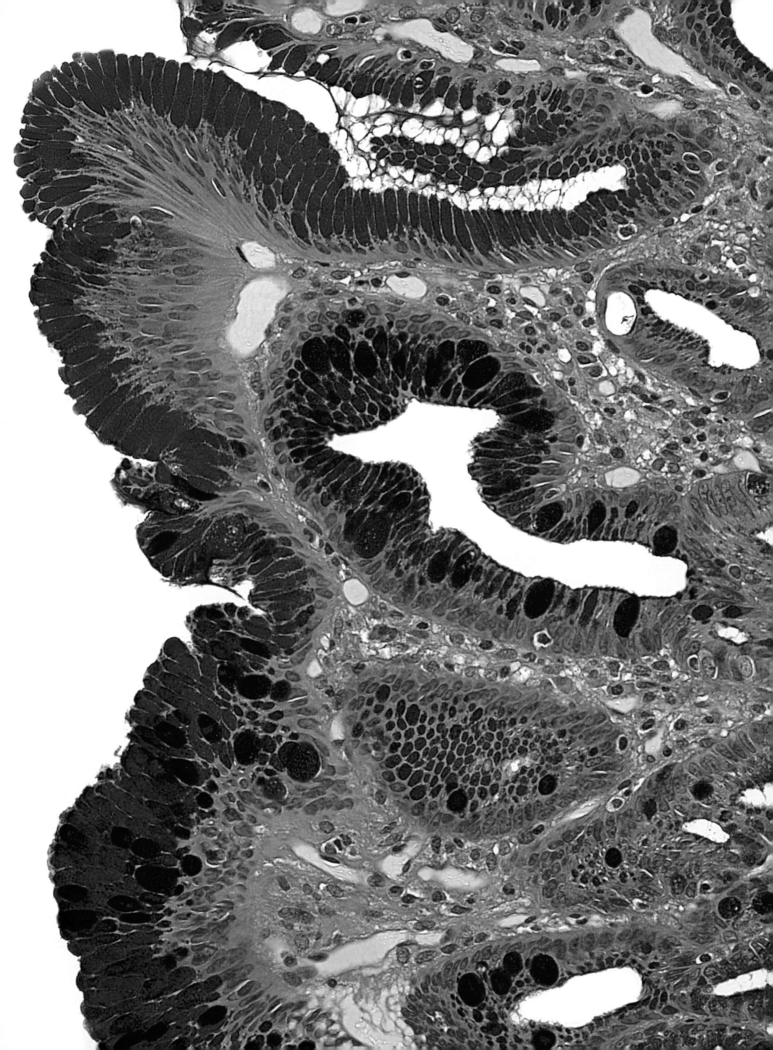

Gastroesophageal reflux disease and Barrett's esophagus

The esophagus is a tubular shaped organ located in the chest that connects the throat to the stomach. When a person swallows food, the muscular wall of the esophagus rhythmically contracts so that the food is propelled towards the stomach. The stomach then produces acid and enzymes to begin digestion. To protect the delicate esophageal lining from these highly acidic stomach contents, the lower esophagus contains a thickening of the muscular wall called the lower esophageal sphincter. This specialized muscle is closed most of the time, only opening when swallowed food or liquid is moved down the esophagus or when a person belches or vomits. Nonetheless, when acid enters the esophagus it leads to an uncomfortable burning sensation in the chest. This is known as gastroesophageal reflux, or heartburn.

Esophageal manometry is a method to measure the pressure within the esophagus. It not only evaluates the rhythmic contractions of the esophagus but also the pressure of the lower esophageal sphincter. The images on the *following page* are from a patient whose esophagus is being evaluated by this method. Twelve panels are shown, each representing a different moment in time. In each panel, the pressure in the throat is shown at the top left, while pressure in the lower esophageal sphincter is shown at the bottom right. Red corresponds to areas of high pressure during or shortly after swallowing.

Left untreated, gastroesophageal reflux can lead to scarring of the esophageal lining and, in some individuals, a precancerous condition known as Barrett's esophagus. This condition is named for Norman Barrett, a British surgeon doctor who first reported the condition. In Barrett's esophagus, the cells lining the lower esophagus transform from normal esophageal cells to cells that are typically present within the small intestine. This phenomenon is known as "intestinal metaplasia," and is thought to be an attempt of the lower esophagus to protect itself from the chronic exposure to stomach acid. Barrett's esophagus is associated with an increased risk of esophageal cancer. Therefore, once Barrett's esophagus is diagnosed, patients must undergo frequent surveillance for early esophageal cancer. This is best accomplished by biopsying the esophageal lining and examining it under a microscope to look for intestinal metaplasia. Shown in the image to the left, the large blue cells (*known as goblet cells*) are an indication that intestinal metaplasia has occurred in the lower esophagus and that the patient has Barrett's esophagus. *x400*

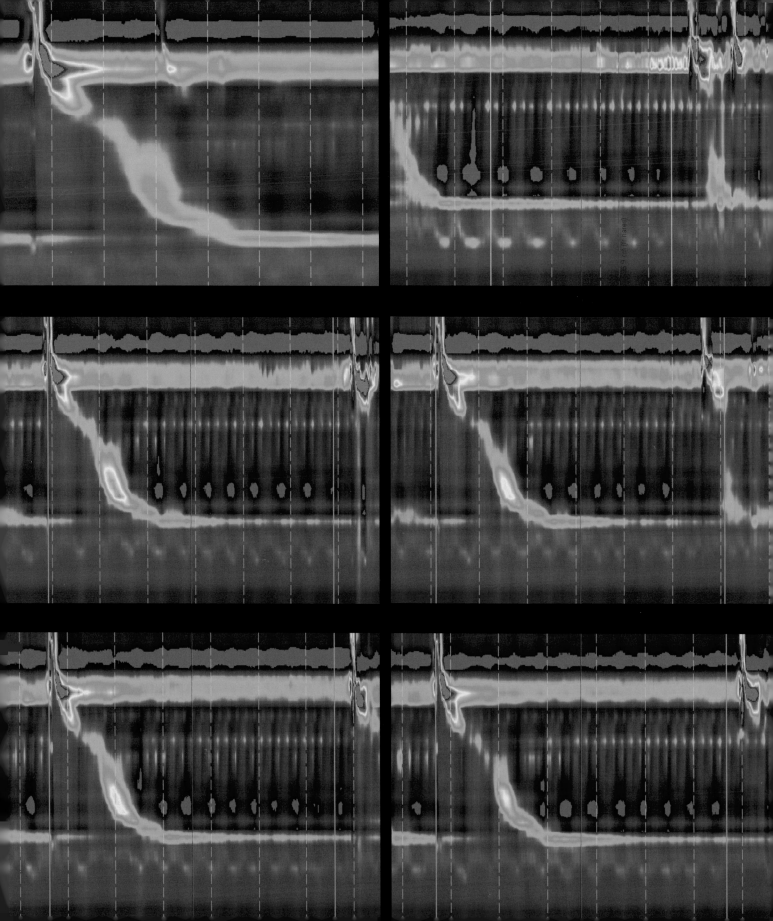

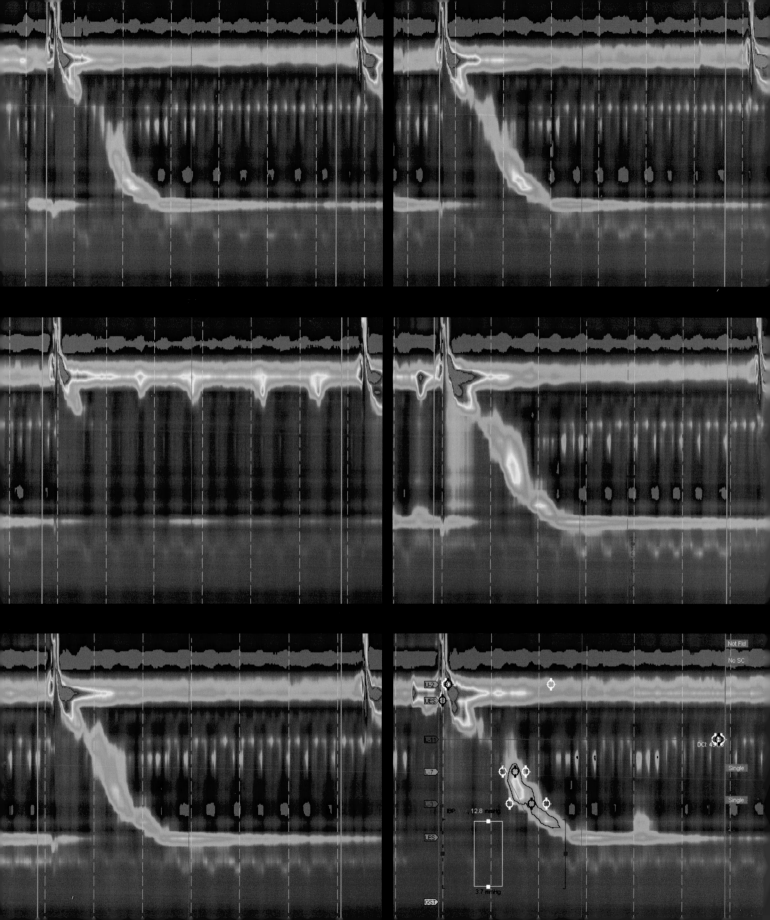

Smoker's lung

We have all been taught that smoking causes lung cancer, but too few realize that cigarette smoking is also responsible for other forms of cancer, including cancers of the larynx (*voice box*), the oral cavity (*mouth*), esophagus (*the tube connecting the mouth to the stomach*) and the urinary bladder. If that isn't bad enough, cigarette smoking also causes emphysema, bronchitis, heart disease and strokes, and, sadly, smoking during pregnancy can cause sudden infant death syndrome (SIDS). Simply put, cigarette smoking causes 1 in 5 deaths in the United States and is the leading cause of preventable death.

Emphysema, pictured on the right, is a disease in which cigarette smoking destroys the alveoli (*small air sacs*) in the lung. As a result, the air-spaces in the lung enlarge abnormally and the exchange of oxygen for carbon dioxide is impaired. Patients suffering with emphysema have difficulty breathing and develop coughing and wheezing. As the disease progresses, patients with emphysema develop weight loss and muscle wasting, and have trouble breathing when lying down. Some patients breath fast (*hyperventilate*) in their struggle for air, giving them the appearance of a "pink puffer."

This section of lung illustrates the destruction of lung tissue that is characteristic of emphysema. Note the areas where the light shines through the lung, as well as black spots representing carbon accumulation from years of smoking. *x4*

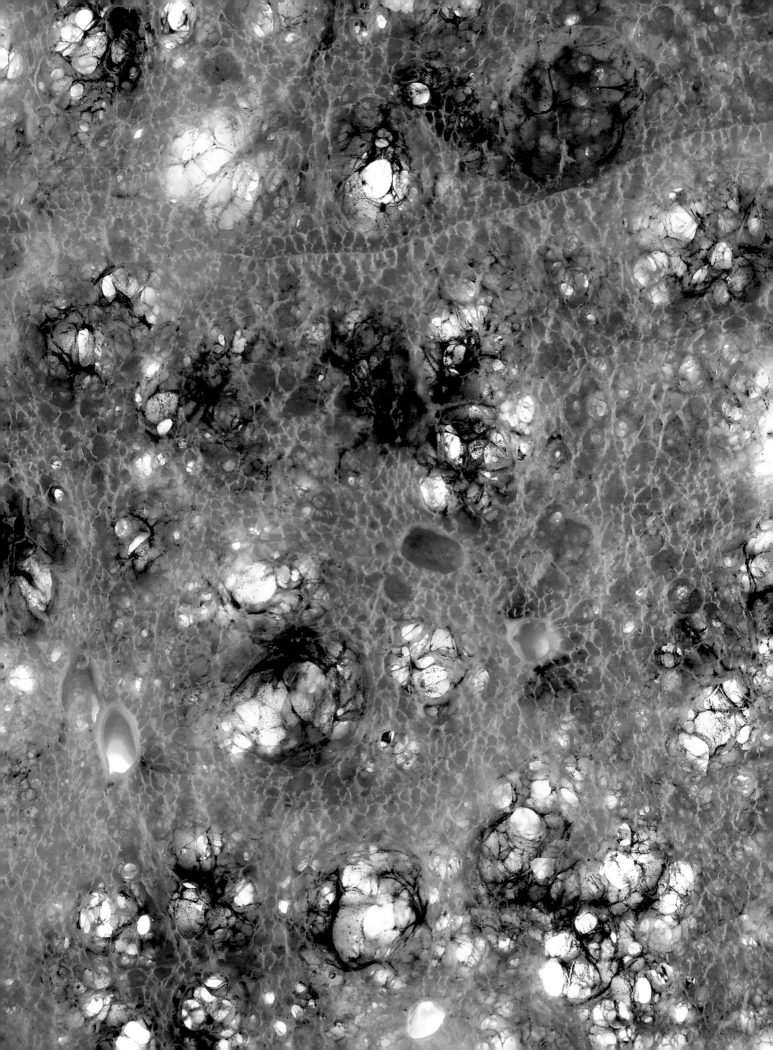

Lung cancer cell culture

Lung cancer is the number one cause of cancer-related death in both men and women in the United States. The most common cause of lung cancer is long-term exposure to tobacco smoke. Repeated exposure to carcinogens in the tobacco smoke causes the cells within the lung to grow abnormally, leading to cancer. One powerful method to study lung cancer is to obtain cancer cells from a patient's tumor and grow them in culture dishes in a laboratory. Incredibly, even outside the patient these cells continue to grow and divide, provided they are grown in solutions that provide nutrients and are kept in special incubators that maintain the human body temperature of 98.6°. Scientists can then use these cells to test the effects of new drugs as they are developed, or to understand the many changes that caused the patient's normal lung cells to transform into cancer cells. The image at right is an example of one such lung cancer that is growing in cell culture. When viewed under a microscope, the cells take on the appearance of an irregular cobblestone road, a feature they retained from when they were normal cells lining an airway within the patient's lung. *x200*

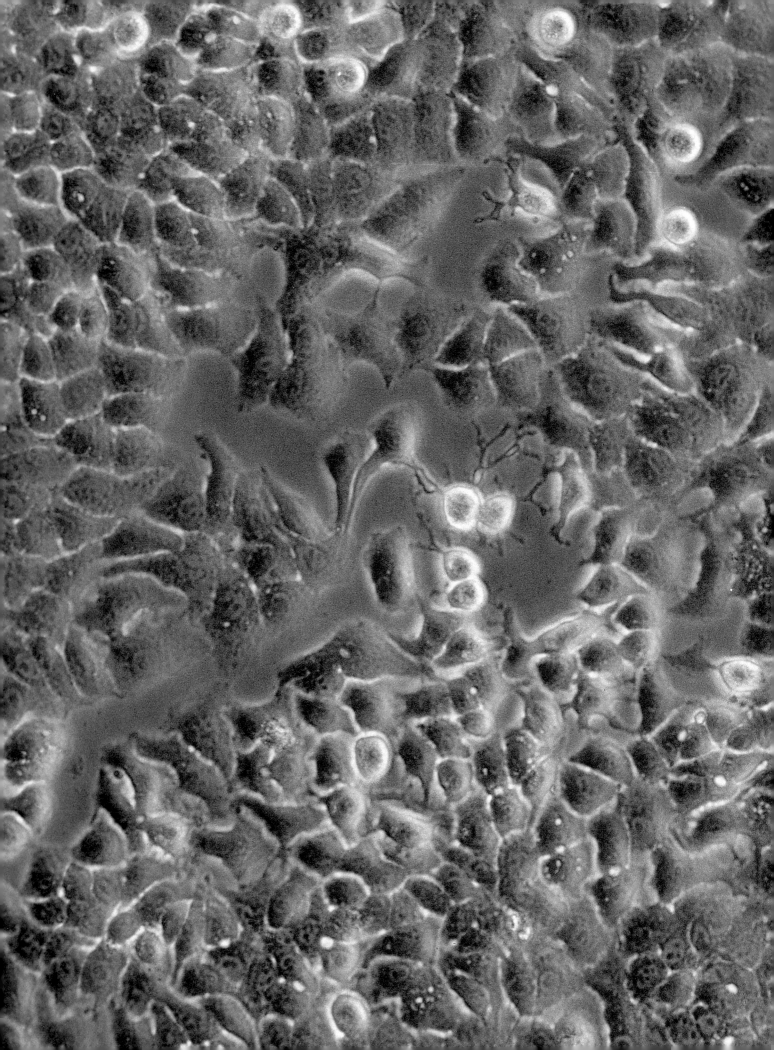

Tuberculosis

More than 125 years after its discovery, *Mycobacterium tuberculosis*, the bacterium that causes tuberculosis (TB), is still surging with 8.8 and 1.5 million new cases of TB and deaths, respectively. Of the more than 2 billion people latently infected with *M. tuberculosis*, many develop reactivation disease (*relapse*), years after the initial infection. *M. tuberculosis* spreads when bacteria coughed up by a diseased person with active TB are breathed into the lungs of an uninfected person. Subsequently, the host immune system develops lesions called granulomas in the lungs, which surround the bacteria. As the granuloma develops, host cells in the center of the granuloma die and form necrotic areas, classically called "caseous" as they resemble *caseum* which means "cheese" in Latin. These caseous lesions are the hallmark of human TB.

The colored lesions in this image represent granulomas from a live mouse (*C3HeB/FeJ strain*), which, similar to humans, develop caseous lesions in response to infection by *M. tuberculosis*. The lesions were imaged using [18F] 2-fluoro-deoxy-D-glucose (FDG)—positron emission tomography (PET) scan—an imaging technique used mostly to diagnose and monitor cancers. The brightness of the lesion represents its activity, with brighter lesions being more active. The bony structure (*rib cage and scapula*), shown in grey, was imaged using a computed tomography (CT) scan, performed at the same time.

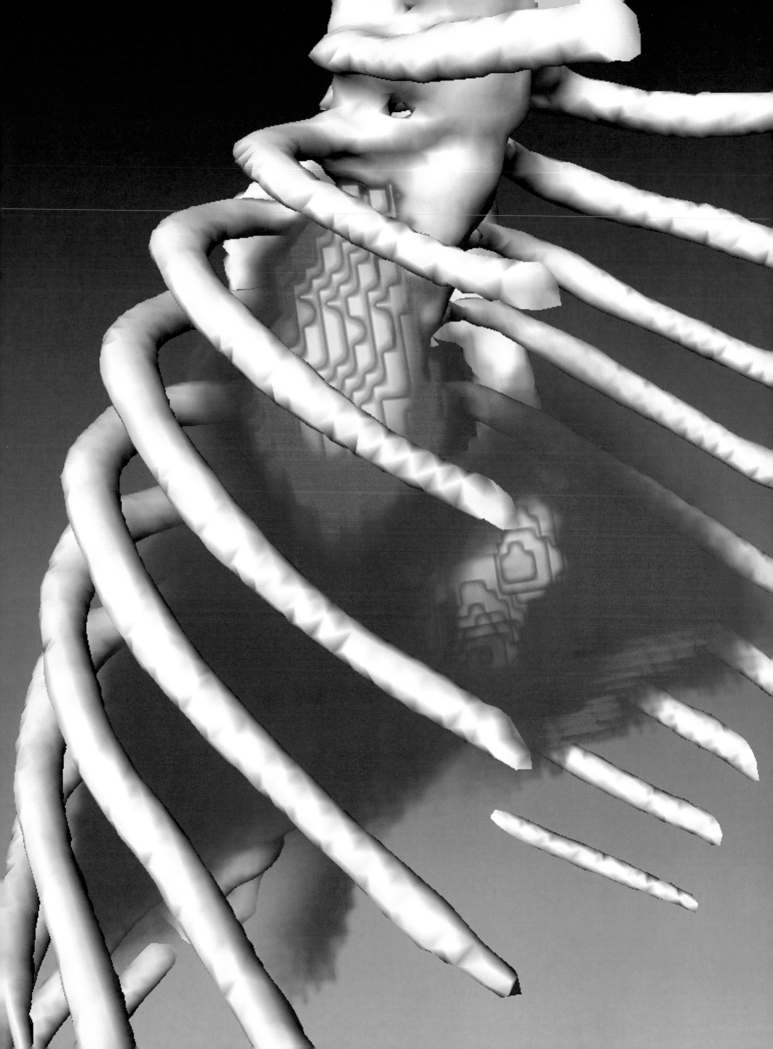

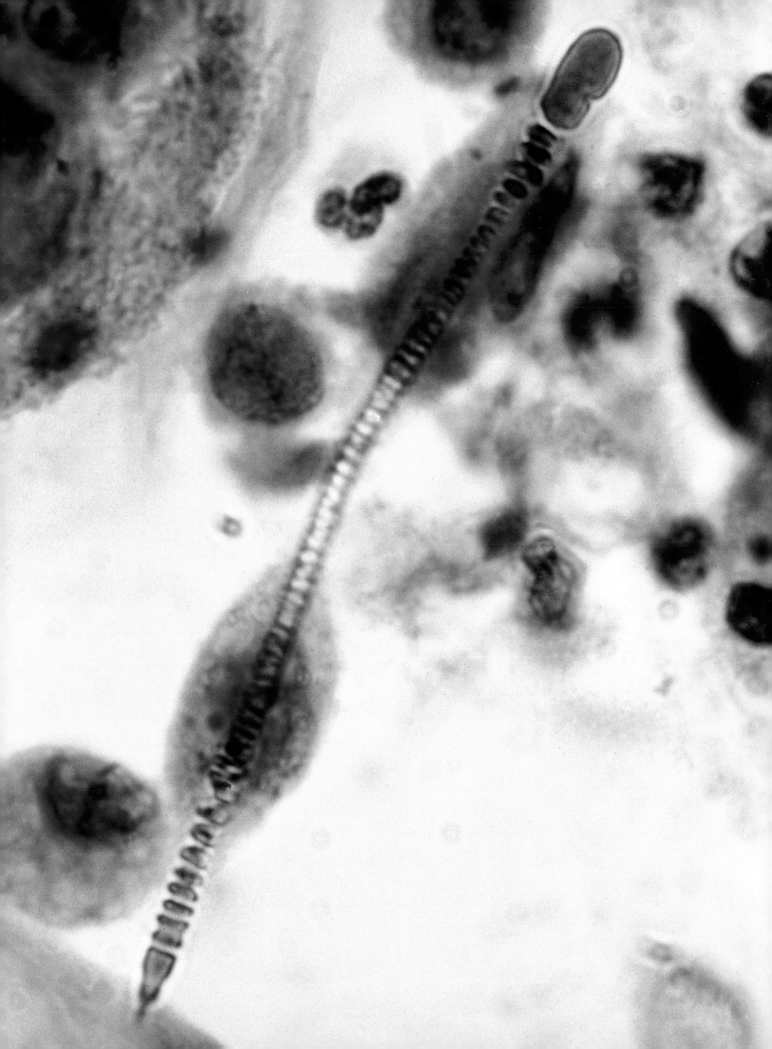

Asbestos body in the lung

At first look, asbestos seems like a fantastic material. It is lightweight, naturally occurring, does not burn and can be woven into fabric. There is one important drawback however—exposure to asbestos puts people at risk for serious lung disease. Many people are surprised to discover that asbestos has been in use for at least 2,000 years. It is even more surprising to note that ancient Greeks and Romans knew about the health risks of asbestos, as they recorded observations of weavers who worked with asbestos suffering from pulmonary illnesses. Specifically, asbestos exposure is associated with the development of malignant mesothelioma (*a neoplasm derived from the pleural lining of the lungs*), pulmonary fibrosis (*asbestosis*) and lung carcinomas (the latter particularly in patients who smoke). The risk of developing asbestos-related lung disease is correlated with the level of exposure to these fibers, the fiber dimensions and the fiber persistence in the lung/pleura. Long thin asbestos fibers are known as "amphiboles," and serpentine feathery fibers are given the elegant name of "chrysotiles." Asbestos bodies are distinguished by their "beaded" appearance, by their thin, translucent, yellow-white core and by their clubbed ends. This image shows a microscopic snake-like asbestos body in fluid from a bronchoalveolar lavage (*fluid used to "rinse" a diseased lung*), stained for iron. The blue and red forms in the background are cells from the patient's lung. *x600*

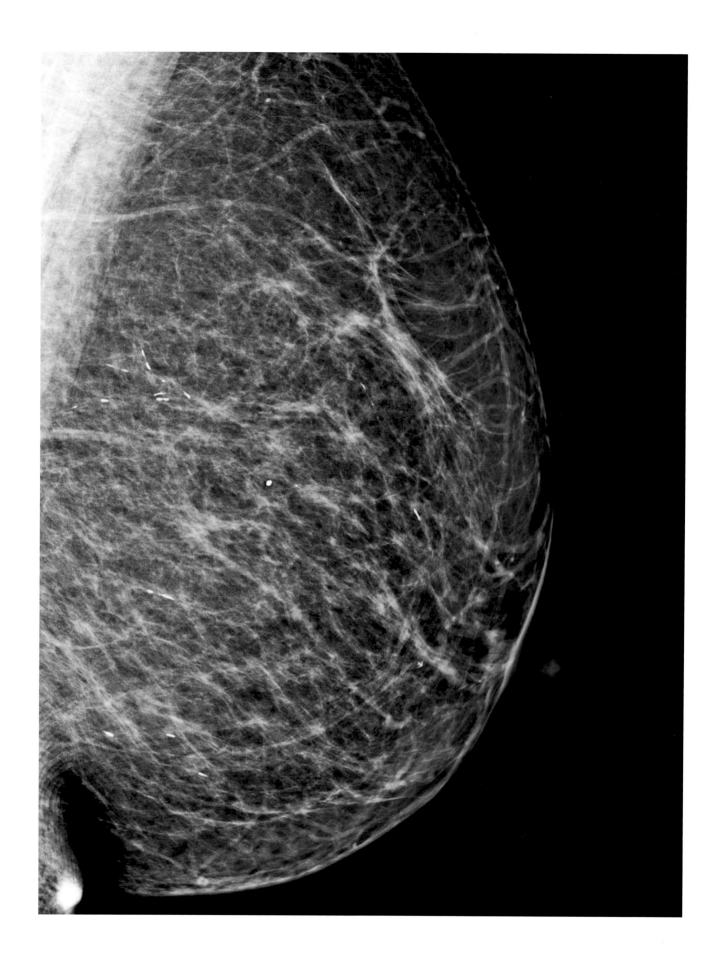

Mammography

Breast cancer is the most common cancer and the second leading cause of cancer death in women. The goal of screening mammography is the early detection of breast cancer, so that treatment can start before the cancer spreads elsewhere in the body and becomes incurable. Mammography is a special radiographic technique that uses low dose x-rays to detect the tiny calcifications, discrete mass, or architectural distortion of breast tissue that may signify a cancer. Radiologists, the doctors who read mammograms, have extensive training in evaluating these signs of cancer, which are often very subtle. Additionally, there are many other causes of calcifications or masses within the breast which are not worrisome for cancer (*for example, the smooth rod-like calcifications seen in this mammogram are benign*). Mammography is just one of several different imaging modalities used by radiologists to evaluate breast disease—others include ultrasound, MRI and PEM (*Positive Emission Mamography*). Each type of imaging test has unique advantages in evaluating the breast tissue, and the most appropriate one depends on patient-specific clinical circumstances.

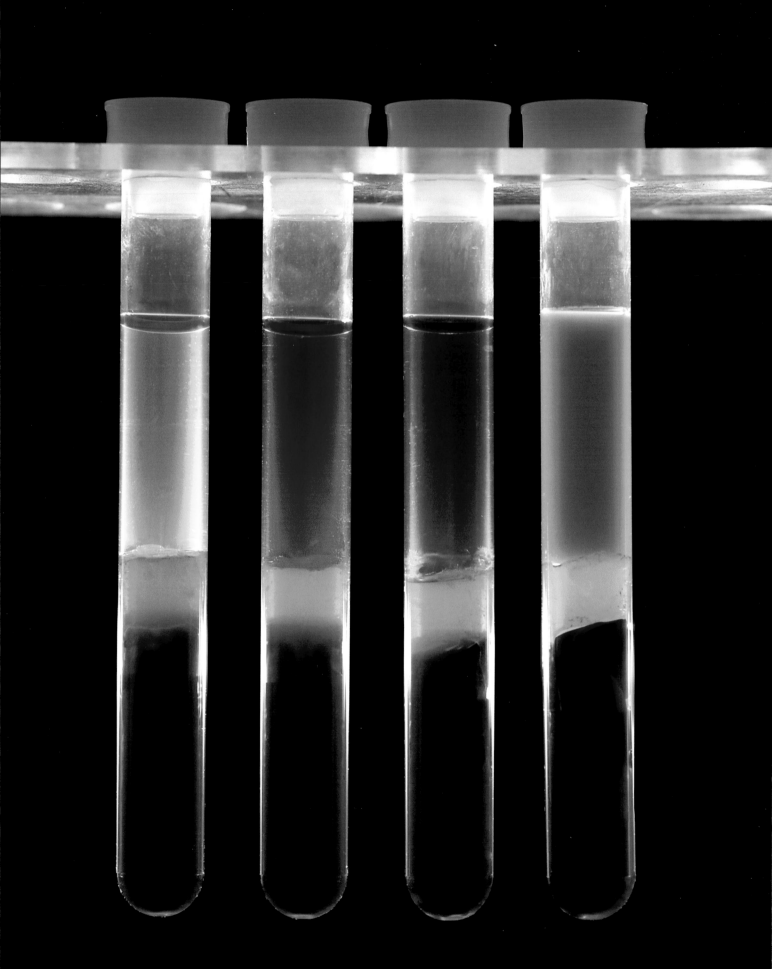

Clinical laboratory testing

Blood consists of red blood cells that carry oxygen, white blood cells that fight infections, and plasma, the liquid portion that the cells are suspended in. Plasma can be further separated into serum and clotting proteins. The picture on the left shows what blood components look like when separated by centrifugation into serum on the top and the clotted blood cells on the bottom. A large number of substances can be measured in serum to assess renal (*kidney*), hepatic (*liver*) and digestive, endocrine (*hormones*), fluid and electrolyte (*sodium, potassium, etc.*), acid-base (*blood gases*), cardiovascular and nutritional status, and to diagnose and monitor disease. Some commonly measured analytes include glucose, to diagnose diabetes, cholesterol, a risk factor for heart disease and PSA, or prostate-specific antigen, for the early detection and monitoring of prostate cancer. However, just the color of serum can often indicate disease. The tube on the left shows a typical serum sample from a healthy person that is light yellow in color. The second sample is hemolyzed and is red due to the release of hemoglobin from damaged red blood cells. Hemolysis can occur within the body and can also be an artifact resulting from specimen collection. The third sample is icteric, its yellowish and greenish color (*jaundice*) is due to elevated concentrations of bilirubin, a breakdown product of heme in hemoglobin. This elevation is typically indicative of liver disease or injury. The fourth sample has lipemia from high concentrations of triglycerides or fat which causes the milky-white opaque appearance. Lipids can appear in blood after eating a meal high in fat content or result from a metabolic disorder.

Foreign body in human lung, polarized light

A young male with a history of intravenous drug abuse was noted to have a miliary (*seed-like*) nodular pattern on chest radiographs. Following a work-up which failed to reveal an infectious source, a lung biopsy was performed. Polarized light reveals refractile foreign material within the nodules consistent with an inert substance (*such as talcum powder*) used to "cut" or dilute the amount of drugs. The combined radiographic and pathologic picture is referred to as "talc granulomatosis." *x200*

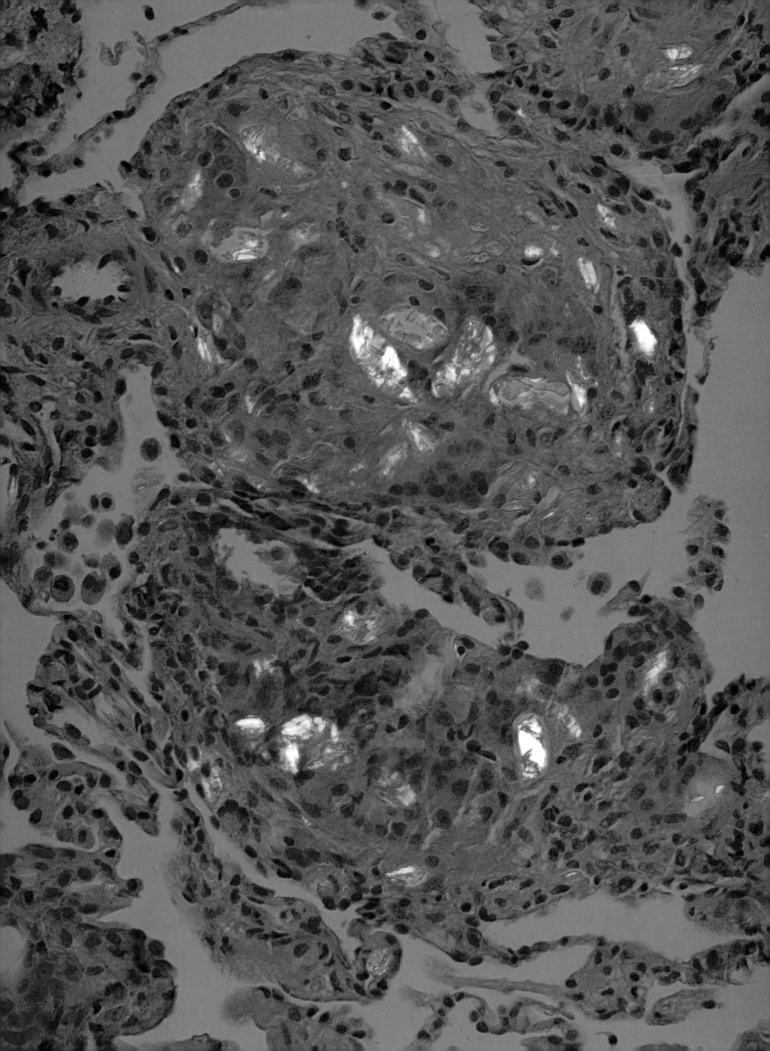

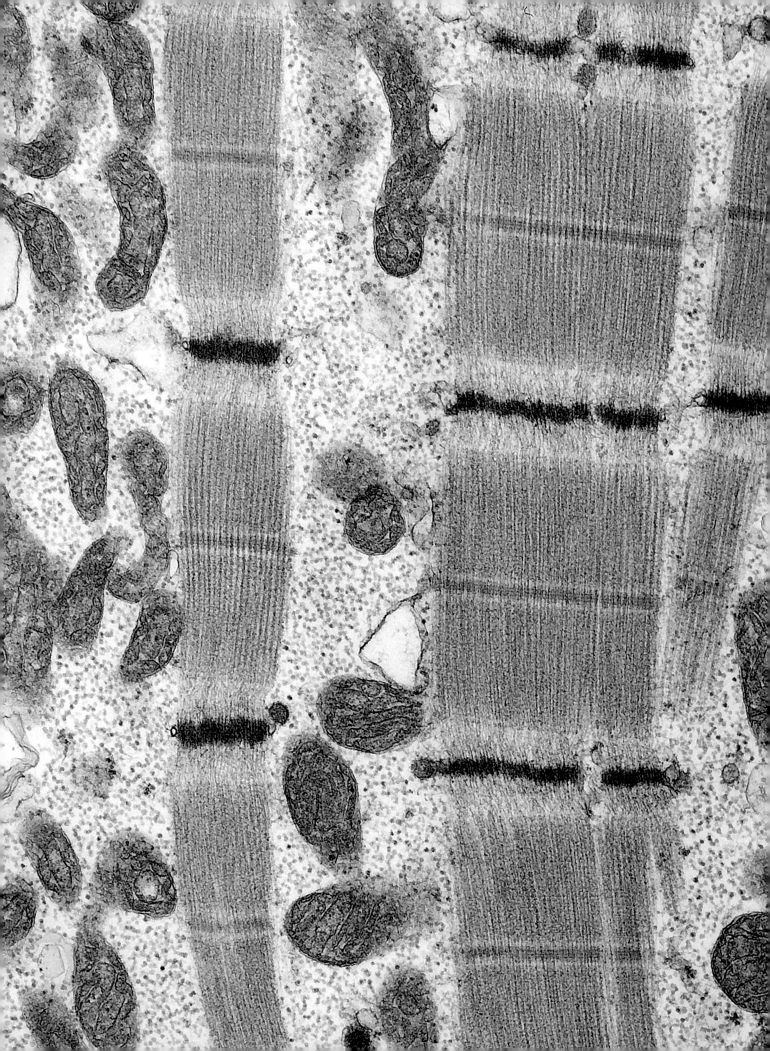

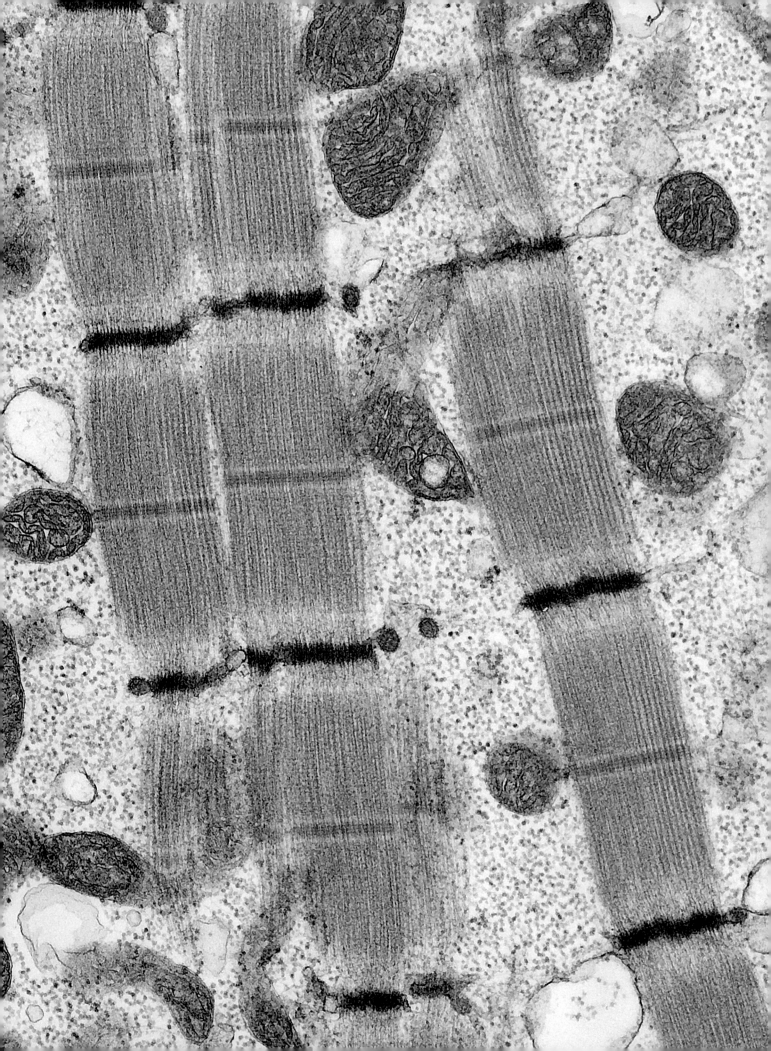

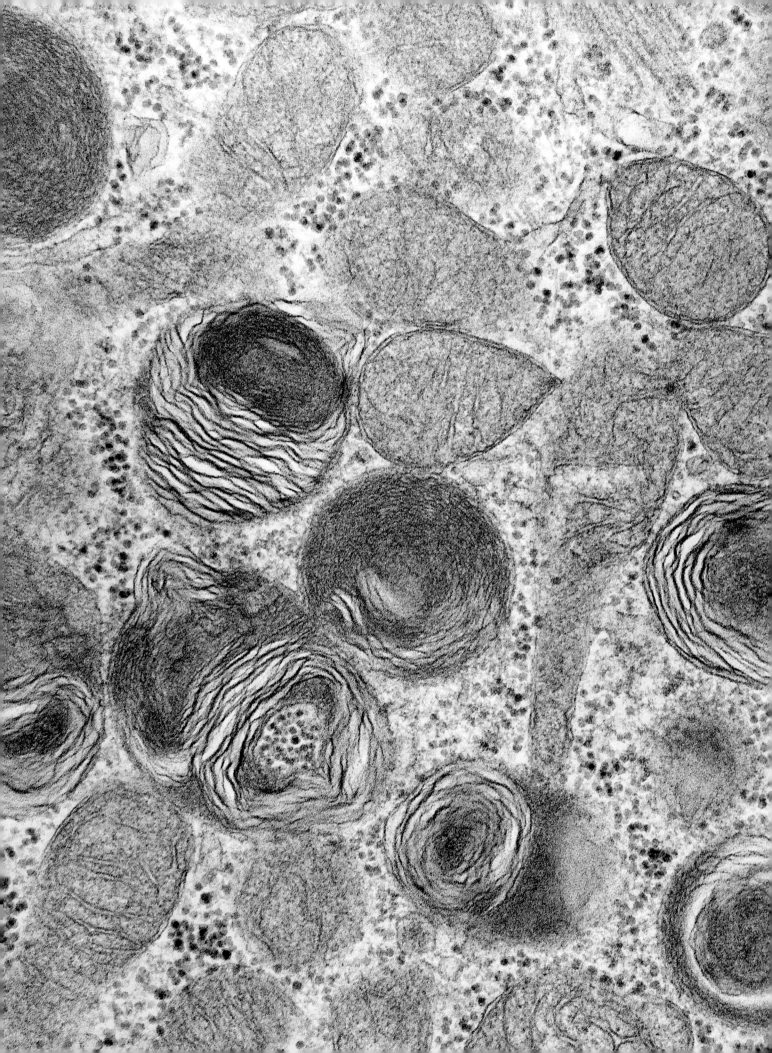

Ultrastructure of a heart myocyte and myelin figures

The beating of the heart is the result of a complex interplay of cardiac muscle cells and nerve stimulation. Healthy heart muscle cells, as seen on the overleaf (*x14,000*), are primarily composed of myofibrils and mitochondria. Myofibrils are repetitive strands of bamboo-like structures that extend the length of the cell. These myofibrils contract and expand 80 to 100 times every minute, with long protein complexes pulling on each other like a tug of war, then releasing. The mitochondria, small ovoid structures with folded membranes called cristae, are the engines that supply energy to move the myofibrils. Scattered amongst these two main structures are tiny balls of glycogen, the raw ingredient that powers the mitochondrial engines.

In certain diseases of the heart other structures can appear. Myelin figures, or "Zebroid bodies" (*opposite, x28,000*) are so named because of their concentric structure similar to the myelination of peripheral nerves. They look like a sliced open ball of wire. Here they are interspersed with mitochondria of similar size and glycogen granules. Interestingly, myelin figures are seen in two unrelated diseases. One is a genetic disorder called Fabry disease and the second is chronic exposure to some medications. Myelin figures interfere with the normal function of the myocyte, causing the heart to stiffen, which in turn reduces the power of each heartbeat.

Telomere fluorescent in situ hybridization (TEL-FISH)

Telomeres are segments of repetitive DNA located at the ends of chromosomes that protect the ends of the chromosome from being destroyed. If cells divided without telomeres, they would lose the end of their chromosomes, and the necessary information this DNA encodes for. Thus, an important role of telomere DNA is to limit the number of divisions a cell goes through, thereby controlling the aging process and affecting an individual's lifespan. Telomeres also protect the ends of different chromosomes from fusing with each other, leading to chromosome rearrangements. These chromosome rearrangements can lead to cancer, so cells are normally destroyed when telomeres are consumed. Many human cancers may develop when cells bypass this important control, leading scientists to speculate that this mechanism is a trade-off between aging and cancer. One way to study telomeres in normal and cancer cells is to use fluorescently labeled DNA molecules that specifically fuse with telomeric DNA. This method is known as telomere fluorescent in situ hybridization. When applied to samples of breast cancer (*opposite*) or testis cancer (*overleaf*), the remarkable expansion of telomere DNA in the cancer cells is seen as a sea of red speckles, in contrast to normal cells in which the telomere DNA is imperceptible. *x400*

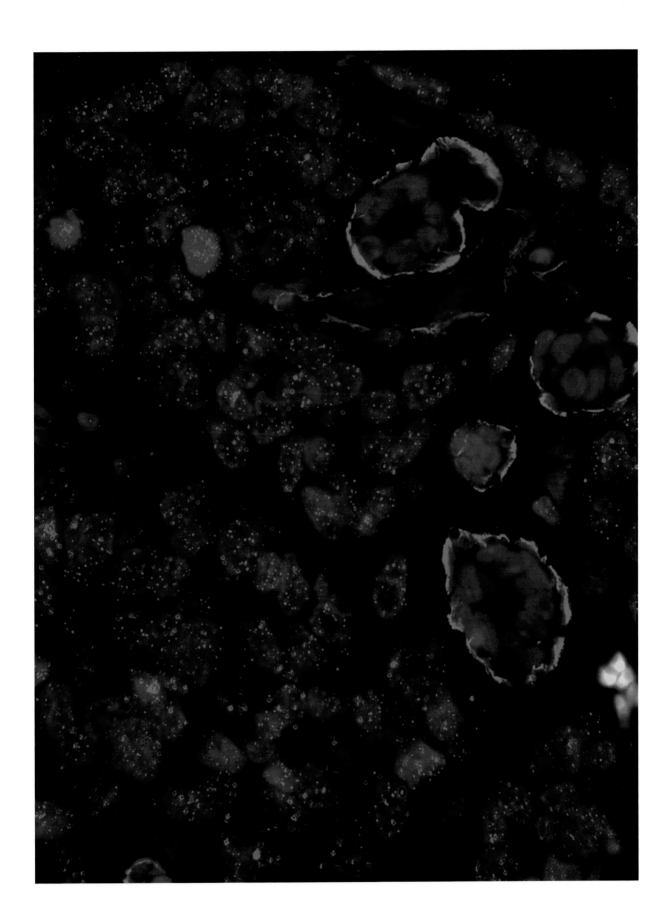

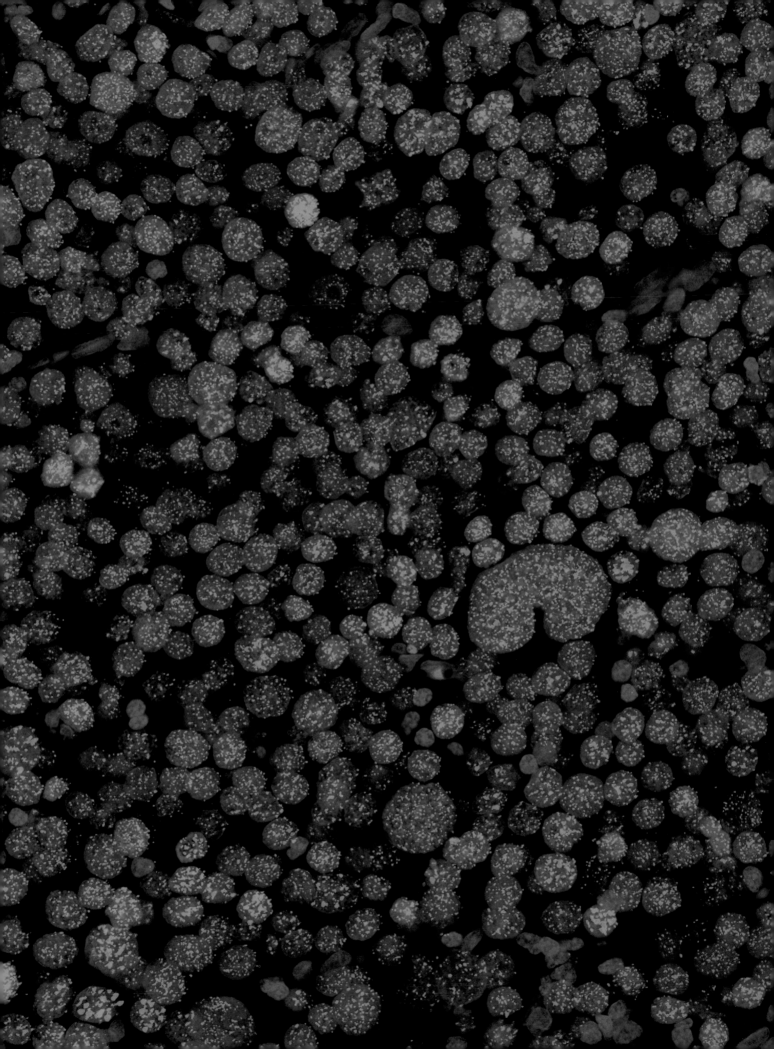

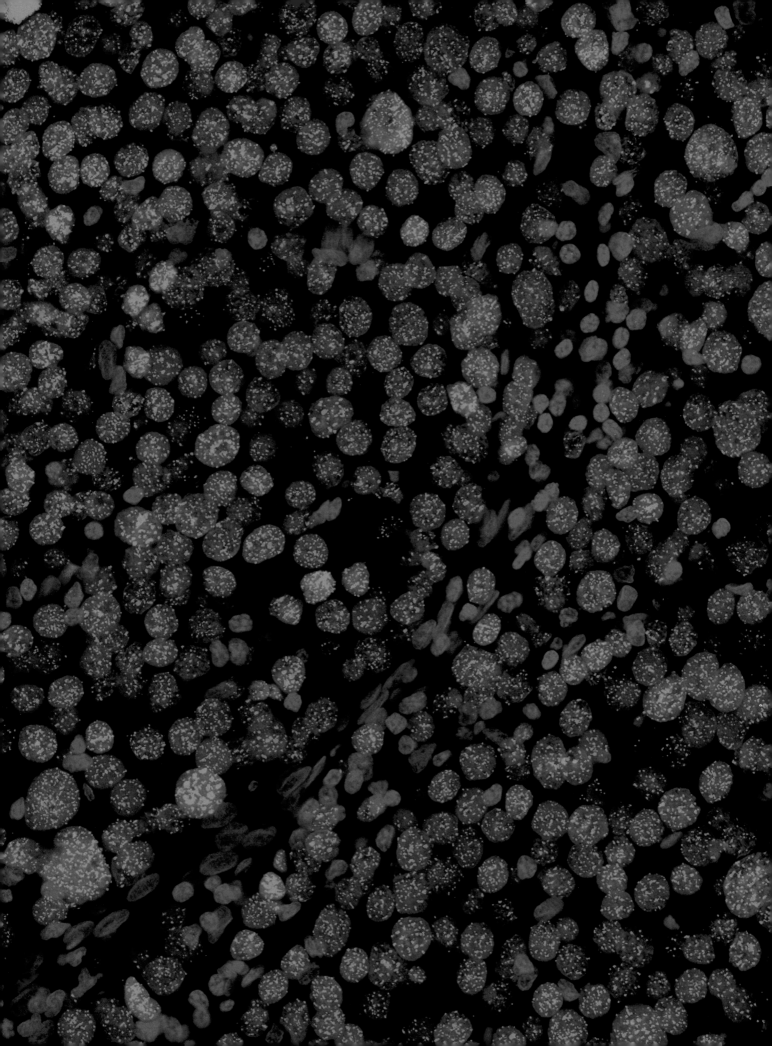

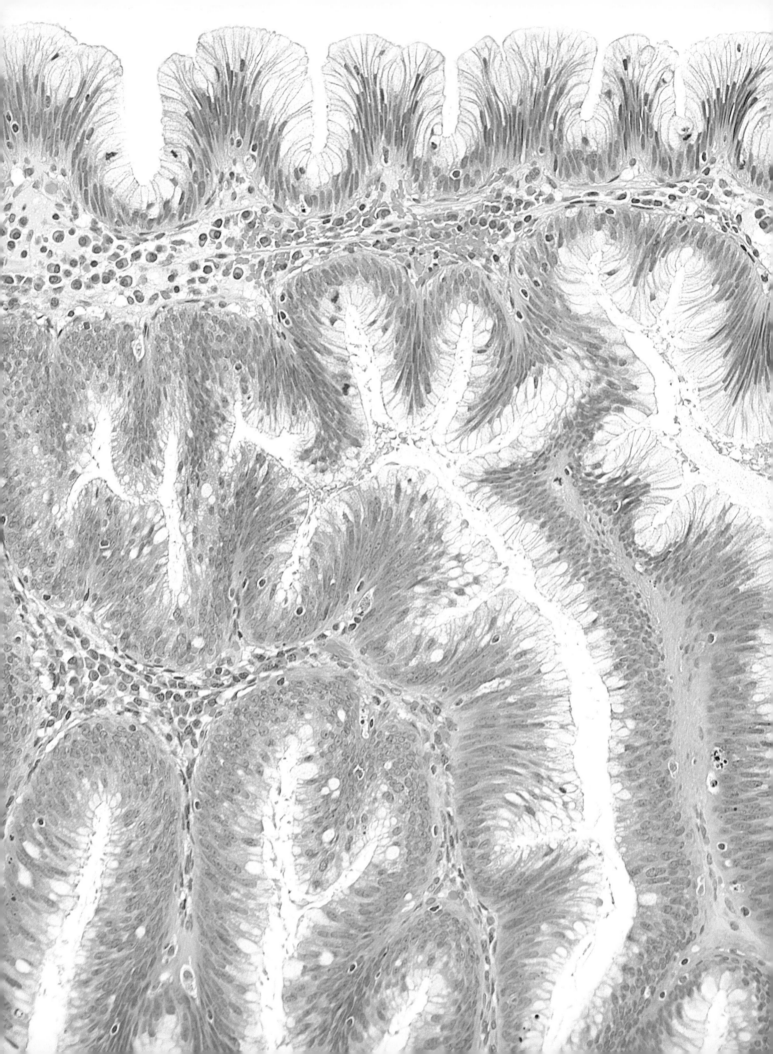

Abdomen

Salmonella enteritidis

The *Salmonella* species of bacteria, named for the veterinary pathologist Daniel Elmer Salmon, are represented by more than 1000 different variants. They are found throughout the environment, and in both warm and cold-blooded animals, including humans. Most forms of Salmonella have never been linked to humans, and in most people, stomach acid can destroy the organisms. However, if eaten in large enough amounts within contaminated or uncooked food, the bacteria can survive within the intestine and cause the ailment commonly known as "food poisoning" that is characterized by diarrhea and abdominal pain. Infants, young children and the elderly are much more susceptible to infection by ingesting a small number of bacteria, as are patients with a weakened immune system. A culture of *Salmonella enteritidis* is shown at right using scanning electron microscopy, allowing it to be magnified 2,750 times from its original size. The bacteria are seen as light green oval shaped organisms, and the darker green filaments are the bacteria's flagellae, i.e., organelles that allow the bacteria to be mobile in their environment.

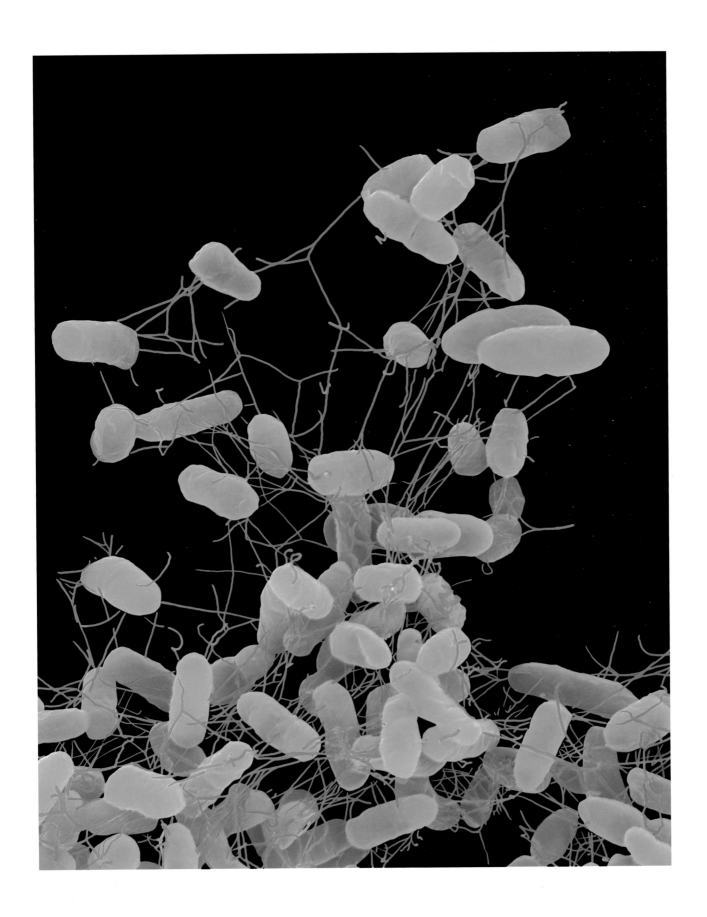

Gallstones

Gallstones are solid crystalline deposits that develop within the gallbladder. More common in women and people of Native American descent, gallstones can be comprised of many different primary compounds, which allows for a great deal of variability in color and texture. Some are faceted like cut gems and others have a chalky, cement-like consistency. While they may appear to us as burnished charms, their patina belies their actions, as they are known to cause excruciating pain in many people who harbor them. Such episodes are often referred to as "gallstone attacks," the language expressing the perceived violence in sufferers. While painful, gallstones are not new—they are even mentioned in divination texts from 2000 B.C. According to these texts, the presence of gallstones could represent either a good or bad omen. Today, however, you would be hard-pressed to find a gallstone sufferer holding up his or her disease as auspicious. *x4*

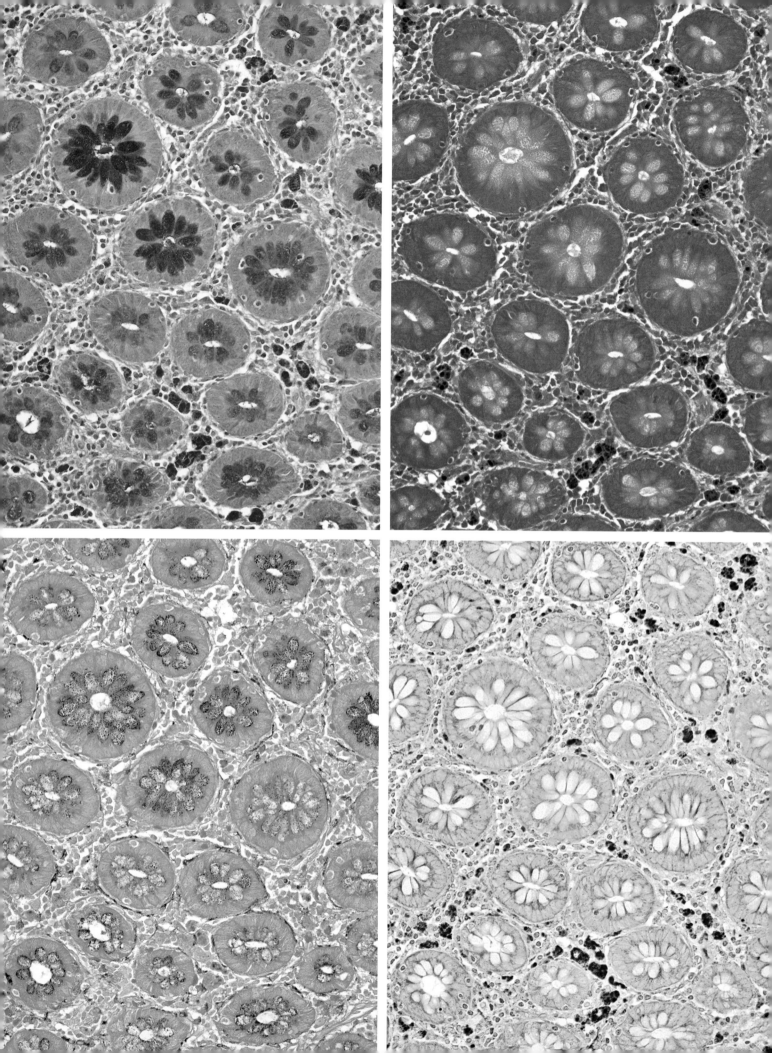

Histological stains

Human tissues, when cut into thin sections for examination under a light microscope, are essentially colorless. Thus, these thin sections are first prepared with different types of histochemical stains to highlight the different molecules of interest within that tissue. The image at right shows a section of the normal colon that is stained with four different histochemical stains, each of which provides different kinds of information to the pathologist who will examine the specimen. Starting clockwise from the top left, these four stains are a Periodic Acid Schiff/Alcian Blue stain, a Diff Quik stain, a Warthin-Starry stain and a Gömöri Methenamine Silver Stain. The Periodic Acid Schiff/Alcian Blue stain, also known as a PAS/Ab stain, is typically used to identify different types of carbohydrates in the tissue, including glycogen. Due to the nature of this stain, the carbohydrates range in color from deep violet to bright magenta. The Diff-Quik stain is used to rapidly stain and differentiate a variety of cell types. In this example, it is particularly useful for determining if bacteria are present within the cobalt blue background of the tissue. Next is the Warthin-Starry stain that is also used to identify microorganisms in tissue, most notably microorganisms called "spirochetes." As a result of this stain, microorganisms are stained black due to deposition of silver and can easily be visualized against the golden yellow background. Finally, the Gömöri Methenamine Silver Stain, or GMS stain, is used to identify different types of fungal organisms in tissue. Incubation of the tissue sections allows penetration of the walls of the fungal organisms by the stain, causing them to turn black against a bright green background. While these are among the most common histochemical stains used, other types of stains are also routinely used to study human tissues. For example, see an example of a Hematoxylin and Eosin stain in *Cytomegalovirus*, or a Masson's Trichrome stain in the image *Cirrhosis of the liver (page 107)*. *x200*

Virtual colonoscopy

Colon cancer is the third most common cancer diagnosed in the United States each year. Most colon cancers develop from tubular adenomas, commonly referred to simply as a "polyp." A colonoscopy is a common procedure used to screen a patient's colon for polyps so that they can be removed before a cancer forms. Although this is not considered a surgical procedure, it nonetheless represents a small medical risk to the patient undergoing the procedure. Recently, a novel technology for screening for colon polyps has been developed that allows a gastroenterologist to examine a patient's colon without performing a colonoscopy. This technology is called a "virtual colonoscopy," and is performed by imaging the colon and then using computer programs to assemble the images into a three-dimensional model of the inside of the colon. An example of the images produced by having a virtual colonoscopy is shown at right.

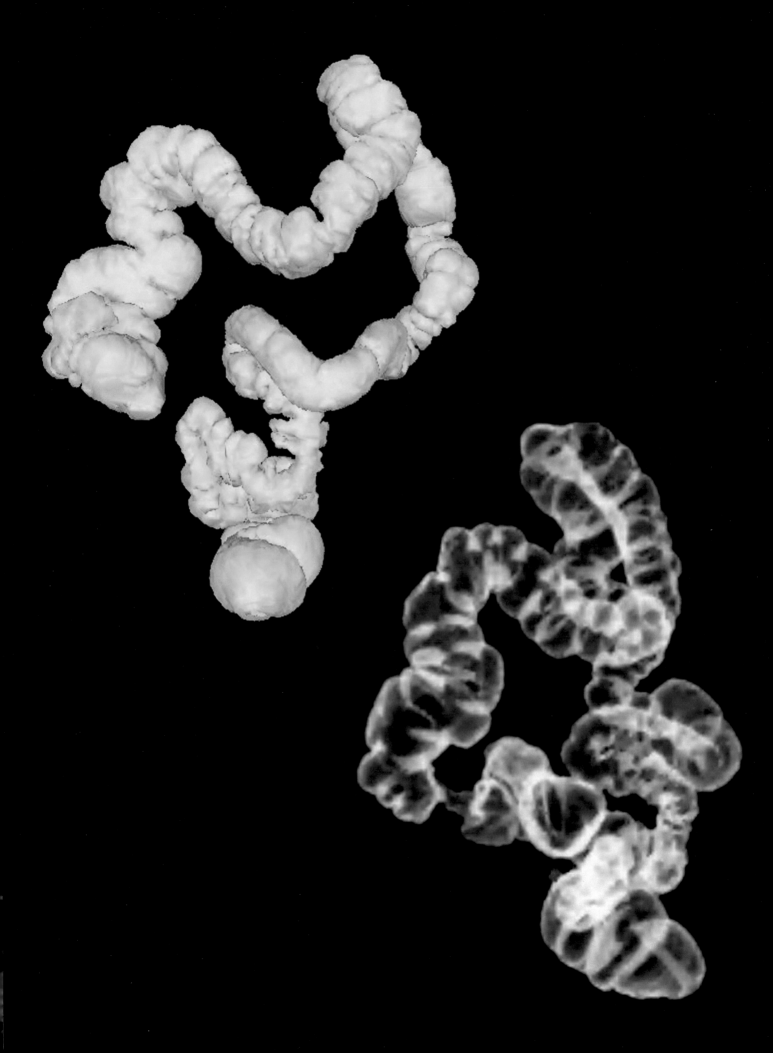

Small intestine, cross section

Contrary to its name, the small intestine accounts for the largest portion of the gastrointestinal tract in humans. Its name is derived from the fact that its caliber in cross section is smaller than that of the large intestine, also known as the colon. The small intestine is located completely within the abdomen where it connects the stomach and the large intestine. The role of the small intestine is to digest food and absorb nutrients. End to end, it measures up to 16 feet long but is roughly only an inch in diameter. Were it only a simple tube though, the surface area of the small intestine for absorption of nutrients would be 17 square feet, sorely deficient for its important role in digestion. To compensate, the inner lining of small intestine contains millions upon millions of finger like projections called villi. Villi increase the surface area 500 fold so that, if the entire surface of the small intestine were flattened out, it would cover an entire tennis court. A complete cross section of a small intestine is shown at right. Note the villi projecting into the lumen. *x20*

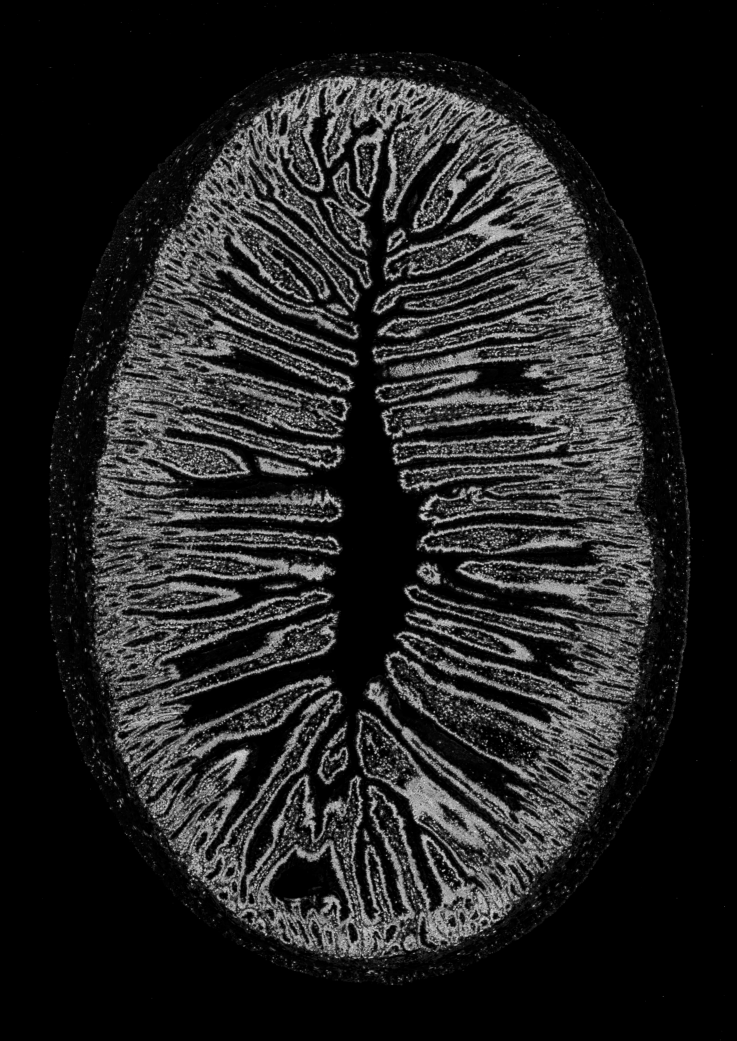

Colorectal neoplasia

Unlike other organs such as the brain or heart that are hailed
for their intricacies and life giving properties, the human colon
is often perceived as occupying a more lowly role among daily
bodily functions. The inner surface of the colon is lined by millions
of shallow test tube shaped pits, called crypts, which precisely
regulate the amount of water, bile and other important fluids that
are excreted with waste products. Patients may survive without
a colon, although their quality of life may be severely affected,
a potent reminder of the vital functions this organ provides.
Shown in the image at right is the surface of the colon as seen
under a microscope. Each crypt is cut in cross section, giving
the appearance of delicate flowers. However, a mutation in the
adenomatous polyposis coli (APC) gene caused the crypt in the
center of the image to transform into a crypt adenoma. Over time,
this crypt adenoma has the potential to develop into a larger villous
adenoma (*overleaf, x40*) and eventually colon cancer, among the
most common causes of cancer deaths in the United States. *x400*

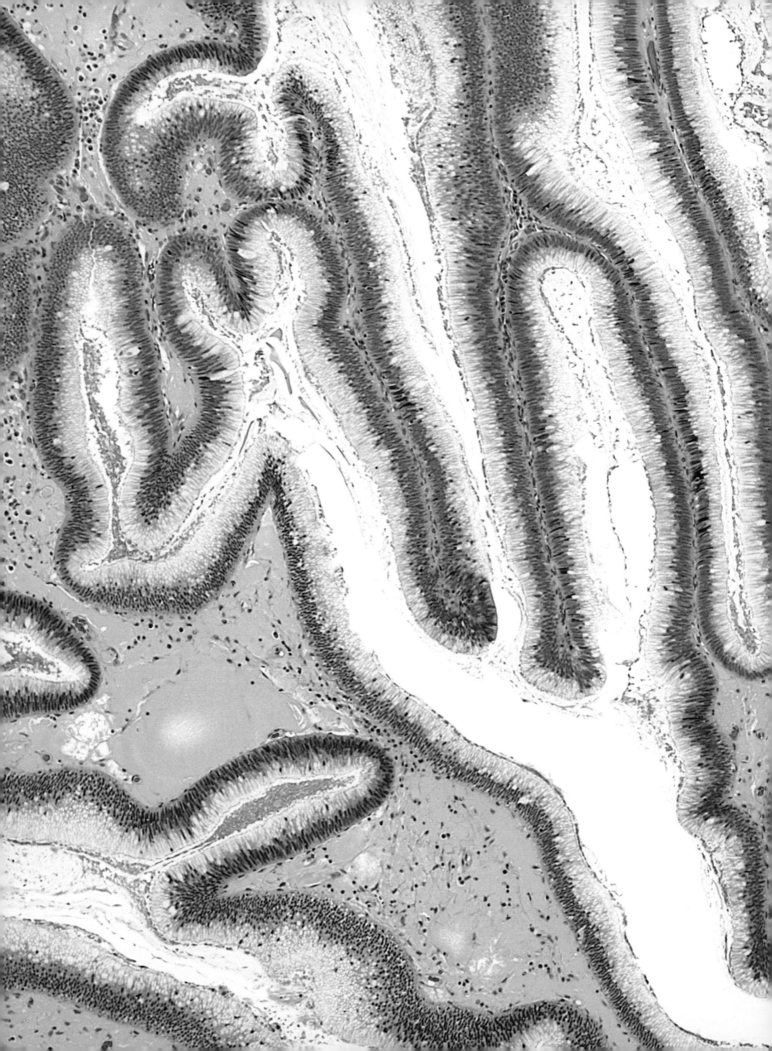

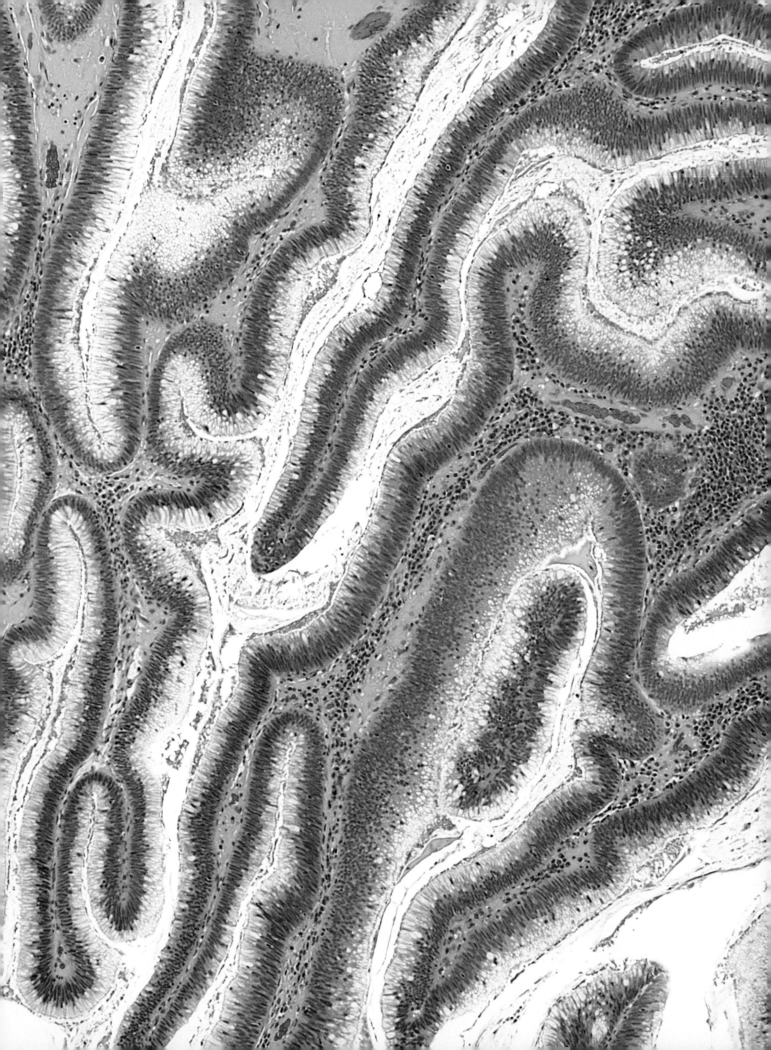

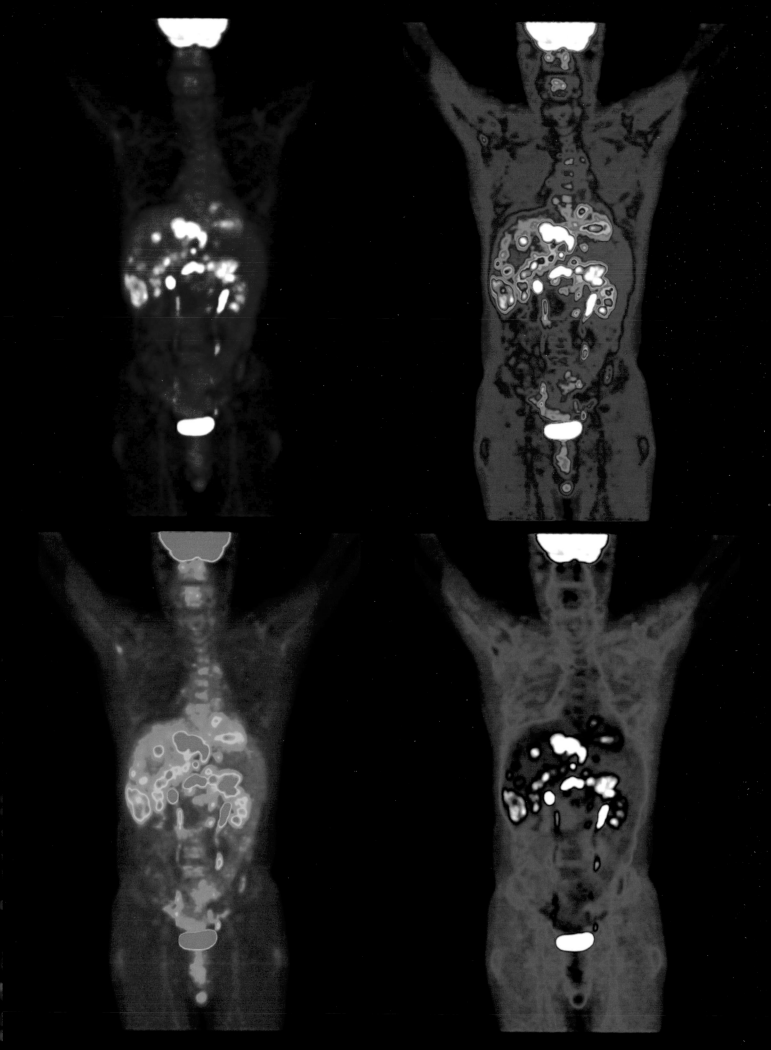

Positron emission tomography

Positron Emission Tomography, also known as a PET scan, is a type of imaging that uses small amounts of radiotracer material to diagnose a variety of diseases. A PET scan measures bodily functions such as blood flow, oxygen use and sugar (*glucose*) metabolism, to help doctors evaluate how well organs and tissues are functioning. PET scans are often performed in association with an MRI scan or CT scan. When done together, the information from the two different studies can be correlated and interpreted as a single image, leading to more precise information about the patient's anatomy and function and thus more accurate diagnoses by the radiologist. The image at left is an example of a PET scan that was used to diagnose metastatic pancreatic cancer. Areas of highest metabolism, seen as bright white or orange, signal and correspond to the anatomic regions of the pancreas and liver with high metabolic activity corresponding to the cancer cells involving the pancreas and liver. By contrast, the bladder and brain also show bright signals, in these instances corresponding to the normally high metabolic levels of the brain and excretion of radioactive material in the bladder at the time of the imaging.

Cirrhosis of the liver

The liver, one of the largest organs, occupies the upper right of the abdomen where it clears our blood of impurities, produces many important clotting factors for our blood and metabolizes drugs. It is one of the few organs that can renew itself after part of it is surgically removed, indicating its enormous capacity for regeneration. The most common causes of chronic injury to the liver are excessive alcohol intake and hepatitis B or hepatitis C infection. Although in most people the liver can effectively handle the damage caused by alcohol or viral infection, others are not as fortunate and develop a condition known as cirrhosis, shown at right. Cirrhosis of the liver occurs when the liver tissue (*stained red*) is replaced by fibrous tissue (*stained blue*). In an attempt to regenerate itself, the liver cells proliferate but are constrained by the fibrous tissue, resulting in the formation of nodules. In end-stage cirrhosis, the liver may shrink to half its normal size and be comprised of dense fibrosis within which nodules of liver tissue remain. *x60*

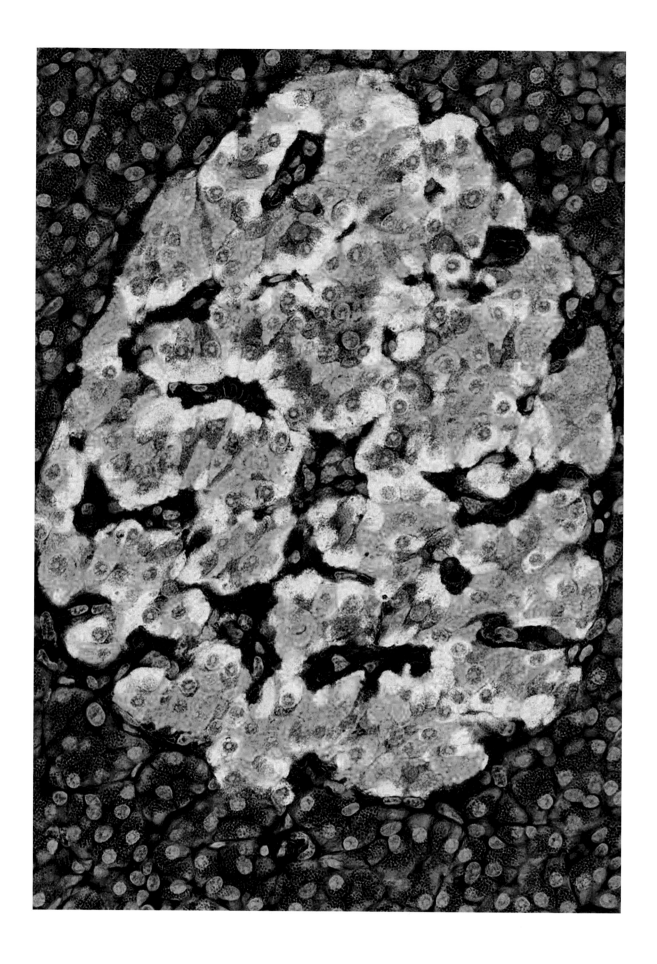

Pancreatic islet

The human pancreas contains two distinctly functioning tissue types, and is in essence two organs in one. The first is known as the exocrine pancreas and is comprised of cells that secrete digestive enzymes into the small intestine via a ductal system to aid in digestion. The second tissue type, known as the endocrine pancreas, is represented by microscopic collections of cells dispersed throughout the pancreas. These cell collections are known as Islets of Langerhans, named for the German anatomist Paul Langerhans who likened them to small islands within the pancreatic tissue when viewed under a microscope. An example of an islet is shown in the figure at right surrounded by cells of the exocrine pancreas. Cells within these islets produce a variety of hormones that are secreted directly into the blood stream, the most important of which is insulin. Insulin is essential to maintaining normal levels of glucose within the blood stream, and loss of insulin leads to a condition known as diabetes. Insulin levels may decline due to a direct injury to the islets in juvenile diabetes (*Type I diabetes*), or in some patients to a dysfunction of the insulin producing cells within the islets (*Type II diabetes*). *x400*

Neuroendocrine tumor

While the majority of our organs exist as a recognizable structure within our bodies, the neuroendocrine system is diffusely distributed throughout our cells and tissues. But don't let its ethereal nature fool you—the neuroendocrine system performs critical functions for which we are dependent on to live. The role of this system is indicating by its name, which is to integrate the function of the nervous system and the endocrine system. Neuroendocrine cells function by releasing hormones into the bloodstream when stimulated by special neurons within the nervous system. These hormones then travel through the bloodstream until they reach their target cell and stimulate, block or maintain the target cell's function. The neuroendocrine system was first recognized with the discovery that secretions from the pituitary gland, a pea sized gland located deep within our head, are closely controlled by special neurons within the brain.

As with virtually all cell types in our body, neuroendocrine cells may give rise to tumors. Because neuroendocrine cells are located throughout the body, tumors that arise from neuroendocrine cells may occur anywhere but are most often seen in the lungs or the gastrointestinal tract. Neuroendocrine tumors are often referred to as carcinoid tumors (*carcinoma-like*) based on a description by the German pathologist Siegfried Oberndorfer who noted that they behaved like a benign tumor despite appearing as a carcinoma under the microscope. In fact, carcinoid tumors often display an incredible range of appearances under the microscope as illustrated in the example shown at right. *x400*

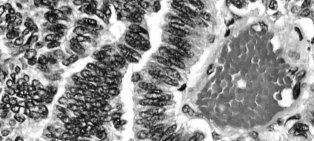
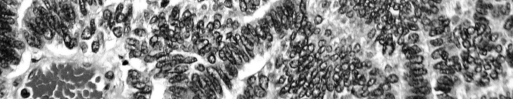

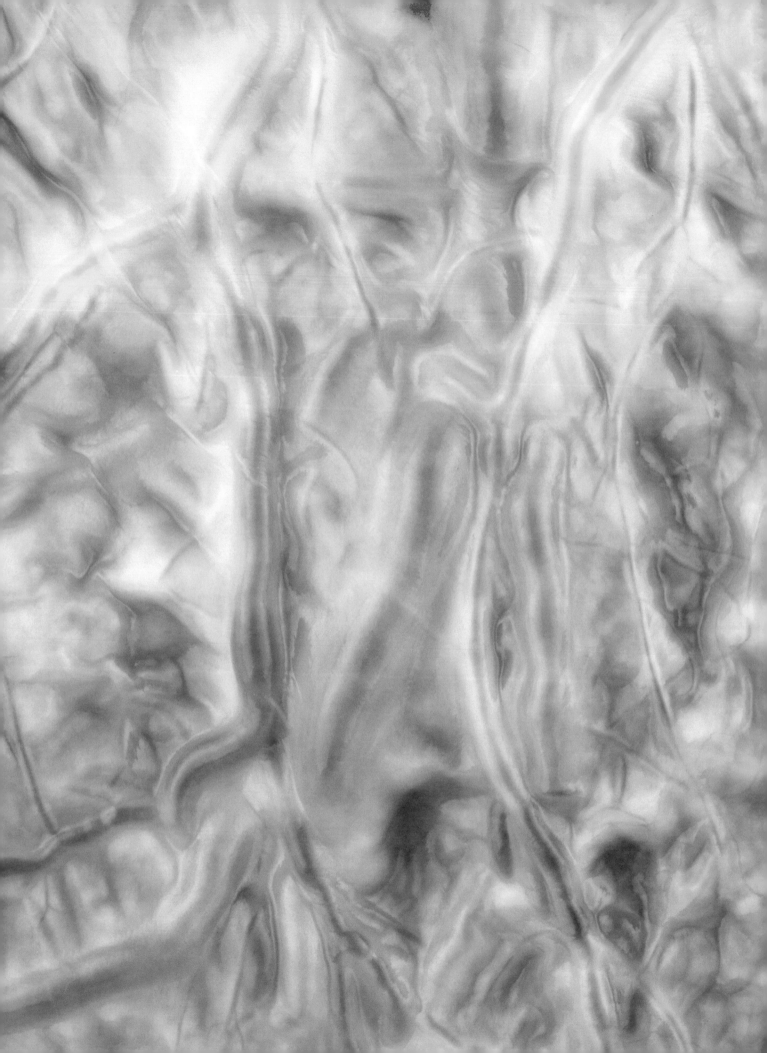

Pelvis

Kidney

The two nodules that flank our spine are more important than their legume-like silhouette may indicate. The kidney is the renaissance organ, multi-tasking continuously in several fields of biological work. The kidneys keep our fluid balance in check, regulate our salt balance, remove waste products and even produce hormones. These rarely lauded workhorses bravely hold their place in the shadows of our spinal column, just behind the limelight of the abdominal cavity. The globular creatures pictured on the following page, the ones that look like strange balls of yarn—are actually important kidney structures called glomeruli. These glomeruli are made of specialized blood vessels that help carry on the kidneys' work by filtering our blood. While the glomeruli may look large here, they are actually so small that a microscope is needed to see them well (see image *The modern microscope, page 28*). The glomerular filtrate then passes through a series of tubules that concentrate the solution and add or remove electrolytes *(opposite)*, and what remains passes out of the kidneys as urine. Many kidney diseases specifically affect the glomeruli or the tubules, causing functional problems. Like other underappreciated personnel, the contribution of the kidney is frequently overlooked unless it malfunctions. When this happens, the patient may be tethered to a cold substitute: the dialysis machine. Another possibility exists, however, for those with serious kidney disease that cannot be ameliorated with current medical technology—these people can accept an organ from another person. The noble transplanted kidney generously performs its functions for a new host. *x400*

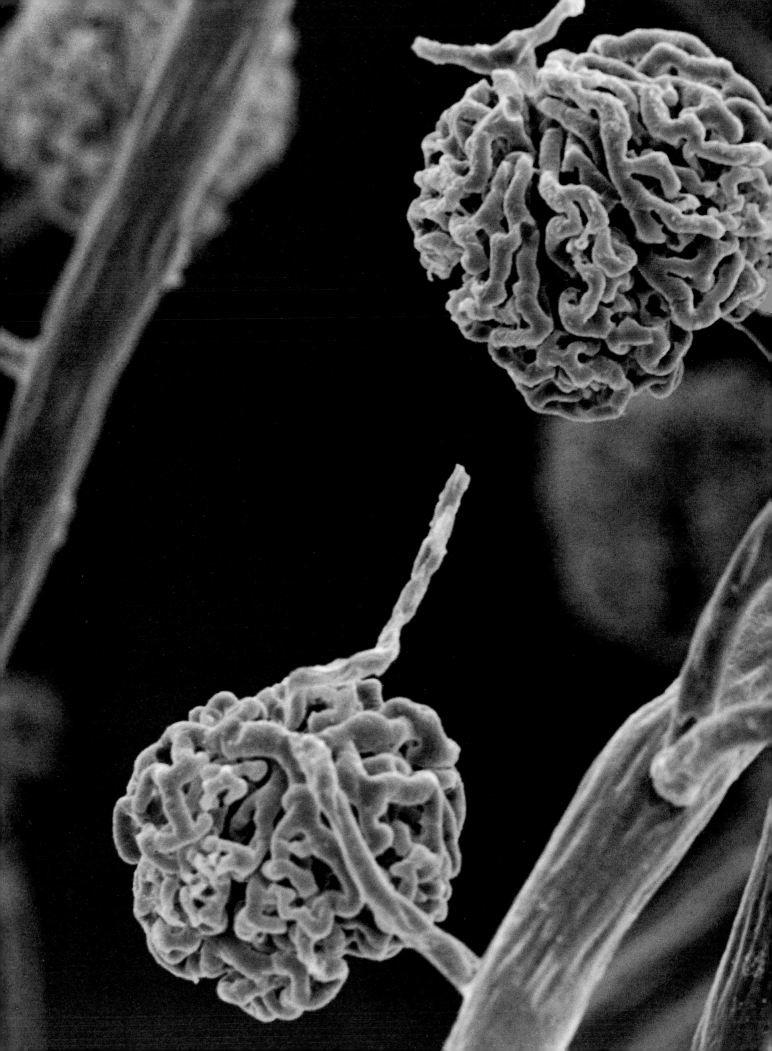

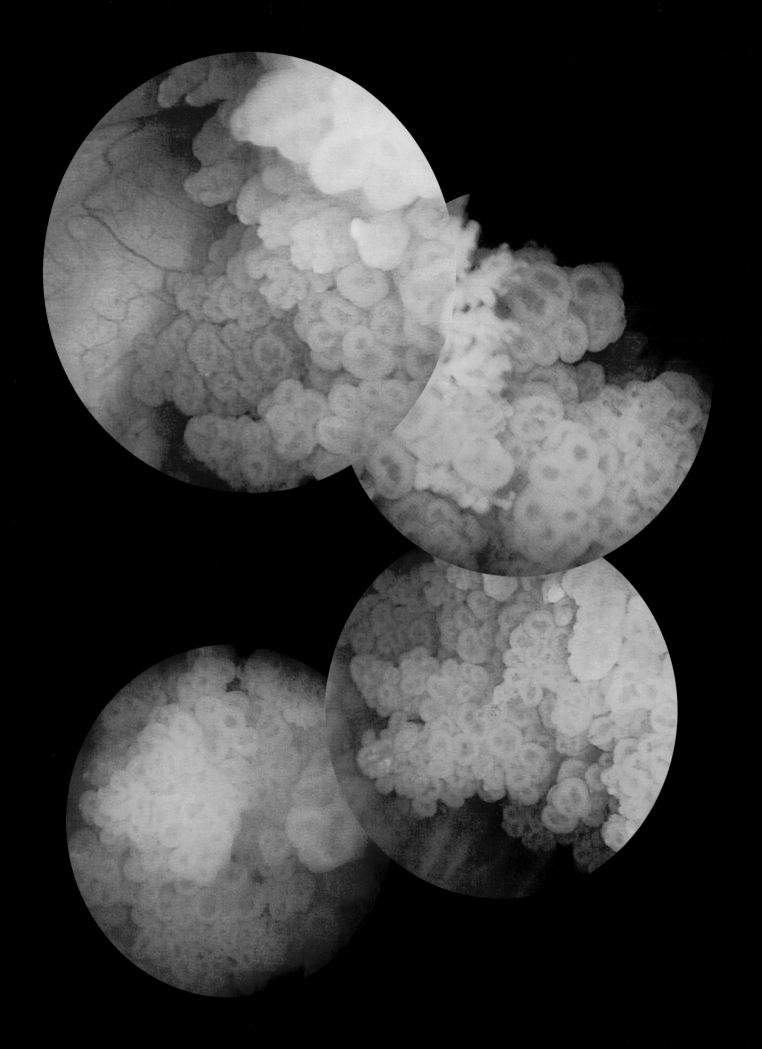

Bladder cancer

The bladder is a balloon-shaped organ in your pelvic area that stores urine. Bladder cancer develops from the cells that line the inside of the bladder. Bladder cancer most often occurs in older adults, although it can affect individuals at any age. The great majority of bladder cancers are diagnosed at an early stage when it is highly treatable. However, even early-stage bladder cancer is likely to recur. For this reason, bladder cancer survivors often undergo frequent follow-up screening tests for years after their first diagnosis. This is typically performed by a simple procedure called cystoscopy, a test that allows a urologist to look at the inside of the bladder and the urethra using a thin, lighted instrument called a cystoscope. To perform an effective cystoscopy, the bladder must be distended with saline so that the urologist can examine the entire surface of the bladder. This results in the bladder tumors appearing as delicate sea anemone floating at the bottom of the ocean. *x10*

Prostate

Deep within the male pelvis, situated beneath the
bladder, lies a walnut sized organ called the prostate. The
prostate contains two predominant tissue types: glandular
structures comprised of epithelial cells that produce
prostatic fluid into which sperm are deposited, and
connective tissue within which these glandular structures
are dispersed. The image at right is of a complete cross
section of a prostate. The lace-like glandular spaces are
seen throughout the gland, surrounding the horseshoe
shaped space of the urethra at its center. As many men
age, the prostate may enlarge due to overgrowth of glands
at the center of the organ, eventually blocking flow of
urine through the urethra. This common condition is
known as benign prostatic hyperplasia or BPH. In others,
cancer may form from the glands at the periphery of the
organ, and this is why prostate cancers can be felt during a
routine rectal examination of the prostate. *x4*

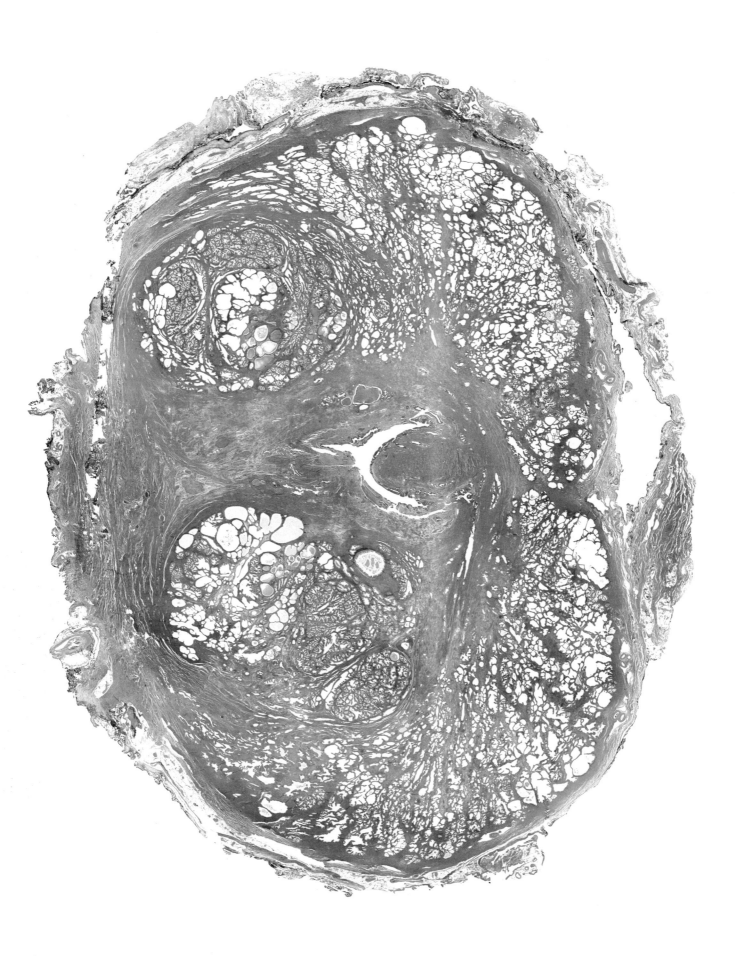

Immunohistochemistry of prostate cancer

Shown at right is a microscopic view of adenocarcinoma of the prostate labeled with a "cocktail" stain marking basal cells (*brown*) and racemase (*red*). In difficult cases, where the pathologist has to distinguish between prostate cancer and one of the many noncancerous mimickers, special studies using antibodies can be utilized. Noncancerous glands have an outer row of cells (*basal cells*) that light up with brown antibody stains for high molecular weight cytokeratin and p63. Prostate cancer glands lack basal cells so that the cancer glands lack any brown staining. However, cancer glands express racemase (*red*), which is absent in the noncancerous glands. The combination of positive staining for racemase and negative staining for basal cells in this case is diagnostic of prostate cancer. *x240*

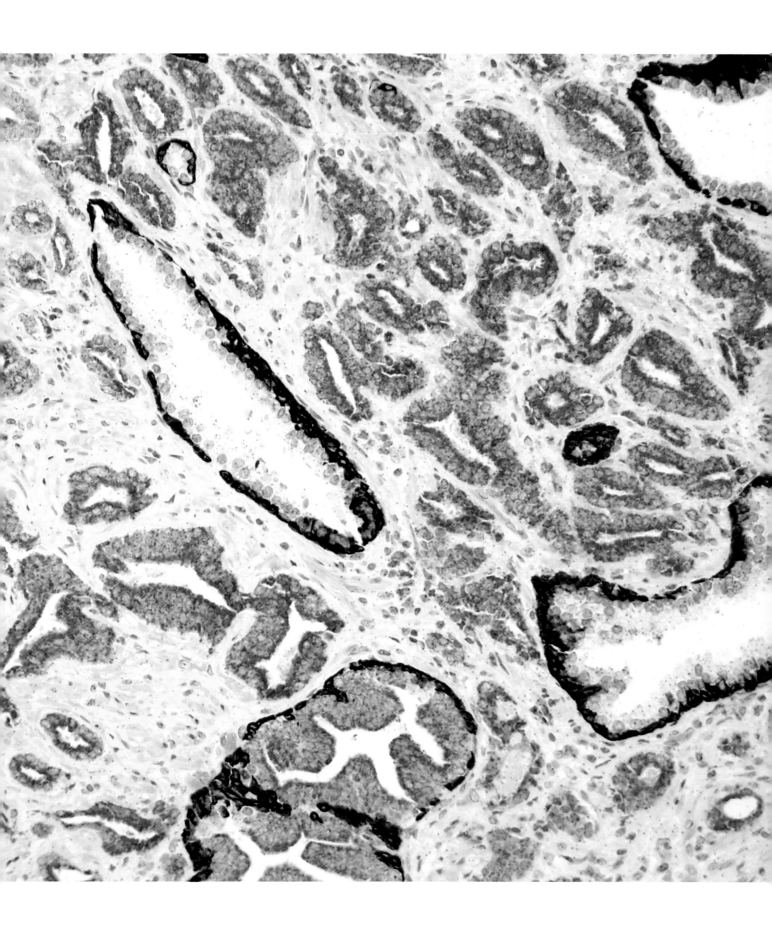

Metastatic prostate cancer

A bone scan, or bone scintigraphy, is a nuclear scanning test to find abnormalities in bone that are caused when bone attempts to heal itself. Bone scans are used to diagnose a variety of conditions of the skeleton such as cancer, inflammation, infection and fractures. Although there are several different types of tests to evaluate bone abnormalities, a bone scan is unique in that it actually measures bone metabolism specifically by osteoblasts, specialized cells that produce new bone in response to injury. A bone scan is performed by injecting a small amount of a radioactive material into the patient, followed by a whole body scan that can detect the radioactive material. At least half of the radioactive material will localize to the bones, and the more active the osteoblasts are near an ongoing injury (*metastatic prostate cancer invasion "injures" the bone*) the more radioactive material that will accumulate in those areas. Although only relatively large metastatic prostate cancer lesions will be seen by this method, those that damage bone and cause increased blood flow and increased osteoblast activity are often detected. The image at right illustrates the use of a bone scan to diagnose metastatic prostate cancer, seen as dark spots within the pale gray outline of the bony skeleton. Aggressive prostate cancers tend to metastasize to bone and thus bone scans are a critical tool to identify these metastatic lesions in affected patients.

Testis *(overleaf)*

Testes are the male counterpart of ovaries in women. The primary functions of the testes are to produce sperm and to produce male hormones, primarily testosterone. Both of these functions are controlled by hormones secreted by the pituitary gland located at the base of the brain. The image on the overleaf illustrates the normal anatomy of the testis when viewed under a microscope. Each round structure is a cross section through the dense coil of tubules, called *seminiferous tubules,* contained within each testis. At the periphery of each section of tubule are round cells called *spermatogonia.* *Spermatogonia* are the primitive cells that give rise to mature sperm, seen as elongated filaments within the center of each tubule. Defective or inadequate sperm production by *spermatogonia* is among the many reasons for male infertility, and neoplasms that arise from *spermatogonia* give rise to testis cancer, the most common solid tumor in young adult males.

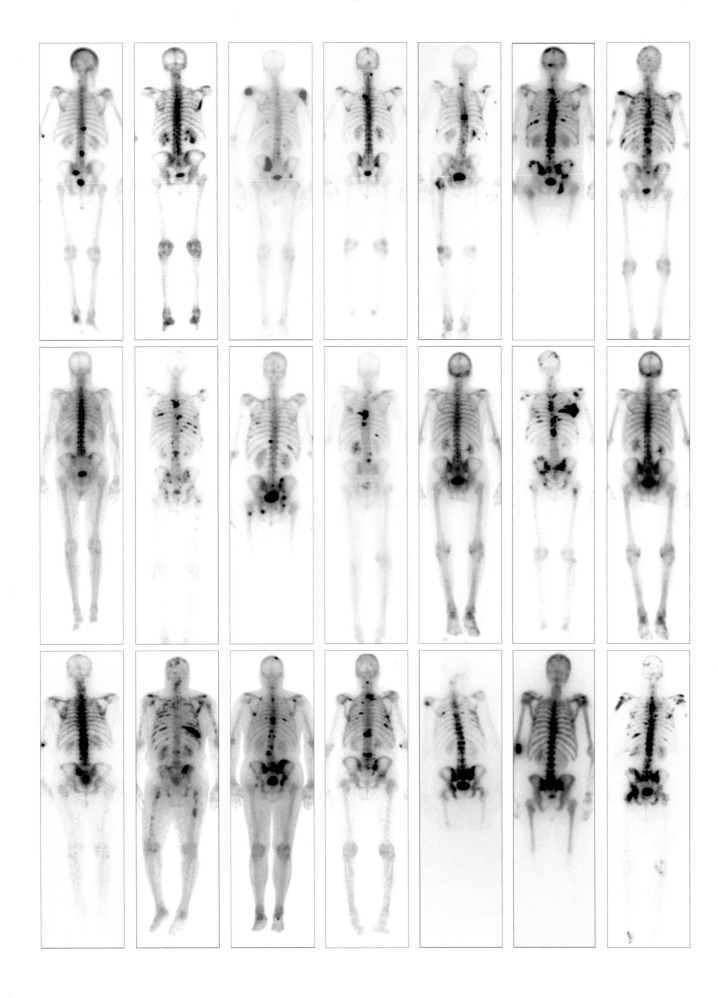

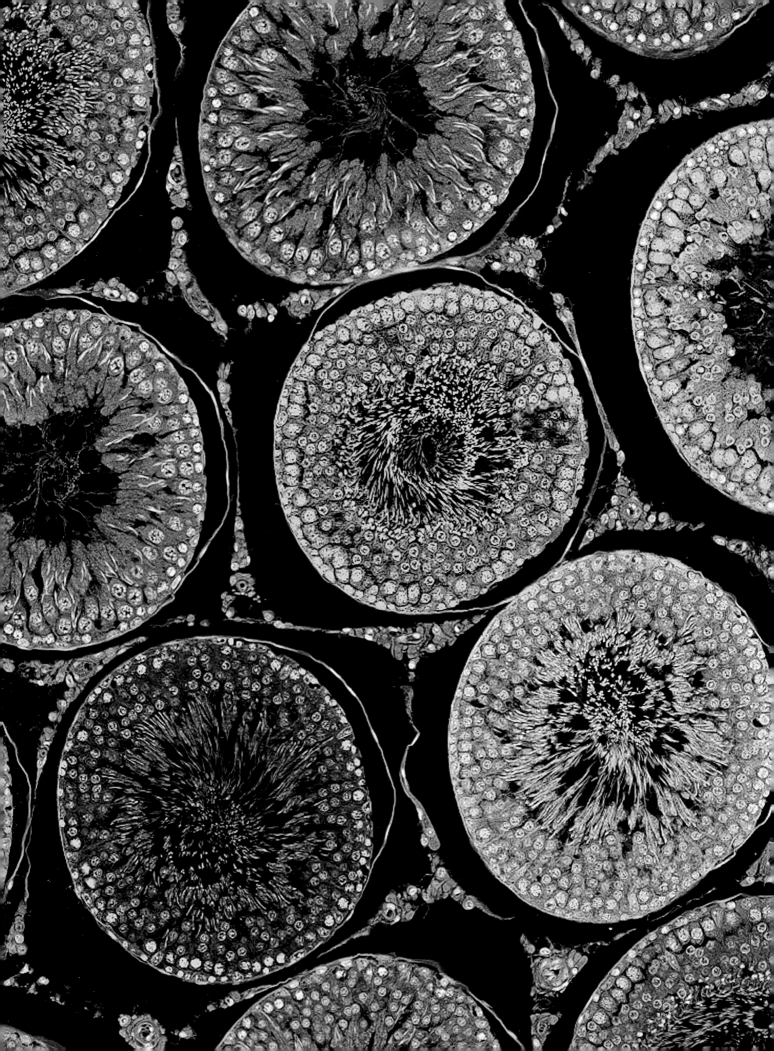

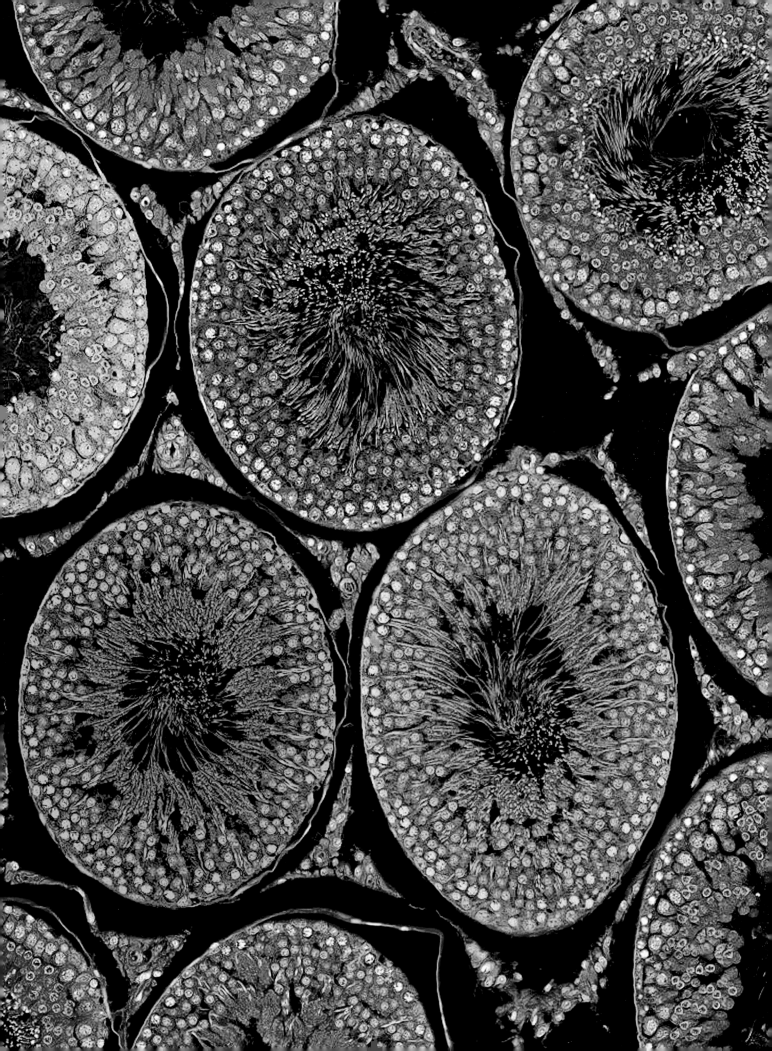

Developing follicle with germ cell ("*human egg*") and a germ cell tumor in an ovary

The human ovary contains numerous germ cells (*the centrally located large pale purple cell surrounded by a rim of pink material*) surrounded by specialized stromal cells. Together, these cells form the follicles that develop on a monthly basis in the ovary. Each month, a dominant follicle develops and extrudes its germ cell "egg" through the ovarian surface in the process referred to as ovulation. If the egg travels along the fallopian tube to the uterus and is not fertilized by a sperm, the uterine lining (*endometrium*) that develops under the influence of hormones is shed (*menstruation*). If, on the other hand, the egg encounters sperm in the fallopian tube and is fertilized, the conceptus implants into the uterine lining where it develops from an embryo into a fetus. There are several types of ovarian cancers, including an uncommon group referred to as germ cell tumors because they are thought to be derived from germ cells in the ovary. One type of germ cell tumor of the ovary is the dysgerminoma, a malignant tumor that occurs in women of reproductive age. It is analogous to a malignant germ cell tumor that occurs in the testis, the seminoma. The collection of primitive-appearing cells arranged in elongated nests in the upper portion of the image is a dysgerminoma. These tumor cells have large pale purple nuclei, prominent reddish nucleoli (*the small round structures within the nuclei*) and abundant pale pinkish to clear cytoplasm (*the substance of the cell that houses the nucleus*). They are reminiscent of the normal germ cell. These tumors are malignant and can metastasize to lymph nodes elsewhere but are highly responsive to therapy and can be cured. *x400*

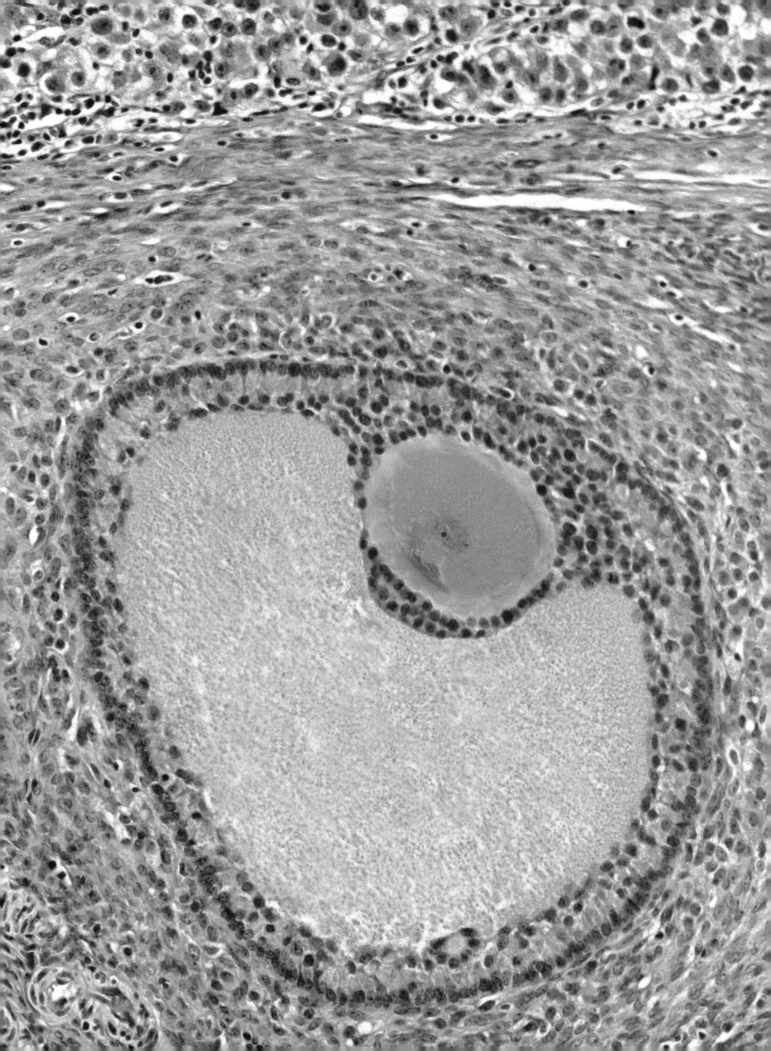

Placenta

Most of our organs are designed to last a lifetime, but the placenta is unceremoniously discarded once its job is done. This organ acts as a mediator between mother and child, carefully regulating the exchange of nutrients and metabolites. Somewhat alien in appearance, the placenta has a raw, red surface that melds with the uterine wall as well as a glistening, pearlescent surface laced with vascular tributaries. This surface, pictured here, faces the developing fetus and serves as the attachment point of the umbilical cord. The cord itself, an unassuming rope about the diameter of an adult woman's index finger, is the universal lifeline, without which we cannot begin to develop. The placenta and its cord represents our first human connection, but also provides the means for our first taste of severance. *x2*

Pap smear *(overleaf)*

Tumbling across the slide like strange confetti, the cells on this cervical Pap smear are presenting themselves for evaluation by a cytologist. In one of the most effective public health activities in history, the widespread use of the cervical Pap smear has allowed us to identify and treat many cervical cancers before they cause harm to the women who harbor them. The festive pink and blue (*and sometimes green and yellow*) colors are imparted by a series of special stains called "Papanicolaou" stains, named after the cytologist who pioneered the technique, Dr. George Papanicolaou. After cells are swiped from the cervix with a special brush or spatula, they are either placed in a preservative solution and then centrifuged onto slides or simply swiped onto slides in the office. Specially trained physicians and technologists scan the cells to look for signs of cancer or indications that one of the viruses that cause cervical cancer are present. The larger "leaf like" cells are the skin or "squamous" cells, while the smaller cells are types of white blood cells, naturally present to protect the tissues in the face of potential infection. Since today there are many effective treatments for cervical cancer, the identification of important changes in the cells seen here represent the ticket to a cure for many women who could otherwise perish from this disease. *x400*

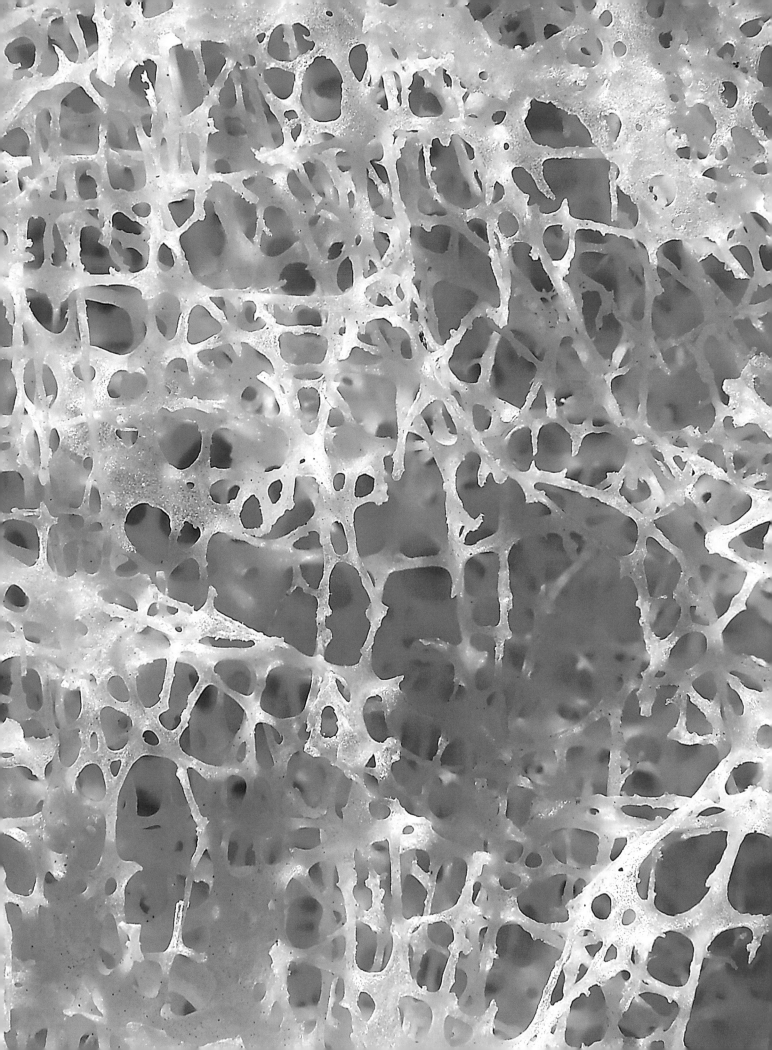

Connective
Tissue

Human cerebrospinal nervous system

This unique photograph of a complete cerebrospinal
nervous system is preserved in the Museum of the
Hahnemann Medical College in Philadelphia. This amazing
dissection was carried out in 1888 by Professor Rufus
Benjamin Weaver, MD, ScD, Professor of Anatomy. He
was one of the foremost American anatomists of the time.
Harriet Cole, who was an African-American scrubwoman
at Hahnemann Medical College, had an interest in
anatomy and willed her body to the medical school. Dr.
Weaver spent five grueling months of twelve hour days
delicately removing flesh and bone from her corpse
leaving only the nervous system and eyes. His dissection
was incredibly meticulous; each strand of nerve was
wrapped in gauze and kept moist with preservative, then
dipped in a white lead-based paint, and finally shellacked.
The entire nervous system was then mounted on a board
with hundreds of tiny pins. His original Cerebro-Spinal
Nervous System dissection is more than five feet tall and
was considered such a feat that the cadaver dissection
was exhibited at the 1893 Worlds Fair, the Colombian
Exposition in Chicago and was awarded a gold medal and
a blue ribbon. Ultimately it became an invaluable teaching
tool for generations of Philadelphia medical students.

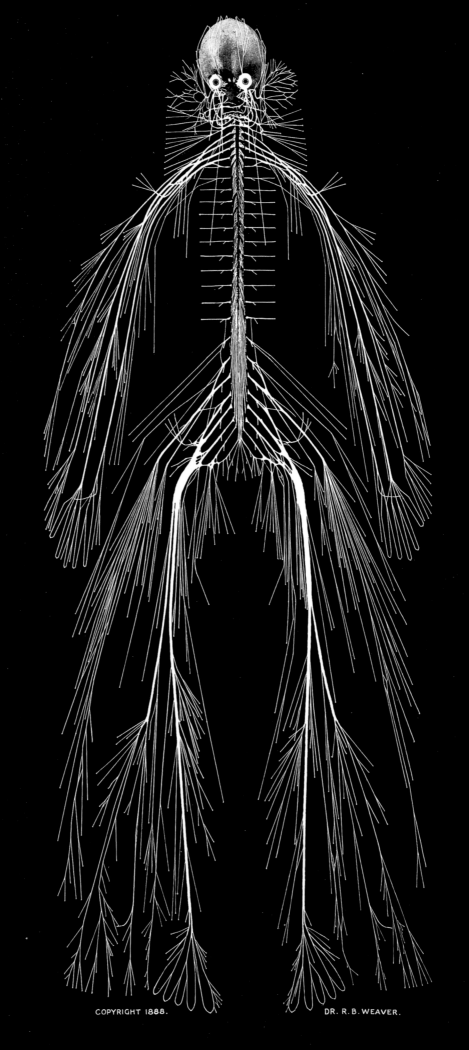

                    DR. R. B. WEAVER.

Skull

This rare exploded, or disarticulated, human skull, also known as a Beauchene skull, was named after the French anatomist Claude Beauchene. He developed this novel method of presenting the skull bones along the suture lines primarily as a teaching aid for anatomical study in the 1850s. Mounted on elaborate stands, the skulls are reminiscent of early arrested motion. The Beauchene technique requires meticulously cleaning a skull, boiling until cranial sutures are loosened, disarticulating its bones by hand while they are wet and mounting them on a stand that is designed to exhibit them at once individually and yet in context. For generations, students of anatomy and illustration have closely studied how the skull comes together with close observation of this model. While Leonardo da Vinci originally introduced the concept of the "exploded" skull in his anatomical drawings, Beauchene's preparation leaves the component parts in their original spatial relationship to one another, making it a wonderful model for studying the complex structure of all twenty-two cranial bones. This beautiful specimen, shown with some of its bones lowered on their movable brass supports, is part of a collection of anatomical models in the Max Brödel Archives of the Department of Art as Applied to Medicine.

Striated muscle (overleaf)

There are three major types of muscle fiber in the body: smooth muscle, striated muscle and cardiac muscle. Smooth muscle is the contractile substance in those organs that are not under voluntary control, such as the walls of the intestines and the muscle of the surrounding blood vessels. Striated muscle is involved in voluntary contractions. The large muscle masses of the body are striated muscles and these are responsible for skeletal movement and work. Striated muscle consists of the tiny contractile proteins of actin and myosin. Actin and myosin are deposited in muscle fibers in very regular ways such that when they are viewed with a special stain, as in this picture, they show varying bands of density according to how much overlap there is in the actin and myosin areas. These bands are responsible for the designation "striated muscle." As muscle undergoes voluntary contraction, these bands become closer together. As muscle relaxes, they become further apart due to the actin and myosin fibers spreading away from each other. A third type of muscle in the body is cardiac muscle. This has striations in it but it is an involuntary muscle similar to the smooth muscle function in the body. x400

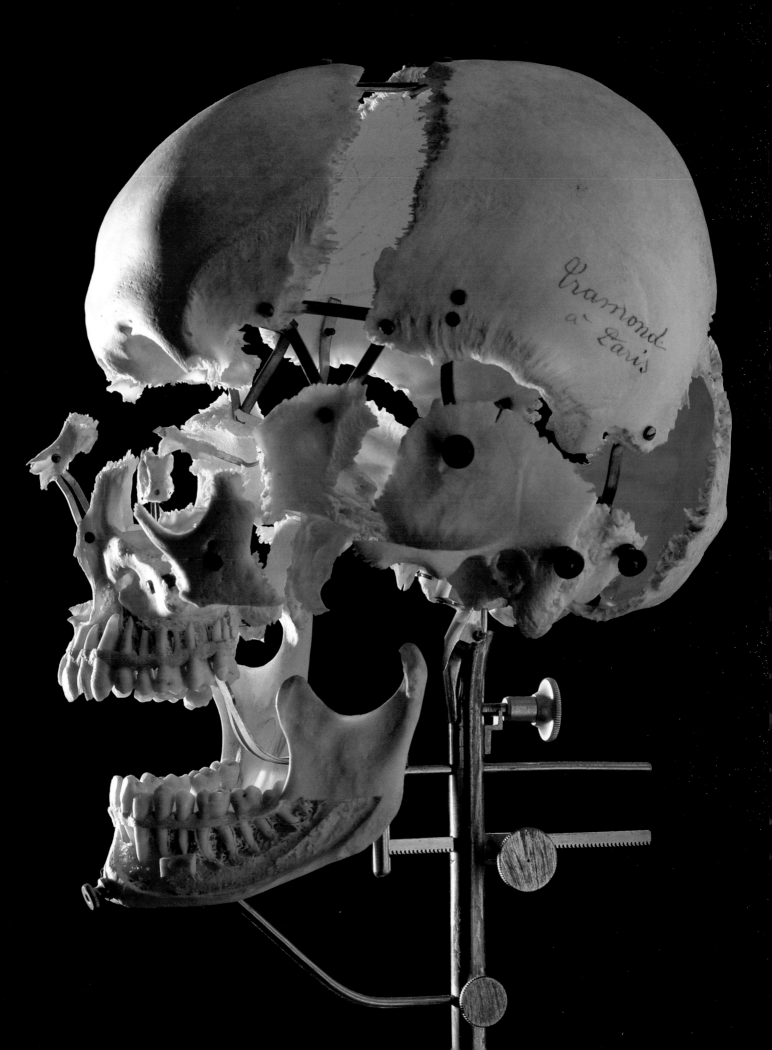

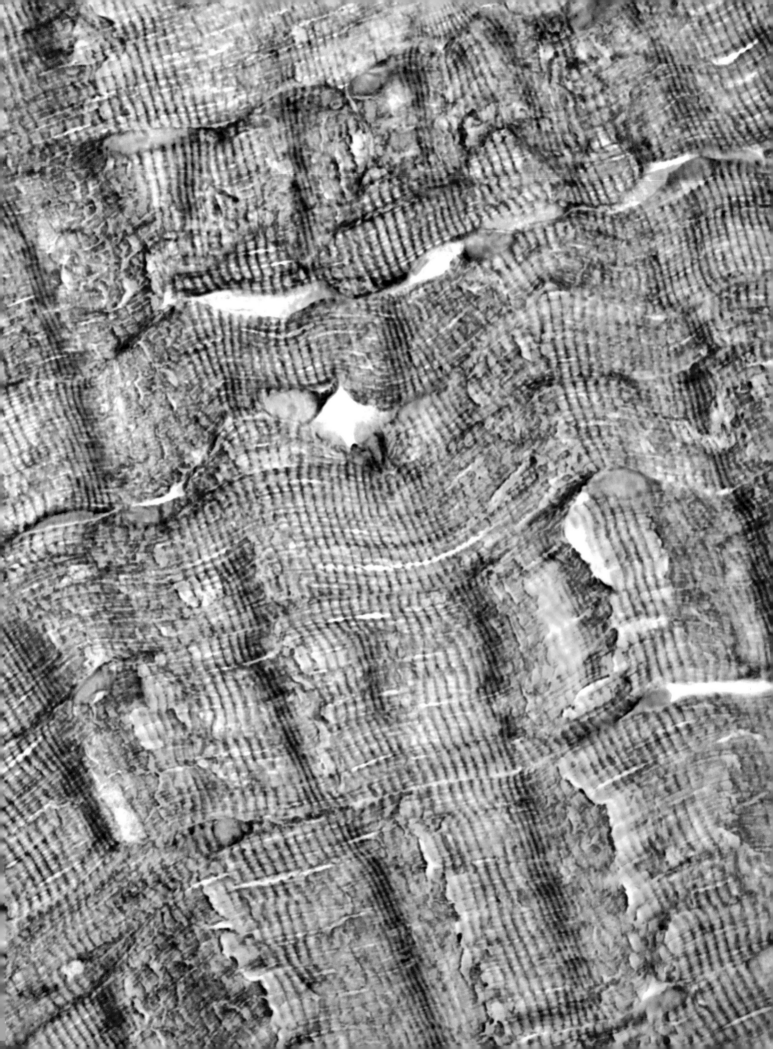

Gene therapy of muscular dystrophy

Muscular dystrophy refers to a group of nine inherited muscle diseases that cause defects in muscle proteins leading to progressive skeletal muscle weakness. The best-known type is Duchenne's muscular dystrophy that is caused by inheritance of an X chromosome, one of the two sex chromosomes, that contains a mutant gene for the dystrophin protein. Because males inherit only one X chromosome whereas females inherit two X chromosomes, males are affected by X-linked genetic disorders much more often than females. However, other forms of muscular dystrophy show different patterns of inheritance unrelated to the sex chromosomes. One group of these are the limb-girdle muscular dystrophies that are due to inherited mutations in one of the four sarcoglycan genes, causing progressive weakness of the upper arms and legs. This image demonstrates an active area of medical research related to the muscular dystrophies, that being gene therapy to restore the function of the causative mutant gene. In this way, scientists hope to slow or even stop the progression of muscular dystrophy. In this example, a modified virus that produces normal sarcoglycan was used to infect a hamster model of limb girdle muscular dystrophy. The virus also produces red fluorescent protein, thus the muscle fibers outlined in red are those in which the virus is also actively producing sarcoglycan protein. *x400*

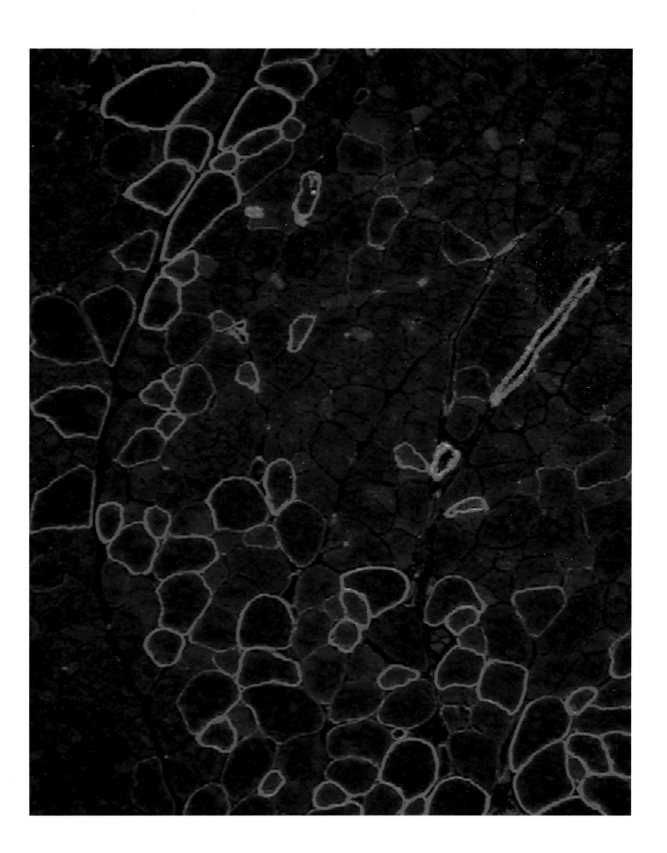

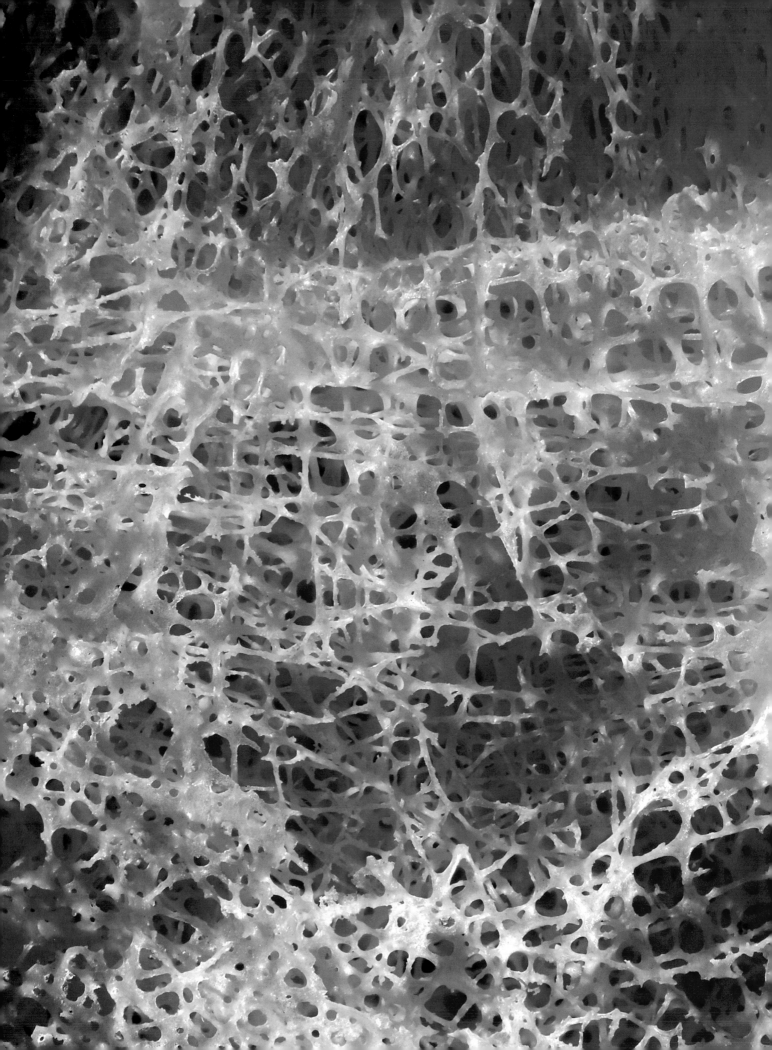

Osteoporosis

The human skeleton provides the framework upon which our organs and tissues are situated. Skeletal bone is not an inert and stony structure but actually a vital and dynamic organ that, in addition to its strength, provides our bodily stores of important minerals such as calcium and phosphorus. This photograph illustrates the appearance of cancellous bone from the femur, the large bone that spans the pelvis to the knee. Cancellous bone, also called trabecular bone or spongy bone, is an elaborate network of slender bone spicules that are interconnected, leading to the resemblance to a delicate sponge. These spicules provide a huge surface area of bone that makes essential minerals available to the body and provide the framework upon which bone marrow cells grow (*not shown in this photograph*). Cancellous bone also provides strength, although the majority of bone strength is from the thick outer layers of the bone that are not seen in this picture. Like other organ systems, the human skeleton is itself affected by many disease processes. One of these diseases is osteoporosis, among the most common causes of bone loss that leads to an increased risk of bone fractures. Osteoporosis is most common in women after menopause but may also develop in men or in individuals with specific hormone disorders, chronic illnesses or long term use of glucocorticoids (*steroids*). Given its influence on the risk of fragility fracture, osteoporosis may significantly affect life expectancy and quality of life. *x5*

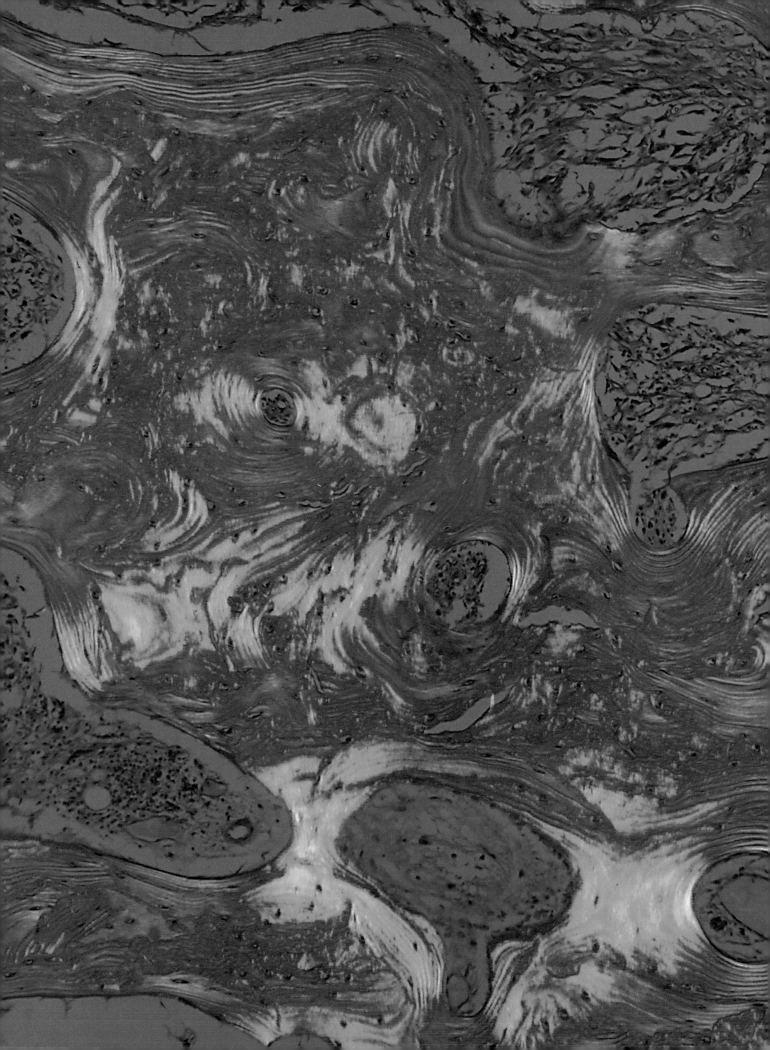

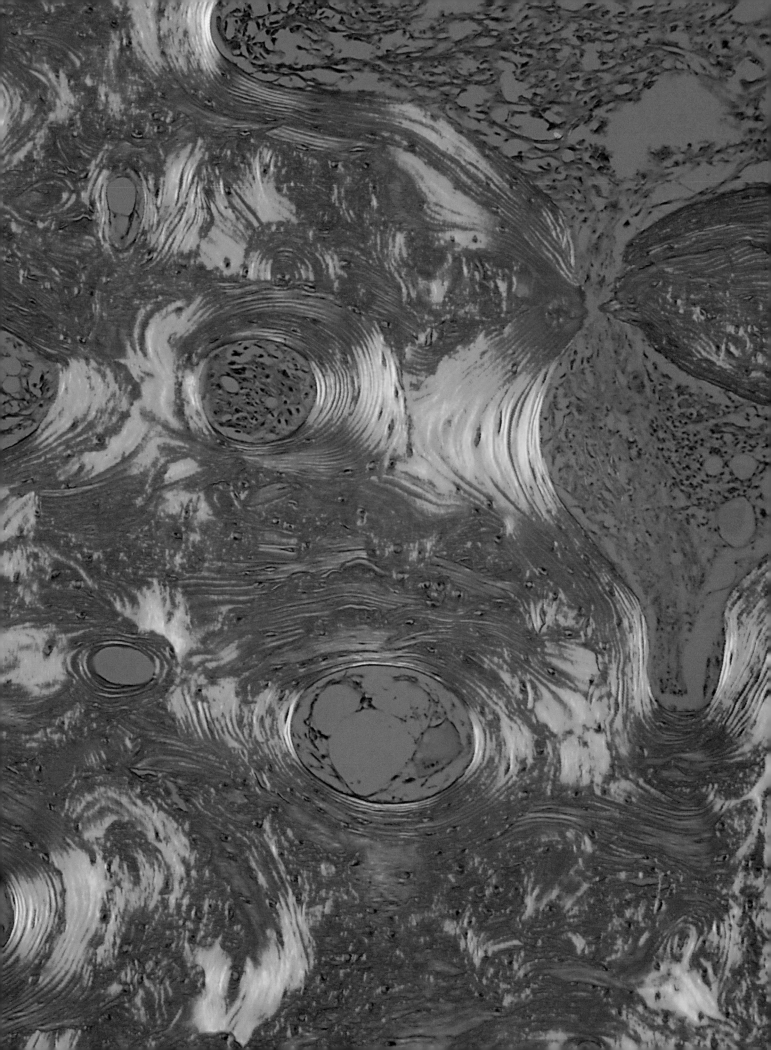

Paget's disease *(overleaf)*

This medium-power polarized light photomicrograph of bone shows the involvement of Paget's disease. Paget's disease is a disorder of exaggerated bone remodeling. Throughout life, the normal skeleton undergoes a process in which old bone is removed and replaced by new bone. This is similar to the process of shedding old dead skin in order to replace it with new skin. This process, called "turnover," is necessary to make sure that organs maintain their resiliency. Bone turnover is at a constant rate of 15% of the skeleton being replaced each year, thus, in 5 years, a normal person will have an entirely new skeleton. If remodeling does not occur, the skeleton will begin to accumulate fatigue micro-fractures and become the consistency of brittle chalk. Paget's disease is a process where the normal remodeling process is amplified over 100 times. There is no orderly sequence to the remodeling process, and the result is chaotic bone turnover. Paget's disease may affect many bones in the skeleton or only a small portion of one bone. Usually the elderly are affected by this disorder. The polarized light highlights the disordered pattern of bone secondary to chaotic remodeling. The bone shows very thin layering called lamellae. Lamellae are orderly lines in the bone caused by orientation of collagen fibers, the main substance of the organic bone matrix. In Paget's disease the intersecting lamellae occur in a very random pattern similar to a mosaic. The lamellae that are perpendicular in the polarized light are orange whereas the parallel lamellae are blue. The end product of Paget's disease is to make bones much more dense than normal. However, despite this increased density, the bones in a Paget's patient are much more brittle. These patients suffer fractures and deformities. *x200*

Mouse tibia

This is a photomicrograph of bony tissue from the proximal tibia (*"shin bone"*) of a mouse. It shows the curved growth plate in the middle of the bone. The bone has been prepared for microscopic study without decalcifying it, and stained with a Von Kossa stain that highlights the presence of calcium in the bone. This preparation enables bone biologists to study how well the bone tissue is calcified. This mouse has a defect in calcification that leads to soft bones. This has parallels with the disease osteomalacia in the adult population. These patients do not get enough vitamin D and therefore do not calcify their bones very well. *x100*

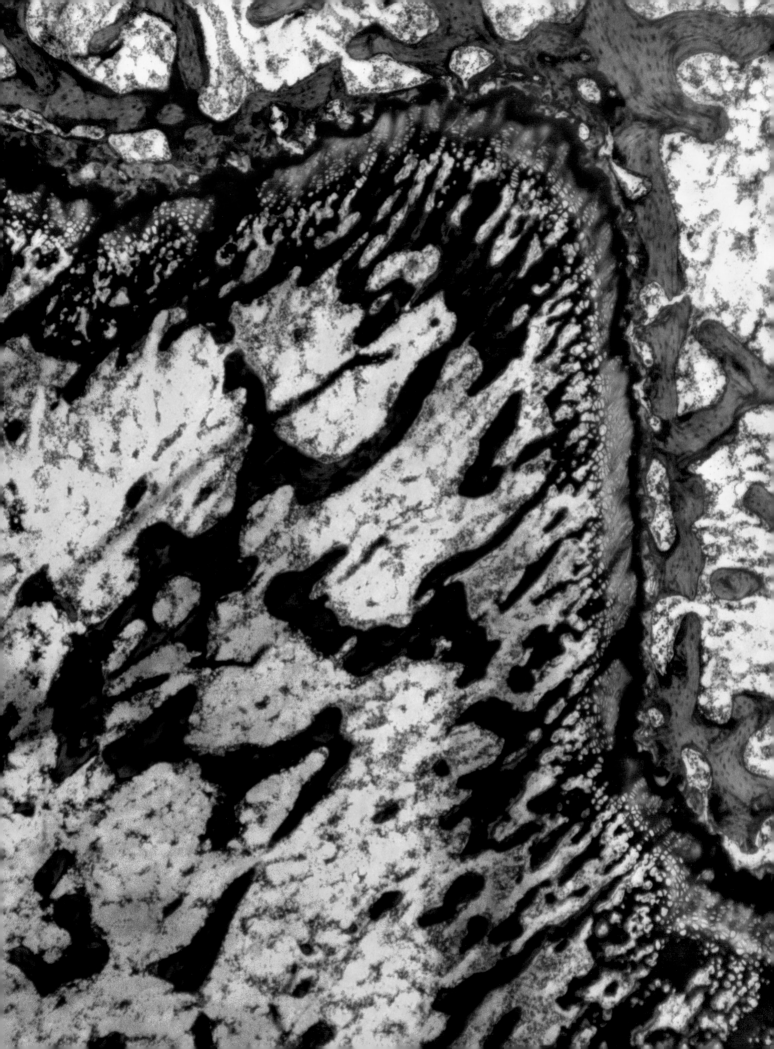

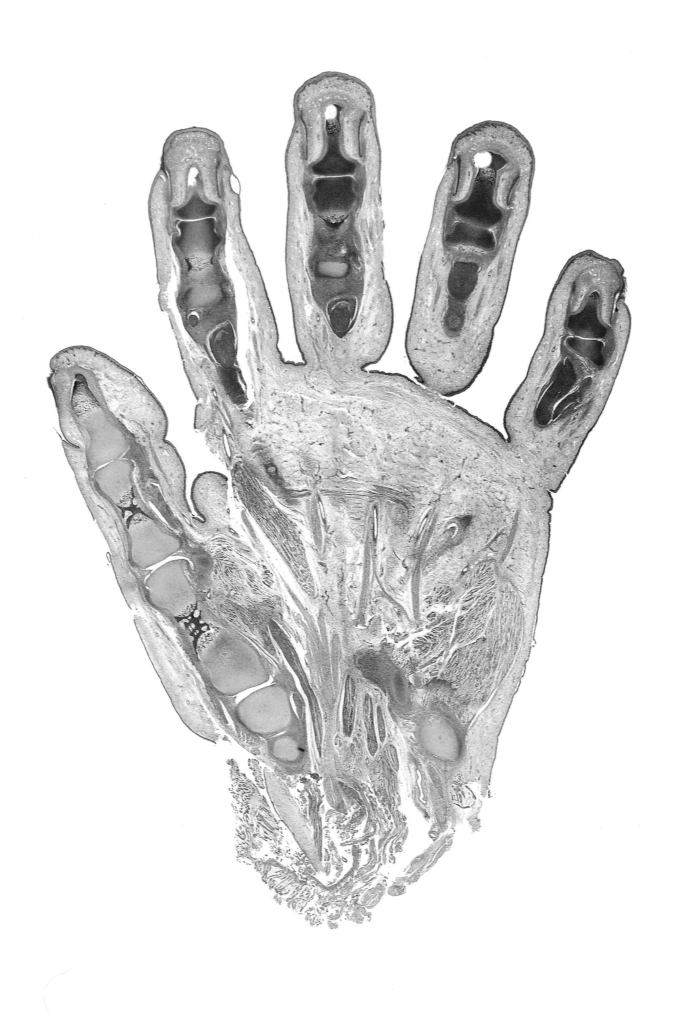

Fetal hand

This fetal hand measures less than one centimeter from
the wrist to the tip of the middle finger. While this fetus
was perfectly formed, he was lodged in his mother's
fallopian tube instead of her uterus. Unfortunately, the
fallopian tube cannot support a pregnancy and the tube
had ruptured, causing life-threatening bleeding requiring
emergency removal of the fetus. Our hands are constant
reminders of our humanity, ever-present in our field
of vision as we go about our lives. Perhaps this is why
the hand is one of the most difficult body parts for new
medical students to dissect in the autopsy lab: like our
faces, our hands are unique and personal reminders of
our corporeal selves. *x6*

Leukemia

Leukemia, derived from the Greek *leukos* and *haima*, literally translates to "white blood." It is a cancer of white blood cells or leukocytes, which are named for the white, creamy layer they form when blood is separated into its components. White blood cells are a critical component of our immune system and include a variety of cells with the ability to fight infection. Most normal white blood cells develop in the bone marrow and then spread via the blood to other parts of the body. Like their normal counterparts, the cancerous white blood cells in leukemia predominantly involve the bone marrow and the blood. Unlike many other cancers, which mostly affect adults, leukemias affect patients of all ages, from newborns to the elderly. In fact, leukemia is the most common cancer in children.

Leukemias arise when a progenitor white blood cell undergoes a transformation into a continuously dividing cancer cell that produces numerous identical daughter cells. The leukemic progenitor cell may grow and divide slowly, resulting in a chronic leukemia, or it may grow and divide rapidly, resulting in an acute leukemia. In both cases, the cancer cells overcrowd normal cells and prevent them from developing appropriately. They thus prevent the body from making the normal components of blood, including red blood cells, which carry oxygen; platelets, which help form blood clots and normal white blood cells. Without their normal cells, patients with leukemia often feel tired and look pale, they bleed easily and they have trouble fighting infections. Ironically, even though they often have an abundance of white blood cells in their blood, these cancerous white blood cells are abnormal and are not able to fight off infections properly. The bone marrow pictured shows a case of chronic myelomonocytic leukemia. Notice how the large pale leukemic cells look very similar to each other in contrast to the heterogenous appearance of residual normal cells in the background. *x600*

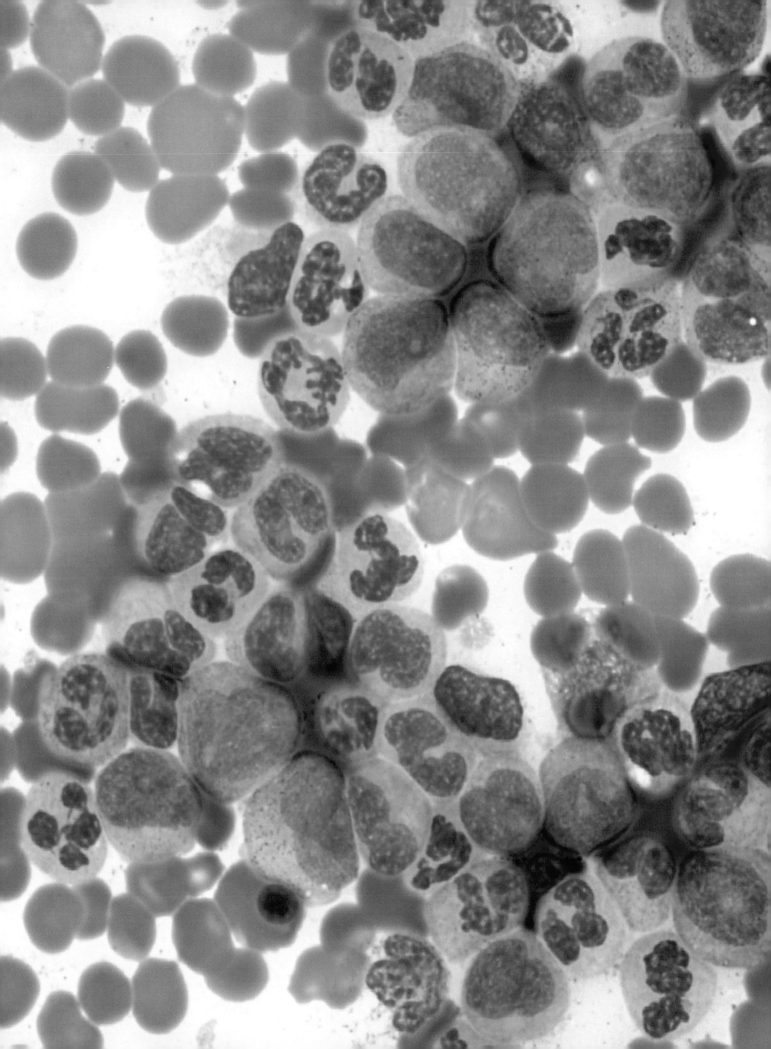

Neuroma

Peripheral nerves are the conduits of communication between the central nervous system (*the brain and spinal cord*) and the rest of the body. These nerves carry instructions from the central nervous system out to the body tissues, such as directing muscles to initiate movement; they also bring information from the body tissues back to the central nervous system, such as recognizing the sensation of touch or temperature. Peripheral nerves are composed of a central nerve axon and its surrounding supportive cells, which include the Schwann cells that make myelin as well as perineurial cells, fibroblasts and dendritic cells. The information carried by the nerve travels down the nerve axon via fluctuations in electrical charges, called action potentials, which are caused by the movement of ions across the cell membrane. The information is passed between nerves as well as between nerves and target tissues through the release of neurotransmitters. The myelin produced by Schwann cells serves as an insulating layer that aids in the swift conduction of the electrical potentials down the axons.

Normally, all of the components of a peripheral nerve are arranged in a neat and orderly fashion, with nerve fibers running in essentially parallel tracts. However, after an injury such as trauma or surgery, nerve fibers may become disorganized as the nerve attempts to regenerate. This benign, non-neoplastic and disordered proliferation of a peripheral nerve is called a neuroma. These traumatic neuromas are small, painful or tender nodules that arise immediately adjacent to an injured nerve. Microscopically, they consist of jumbled masses of nerve bundles embedded in scar tissue and collagen. Under polarized light, both the collagen fibrils as well as the myelin are birefringent and appear shiny yellow or green. The polarized light helps illustrate the many directions in which the collagen fibers and nerve fibers are running. This disarray leads to ineffective nerve conduction at the site of injury and repair. *x400*

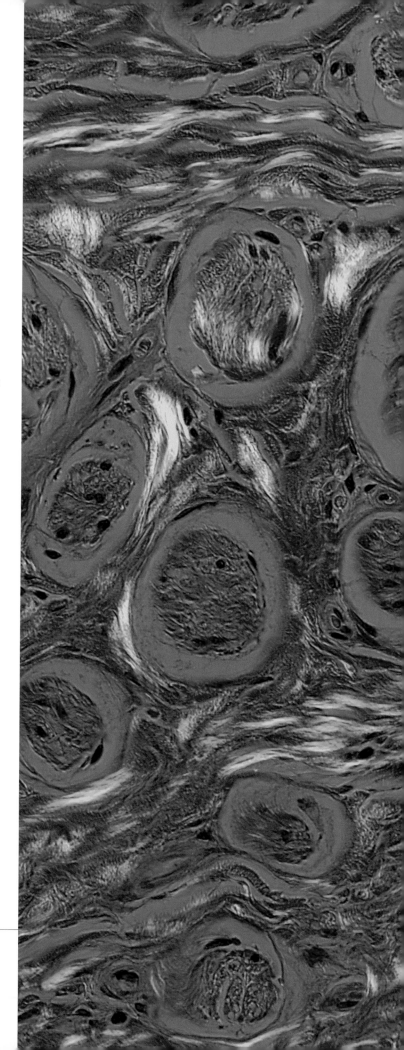

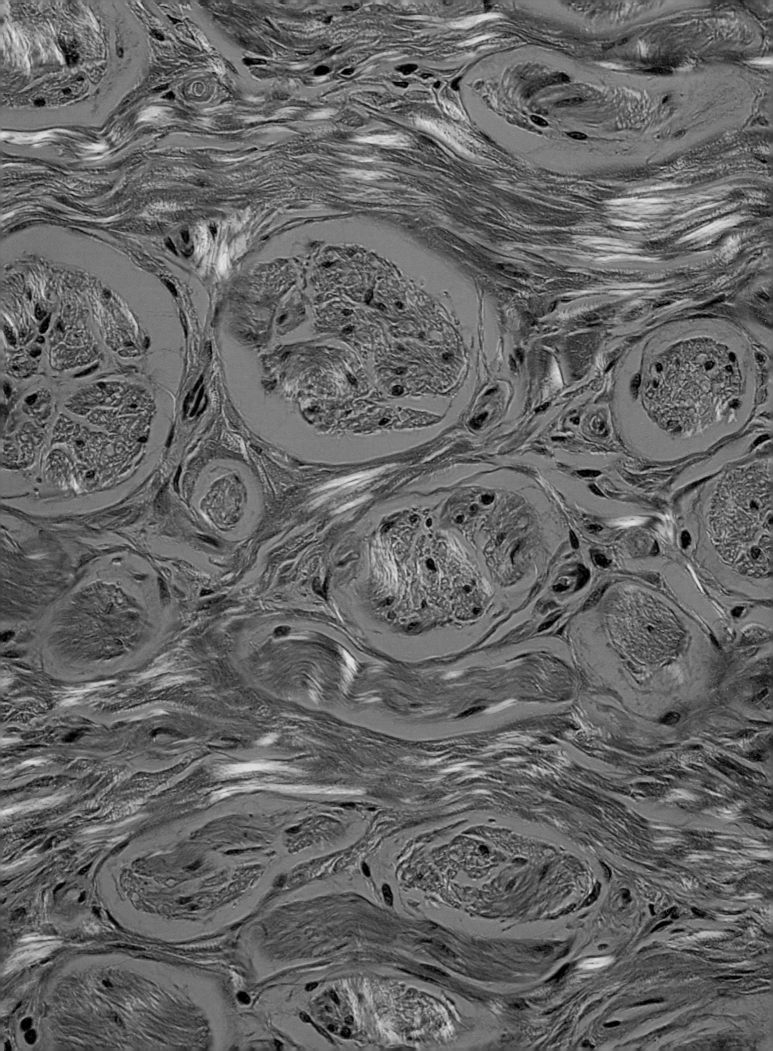

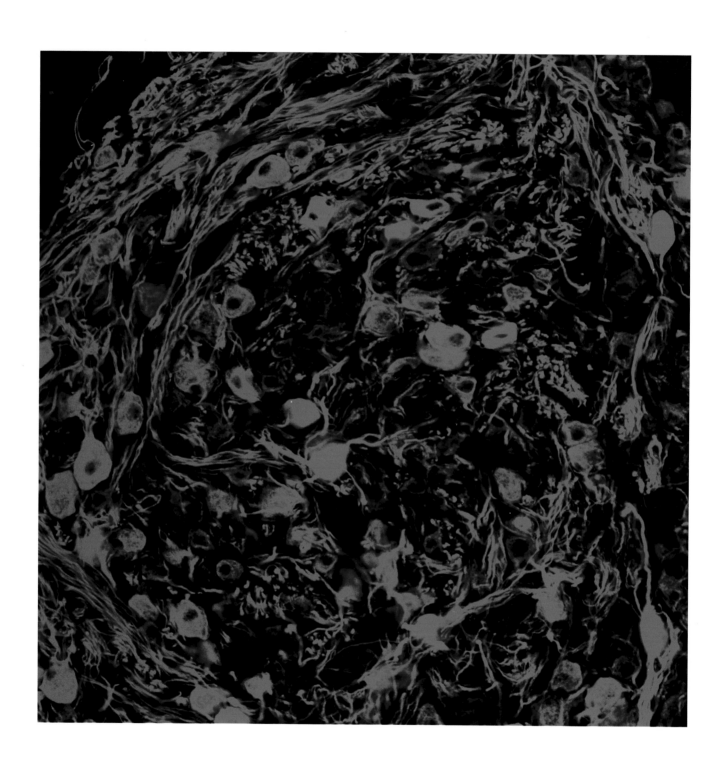

Sympathetic ganglia

Sympathetic neurons are the constituents of a major branch of the peripheral nervous system, which control homeostatic processes such as heart rate, blood pressure, sweat production and pupil dilation. In order to control these events, information must be passed from the spinal cord to sympathetic ganglia located alongside the spinal cord. Axons from the spinal cord contact the sympathetic ganglia via synapses which enable the propagation of information from the CNS (*Central Nervous System*) to the sympathetic nervous system. Activity from the sympathetic ganglia, in turn, control target organs such as the heart. *x750*

Mouse skeleton

Loeys-Dietz syndrome (LDS) is a recently described genetic
connective tissue disorder with similarities to Marfan syndrome
(MFS). The skeletal features of both syndromes often overlap:
for example, LDS patients will also commonly present to an
orthopedic surgeon demonstrating skeletal abnormalities. Unlike
MFS, however, LDS carries a strong risk of aneurysm and dissection
throughout the arterial tree that is often difficult or impossible
to manage surgically, highlighting the need to elucidate disease
pathogenesis and develop medical therapies. To address these
issues of mechanism and treatment, mutant mouse models of LDS
have been created. These mice fully recapitulate the LDS vascular
and musculoskeletal phenotypes, with widespread arterial disease,
including arterial tortuosity, aneurysm and dissection, skeletal
pathology such as kyphoscoliosis (*abnormal curvature of the
spine*) and craniosynostosis. These mice highlight the benefit of
studying disease pathogenesis in mouse models that replicate the
complex physiology of the human condition. Such indicative animal
models may also allow for the trial and development of therapeutic
strategies for genetic disease.

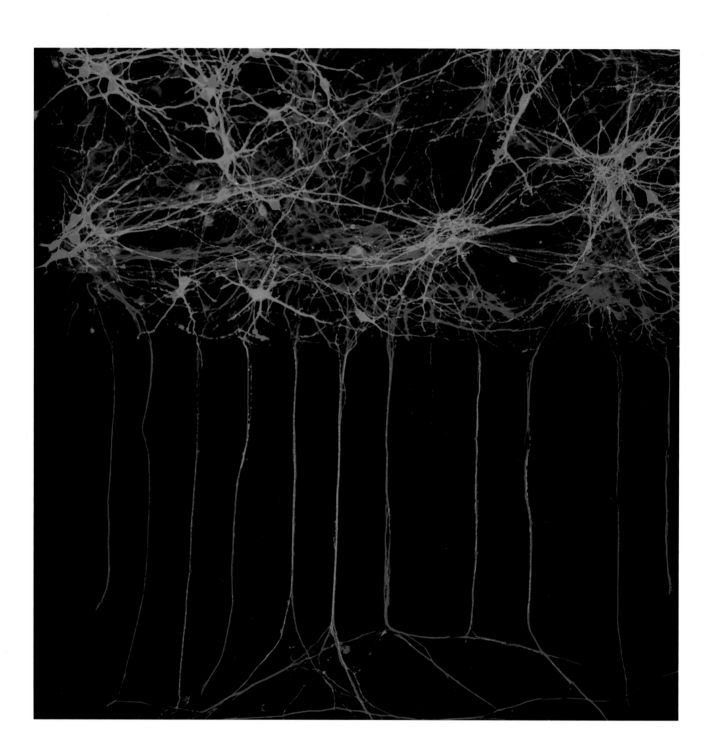

Motor neurons

All of our voluntary movements are controlled by a class of neurons in the spinal cord known as motor neurons. Although the cell bodies of these neurons are located in the spinal cord, they control the activity of the skeletal system by sending electrical impulses along a process, known as the axon, which contacts specific muscles. In humans these axons can extend over one meter away from the cell body. As a result, the local environment of a motor neuron cell body and its axon are distinct. Furthermore, muscles provide the tips of axons with specialized molecules, called trophic factors, which are required for maintaining motor neuron health. If a motor neuron is unable to transport trophic factors back to the cell bodies from the muscles, they will die. Interestingly, several diseases associated with motor neurons, such as Lou Gehrig's Disease, may be due to these axons losing their ability to transport trophic factors from muscles to cell bodies. Recent advances in technologies allow motor neurons to be grown in vitro. *x1000*

Melanoma

The sting of sunburnt skin is frequently the most tangible souvenir of a childhood vacation at the beach. Even though this long-ago sensation remains a distant memory to an adult, those historic blistering sunburns contribute to an increased risk for one of the most sinister diseases of the skin: malignant melanoma. The pathology of melanoma involves the uncontrolled growth of a particular type of cell called the melanocyte. The out-of-control melanocytes proliferate and eventually begin to spread to other locations in the body, where they disrupt normal body functions and destroy normal tissues. Despite extensive research, we still do not have satisfactory treatments for melanoma. Currently, our best hope for people with melanoma lies in the quick and thorough surgical removal of disease, before the cells have had a chance to spread beyond a few millimeters. After the cells begin to spread, or metastasize, there is no cure. Shown at right is a high power microscopic view of a melanoma. The large round structure in the center of the image is a cross section of a hair follicle that is surrounded by the melanoma cells containing brown pigment. *x400*

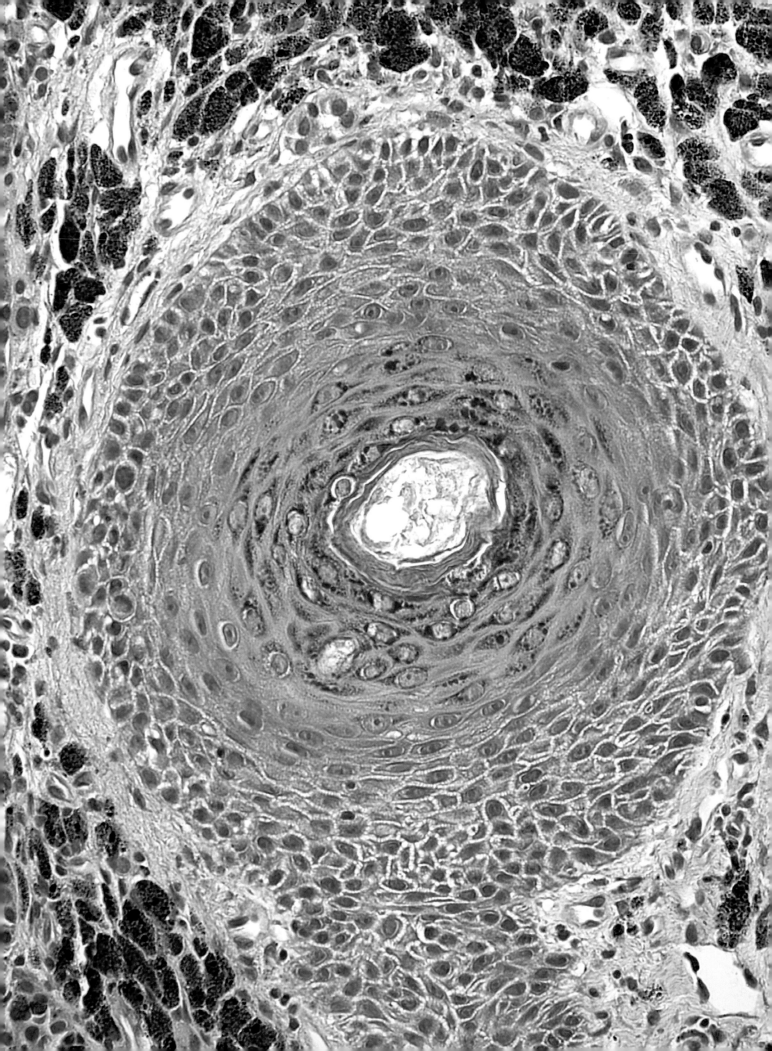

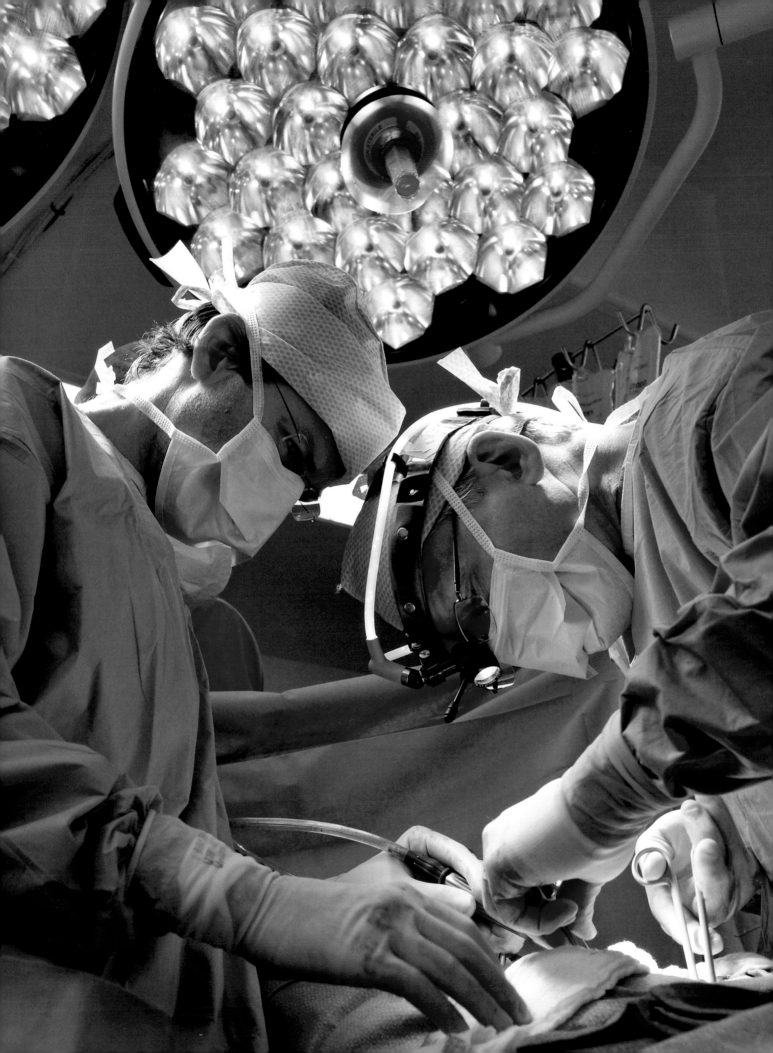

Modern surgery

Surgery can be traced back to antiquity. Archeological finds have demonstrated that Incan surgeons (*called siraks*) successfully practiced trepanation, the burring of a hole in the skull. For many centuries, however, surgery was painful, almost barbaric. In the eighteenth century operating room floors were covered with sawdust to absorb large quantities of blood that were lost, and multiple assistants were needed, not to aid the surgeon with the operation, but to hold the screaming patient down. A good surgeon was a very fast surgeon. Everything changed on October 16, 1846. On this date in Massachusetts General Hospital, William Morton delivered ether to a sleeping patient while John C. Warren painlessly removed a tumor from the angle of the patient's jaw. The modern era of surgery was born.

In the decades that followed, many surgeons continued to operate quickly, even though they now had ample time since the patient was asleep. It wasn't until the end of the nineteenth century that William Stewart Halsted, the first chairman of surgery at Johns Hopkins, established the modern principles of safe, surgery-delicate handling of tissues, careful control of bleeding and prevention of infection; Halsted also established the modern surgery residency training program, and his disciples would promulgate his methods throughout the country. His students would establish new branches of surgery and explore the deeper and inherently more dangerous parts of the body. Halstead's resident, Harvey Cushing, a pioneering neurosurgeon, performed painlessly and meticulously in well-lit extremely clean operating rooms. Absolute care is taken to maintain sterility, to minimize bleeding and to preserve function. Most importantly, surgery is now safe.

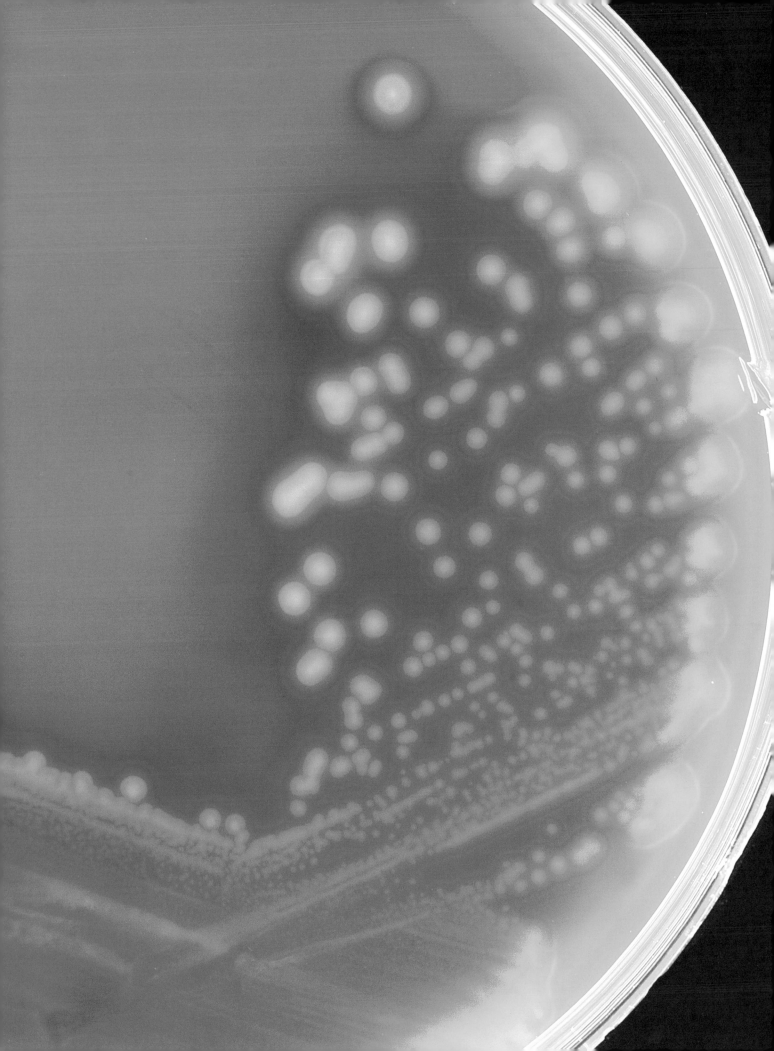

Infection & Inflammation

Lone star tick

This sample was a punch biopsy removed from a patient
who never became sick. The tick that is attached is
Amblyomma americanum, aka "Lone star tick," and this
one is an adult female that is engorged. This tick is best
known as a vector for *Francisella tularensis* (*a bacterium
that causes tularemia*) and for *Ehrlichia chaffeensis* and
Ehrlichia ewingii (*related bacteria that cause "ehrlichiosis"*).
The photograph on the left is particularly interesting
because the histology shows very clearly how the tick
inserts its hypostome (*the syringe like needle nose*)
through the skin surface (*epidermis*) into the underlying
dermis, to create an inflammatory lesion that is also
enriched with blood and fluids that are food for ticks. This
also demonstrates how easily a pathogen that rides along
in the tick saliva can get access to the blood or lymphatics
of an animal, or a person who is bitten. Other interesting
features include some of the tick histology and anatomy,
including: the tick salivary gland, from which pathogens
can enter into the host; the tick hemocele, the "blood"
compartment of the tick and the tick midgut, through
which pathogens obtained from an infected host's
blood must pass before infecting the tick. *x10*

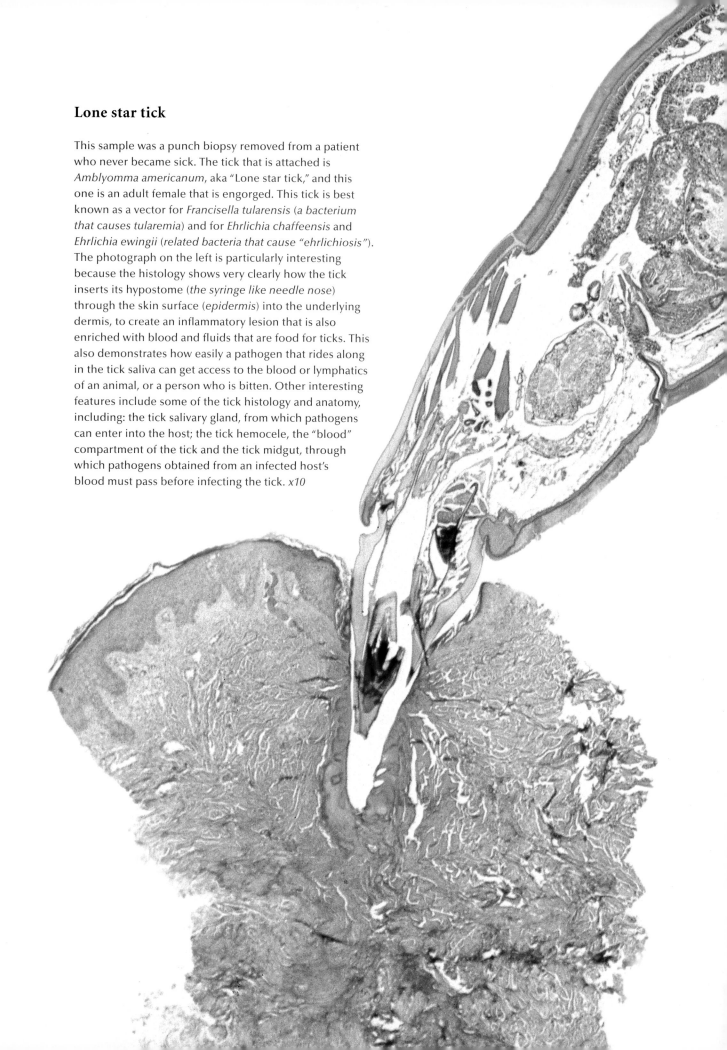

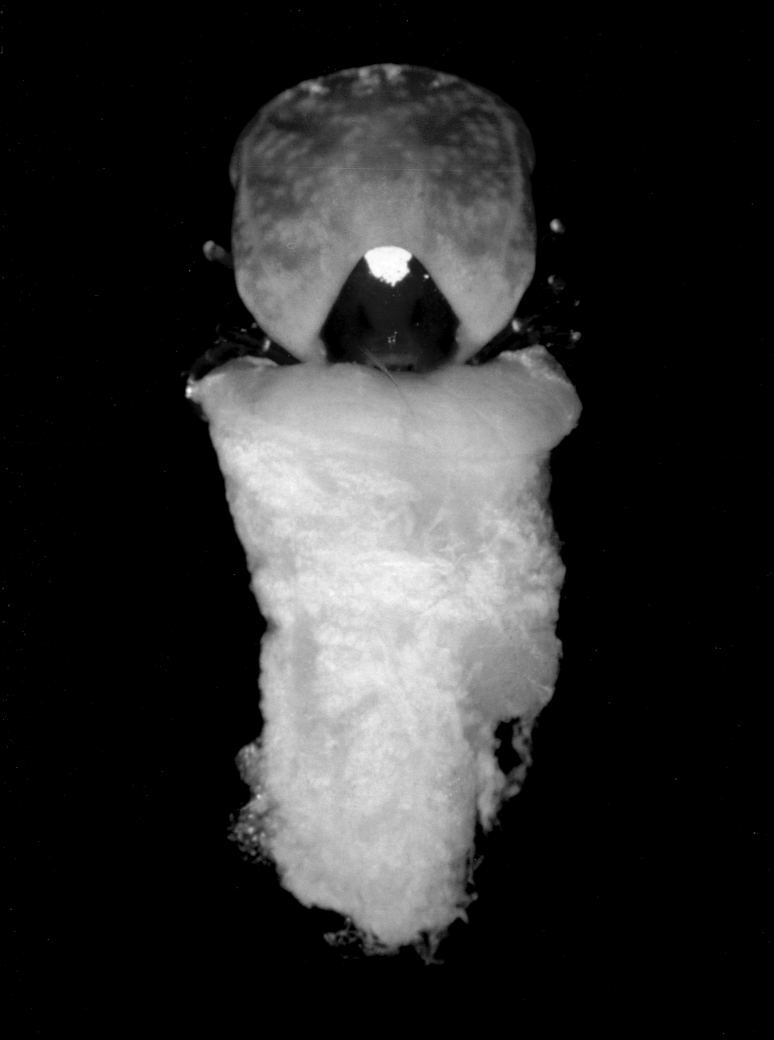

Culture plates

Culture plates illustrate the rich variety of fungi that are present in the environment. The effects of fungi on humans vary as widely as their diversity of color and texture. The great majority of fungi are completely harmless. Some fungal species can colonize the human body, or produce superficial infections like ringworm or athlete's foot. Others, however, can cause serious tissue infections in both normal, immunocompetent individuals, and more often in immunocompromised hosts such as those persons receiving chemotherapy, organ transplants or who are HIV positive. In some patients these fungal infections can be fatal.

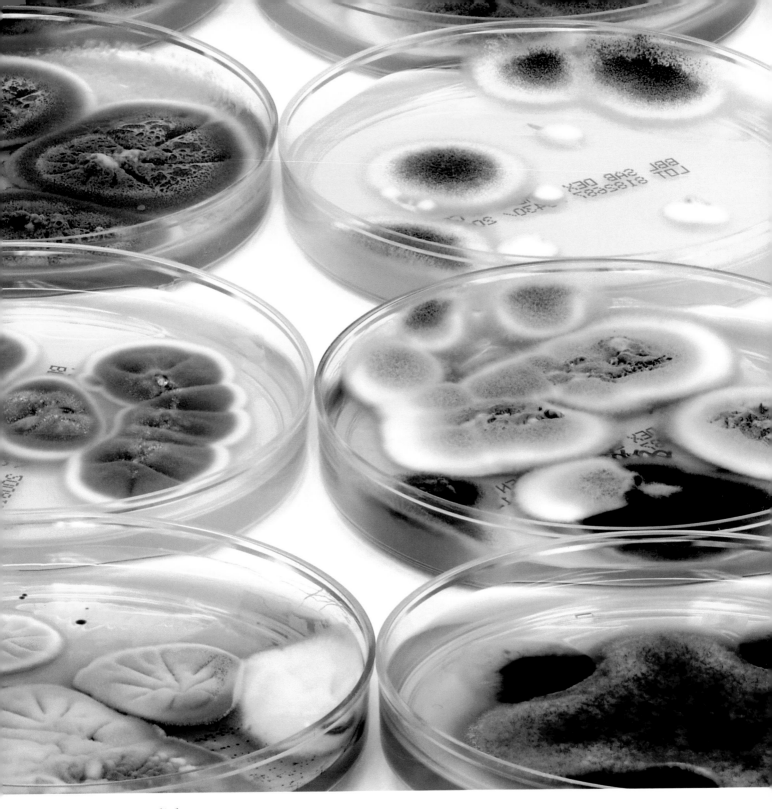

Agar petri dishes *(overleaf)*

Clinical microbiologists use culture plates containing different types of agar-based media to identify bacteria and fungi that cause infections in patients. Pathogenic microorganisms are isolated in the laboratory from clinical specimens on media containing ingredients such as antibiotics, special nutrients, or dyes. These ingredients often enable the organisms to grow better or display a characteristic appearance or color that makes them more easily identified from other organisms.

Cutaneous nerve fibers

Skin, the largest organ of our body, performs many complex life-sustaining functions. It serves as a protective barrier against disease, regulates body temperature, prevents dehydration, produces vitamin D through UV exposure and acts as a communication system through blushing. Bundles of nerves enter the skin in the deep dermal layers and course toward the epidermis, the superficial layer of the skin. The nerves, acting as electrical cables, innervate blood vessels, hair follicles, sweat glands and terminate as free nerve endings. The sensory nerve fibers allow us to feel touch, pain, temperature, vibration and pressure sensations. The hair follicles are closely associated with arrector pili muscles. When these muscles contract, "goose bumps" form, and sebum secreting sebaceous glands oil the surface, which helps waterproof the skin. The Cutaneous Nerve Laboratory of the Johns Hopkins Neurology Department, along with several groups, has developed expertise in the identification and quantitation of cutaneous nerve fibers. The skin punch is a simple non-invasive technique that serves as a sensitive measure of nerve function, and thus helps in identifying patients with sensory neuropathies.

The photomicrograph shown is a section of normal skin as viewed under a microscope. The nerves have been visualized by immunostaining with an antibody directed against PGP 9.5 protein, which is specific to the nerves. A single yellow hair shaft is seen in the dermis and the innervation pattern of the hair follicle is complex. The nerves are wrapped around the base of the follicle and along the shaft of the hair. The rich plexus of nerves in the top layer of epidermis are single unmyelinated (*uninsulated*) sensory nerves. Skin biopsies have changed the way neurologists around the world are looking at peripheral nerves. *x20*

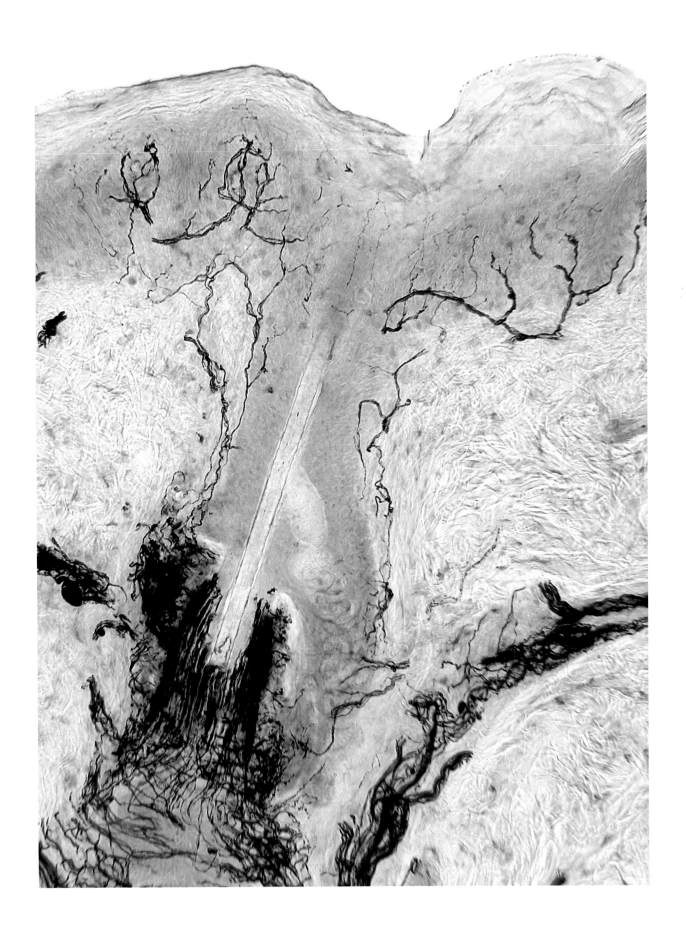

Autoimmune diseases

We are at constant risk from foreign invasion; countless bacteria live on our skin and in our gastrointestinal system, and we can be exposed to numerous viruses and fungi each day. It is our spectacular immune system that protects and defends us from their potentially harmful effects. It is this same immune system, though, that also causes us to feel sick when we are ill. It is the immune system that causes us to have a fever when we have the flu, and it is the same immune system which results in the redness, warmth and pain that we experience after we cut ourselves. Without question, our immune system is absolutely critical to human survival, but it can also be a component of human suffering.

The goal of any immune system, essentially, is to distinguish things that are foreign from things that are not. The immune system in some people, however, is not perfect. When an immune system develops a significant and long-lasting response against substances and tissues normally present in the human body, we medically define these as autoimmune diseases. In these diseases, the body actually targets its own cells because the immune system mistakes some part of our own body as a pathogen and attacks it. There are numerous human diseases classified as autoimmune diseases, and more than 23.5 million Americans today suffer from some type of autoimmune disease. They also have an extraordinary diversity. The process may be restricted to a certain organ (*e.g., in autoimmune thyroiditis and the thyroid*) or involve a particular tissue type (*e.g., in Goodpasture's disease which may affect basement membrane tissue in both the lung and the kidney*). Simply put, no organ or tissue in our body is safe from our own immune system. Some common autoimmune diseases include Lupus (SLE), Multiple Sclerosis, Celiac disease, Diabetes (*type 1*) and Rheumatoid arthritis.

The presence of antinuclear antibodies (ANA) (*pictured to the right*) is the hallmark of patients with systemic autoimmune diseases, such as Lupus (SLE), but it is not necessarily specific for any one disease. These antibodies, when detected, can help establish a diagnosis in a patient with clinical features suggestive of an autoimmune disease or exclude such disorders in patients with limited clinical findings. Additionally, antinuclear antibodies produce a wide range of staining patterns that reflect the presence of antibodies to one, or a combination of, specific nuclear proteins. Many labs today use a fluorescent label to highlight the patient's nuclear antibodies as they adhere to the nuclei of a standardized commercially available cell line known as HEp2 (*human epithelial cell tumor line*). While studies to detect specific types of ANA have largely replaced the need for accurate staining pattern interpretation, the presence of a specific pattern can help support a diagnosis or serve as a clue to guide additional diagnostic studies. The ANA pattern shown to the right is known as a speckled pattern; a pattern that can be seen in SLE but may also be detected in other systemic autoimmune diseases.

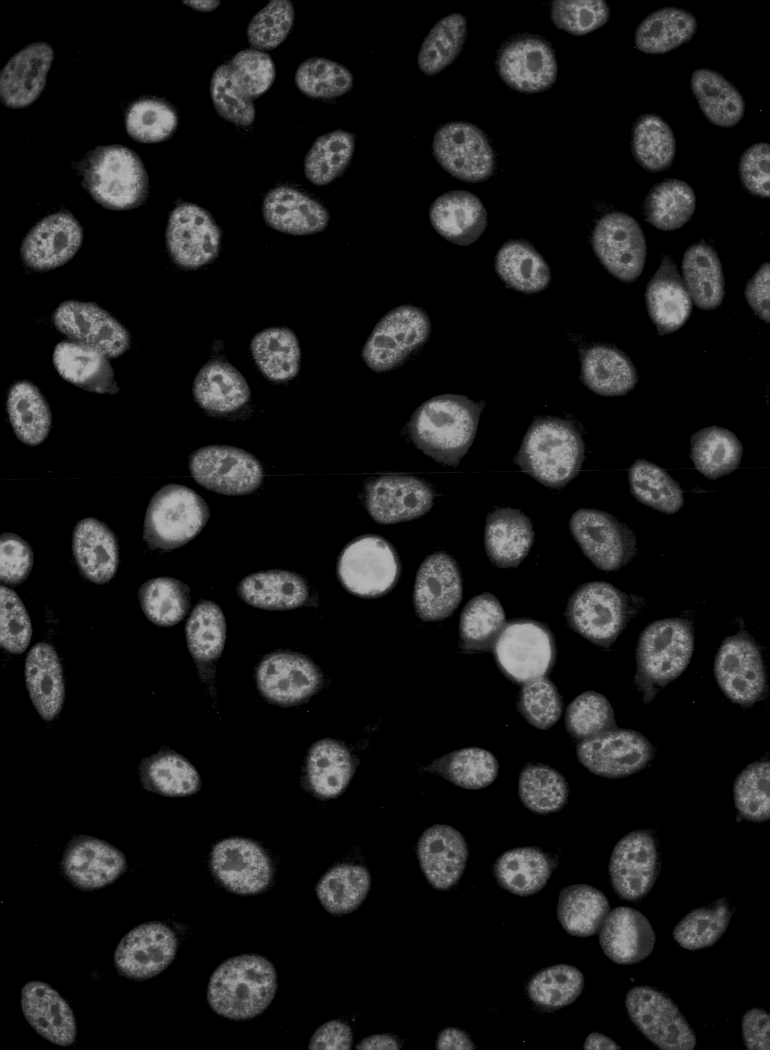

HIV

The first cases of the acquired immune deficiency syndrome (AIDS) were reported in 1981 in gay men in Los Angeles. These men presented with Pneumocystis Carinii pneumonia in association with enlarged lymph nodes and immune deficiency. In 1983, Luc Montaigner and his colleagues in France reported finding a retrovirus in patients with AIDS which was called lymphadenopathy associated virus (LAV). The following year, Robert Gallo and colleagues at the National Institutes of Health in Bethesda Maryland further characterized this retrovirus and identified antibodies in the blood of AIDS patients against the virus; this quickly led to an antibody test to diagnose this infection and protect the blood supply. Gallo's group named the virus HTLV-III, which was later renamed human immunodeficiency virus, or HIV.

The electron micrograph to the right captures the basic pathogenesis of HIV. HIV infects a CD4 positive T cell (*a type of white blood cell*) which then produces more HIV virions, seen in the image at right budding from the T cell surface. This process causes destruction of these cells and infection of additional CD4 positive T cells and macrophages. This constant and dynamic destructive process over nearly a decade leads to CD4 positive lymphocyte depletion resulting in severe immune deficiency. The loss of these critical cells allows opportunistic infections and various cancers to arise that may cause patient death. Fortunately, a number of very effective antiretroviral drugs have been developed since 1987 which have greatly extended the lives of these patients for decades and effectively prevent mother-to-child transmission of HIV. However, because HIV is able to integrate into DNA and remain silent in some types of lymphocytes, eradication of the virus has not been successful. In addition, the extremely high mutation rate of the virus has allowed it to become resistant to multiple antiretiroviral drugs, and escape the attack of both the body's immune response or that generated by experimental vaccines to date. By 2010, approximately 70 million people had died of AIDS worldwide and some 33 million people were living with HIV infection. Hopefully, an effective vaccine will be developed which will prevent HIV infection and greatly reduce the number of people who acquire this deadly infection. *x27,630*

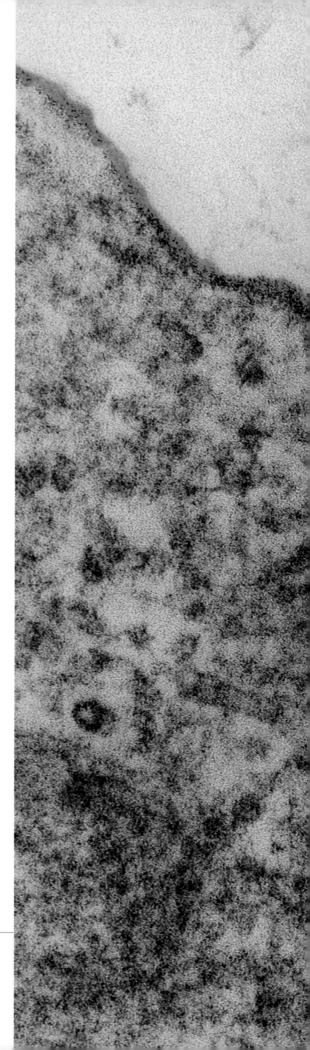

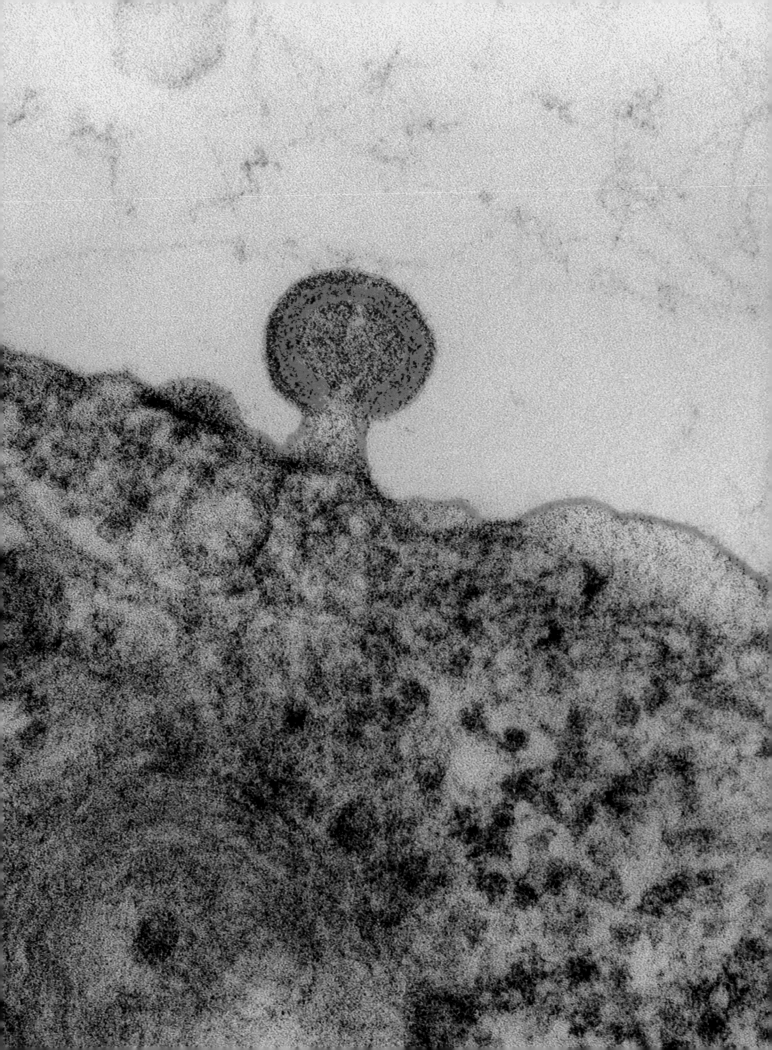

Aspergillus fumigatus

Every day our bodies are bombarded with thousands of microorganisms in the environment, but our immune systems efficiently eliminate them and prevent the development of an infection. One such microorganism is *Aspergillus fumigatus*, a fungus that is found naturally in soil. *Aspergillus* grows on organic debris, aiding in the normal decaying process. In some individuals repeatedly exposed to *Aspergillus* spores from soil, such as farmers, *Aspergillus* may cause mild forms of allergy. However, with the ever increasing number of people who are immunosuppressed following an organ transplant, cancer chemotherapy or infection with HIV, *Aspergillus* is the most prevalent cause of airborne fungal infection, and a common cause of death. *x400*

Candida *(overleaf)*

Candida species are a type of yeast. The most medically significant form of Candida is *Candida albicans* (*C. albicans*), although *C. glabrata* is another form of Candida increasingly recognized as contributing to human disease. These Candida species are normal constituents of the skin, the gastrointestinal and genitourinary tract of humans. Candida are responsible for common conditions such as thrush in infants, athletes foot, jock itch and vaginal yeast infections, all of which are easily treated with antifungal medications. However, in patients with a weakened immune system such as those with HIV infection, in intensive care, cancer, or an organ transplant, Candida may cause an "opportunistic" infection that is life threatening. The image on the overleaf is a high-powered view of an active Candida esophagitis in a patient with acquired immunodeficiency syndrome due to HIV infection. Whereas Candida species normally appear as oval shaped organisms under the microscope, in this patient the yeast forms (*stained black*) have sprouted into branch shaped structures that are invading into the esophageal tissues. *x200*

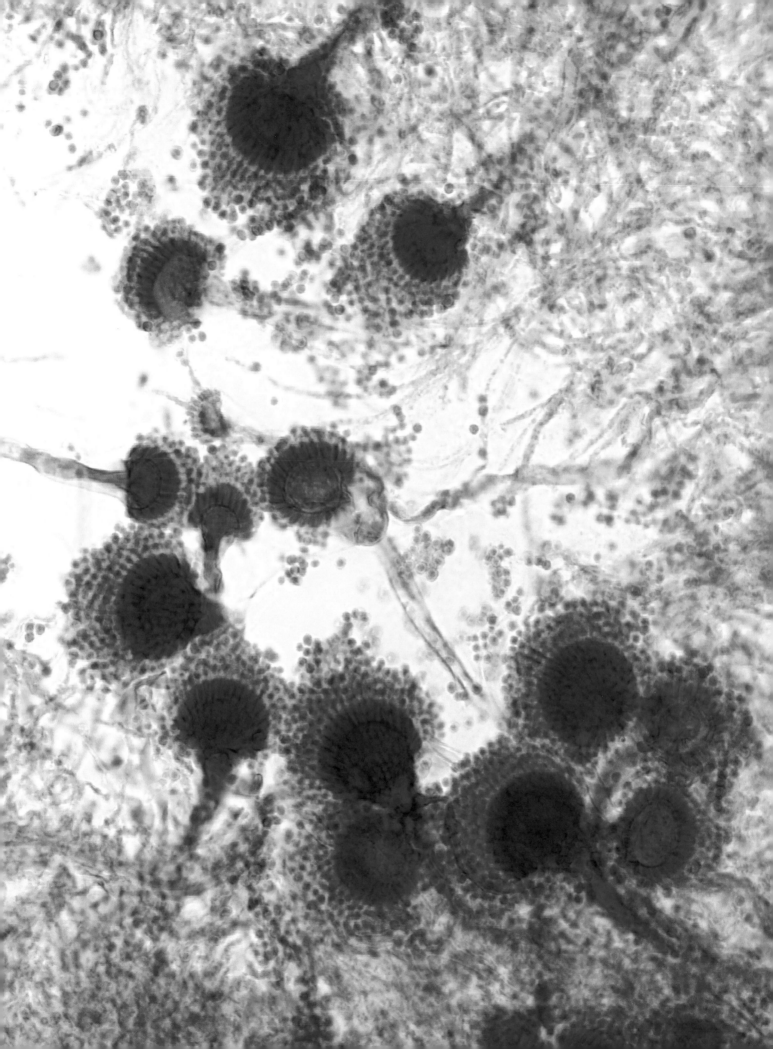

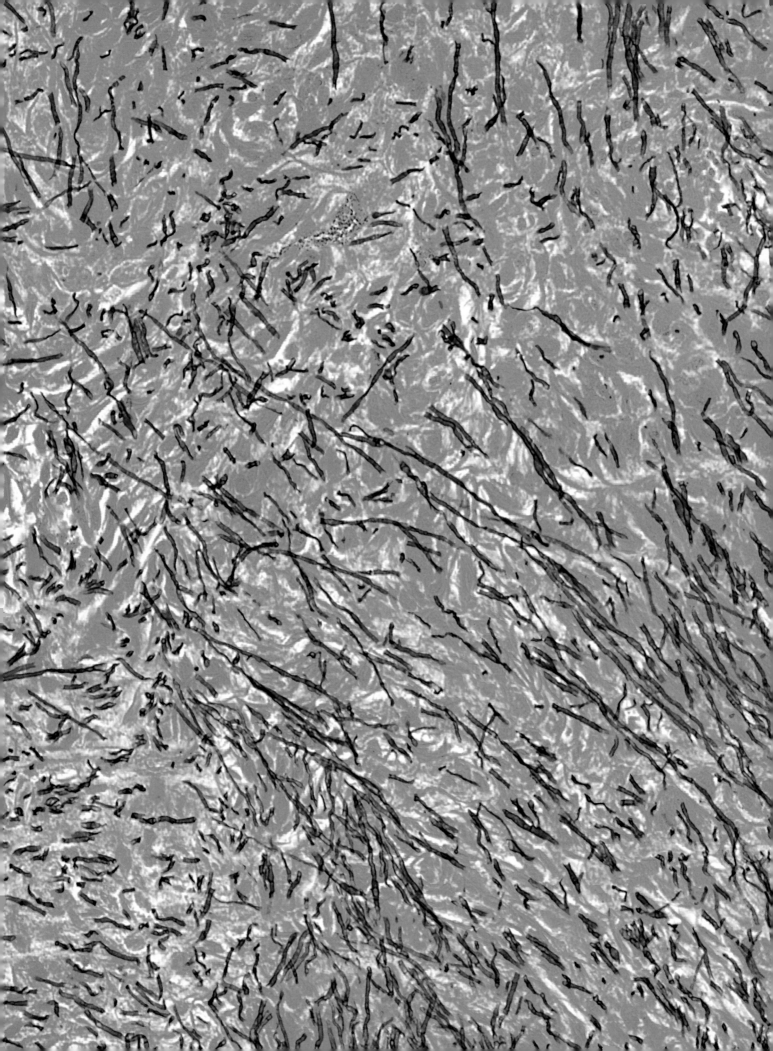

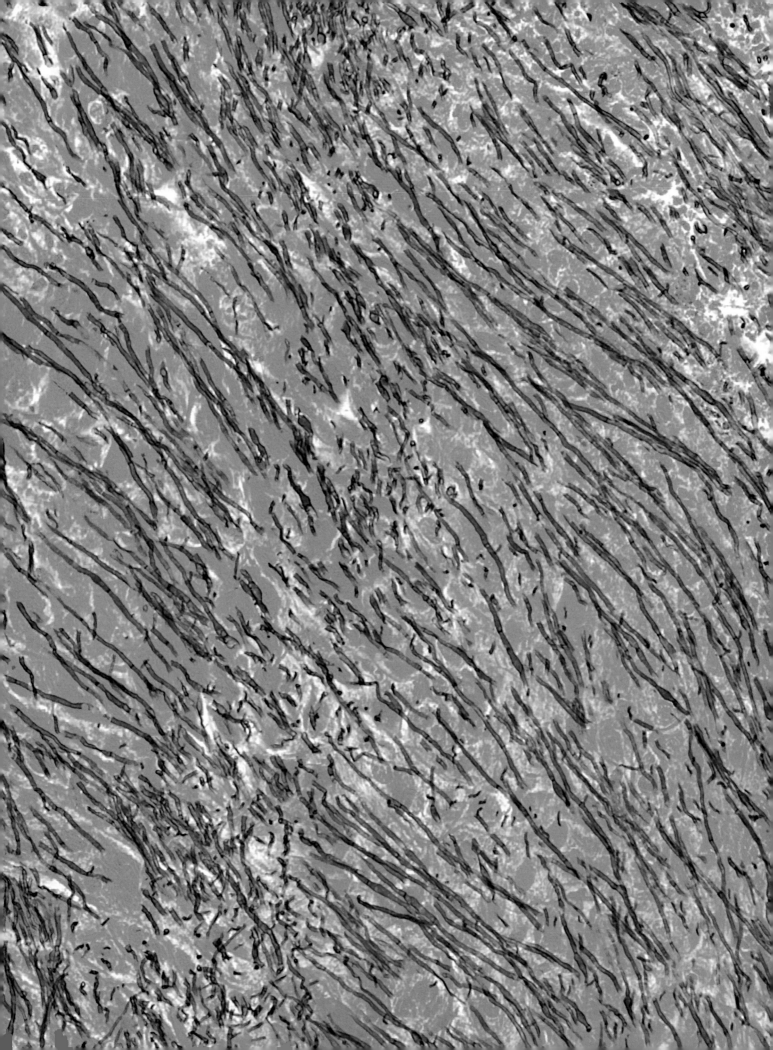

Helicobacter pylori

Helicobacter is a genus of gram-negative bacteria possessing a characteristic helix shape. The most widely known species of this genus is *Helicobactor pylori* which infects up to 50% of the human population. In particular, *Helicobacter pylori* not only survives but thrives in the very acidic stomach of infected individuals by producing large quantities of the enzyme urease that raises the pH of the stomach from ~ 2 to a more biocompatible range of 6 to 7. In biopsies of infected individuals, the stomach contains a characteristic form of inflammation that is typically not seen in the stomachs of noninfected individuals. *H. pylori* organisms are usually susceptible to routinely used antibiotics and can thus be easily treated. However, if untreated *H. pylori* infection can lead to the formation of peptic ulcers, chronic gastritis, stomach cancer and lymphomas of the stomach. The image at right illustrates *Helicobactor pylori* bacteria as seen by scanning electron microscopy. The organisms, seen in shades of yellow and green, are helical (*i.e. spiral shaped*). In some instances delicate filaments are also seen that correspond to the bacterium's flagellae, an organelle that provides motility. *x1600*

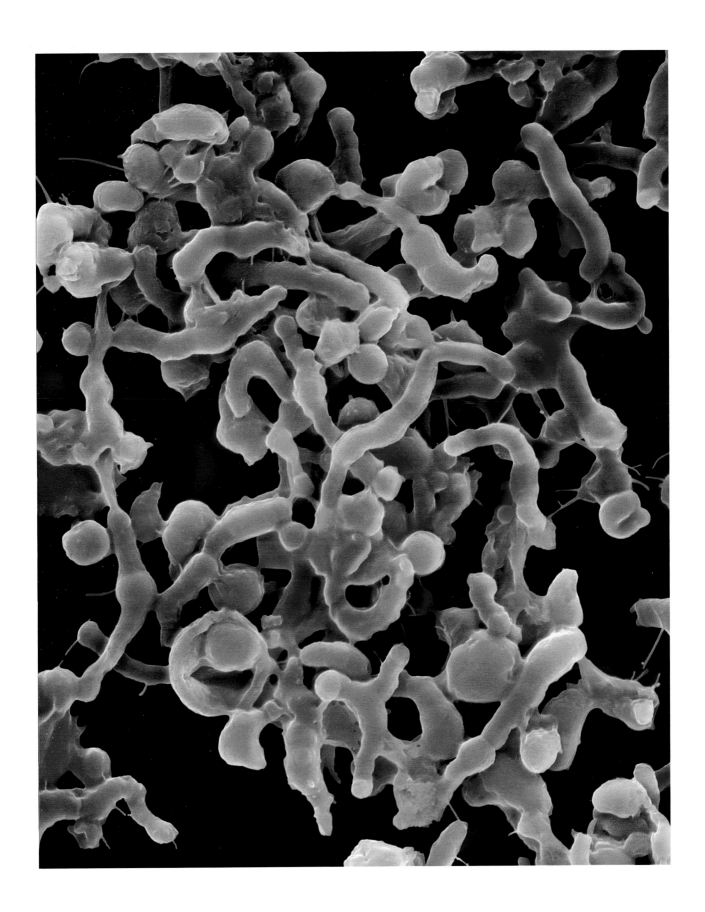

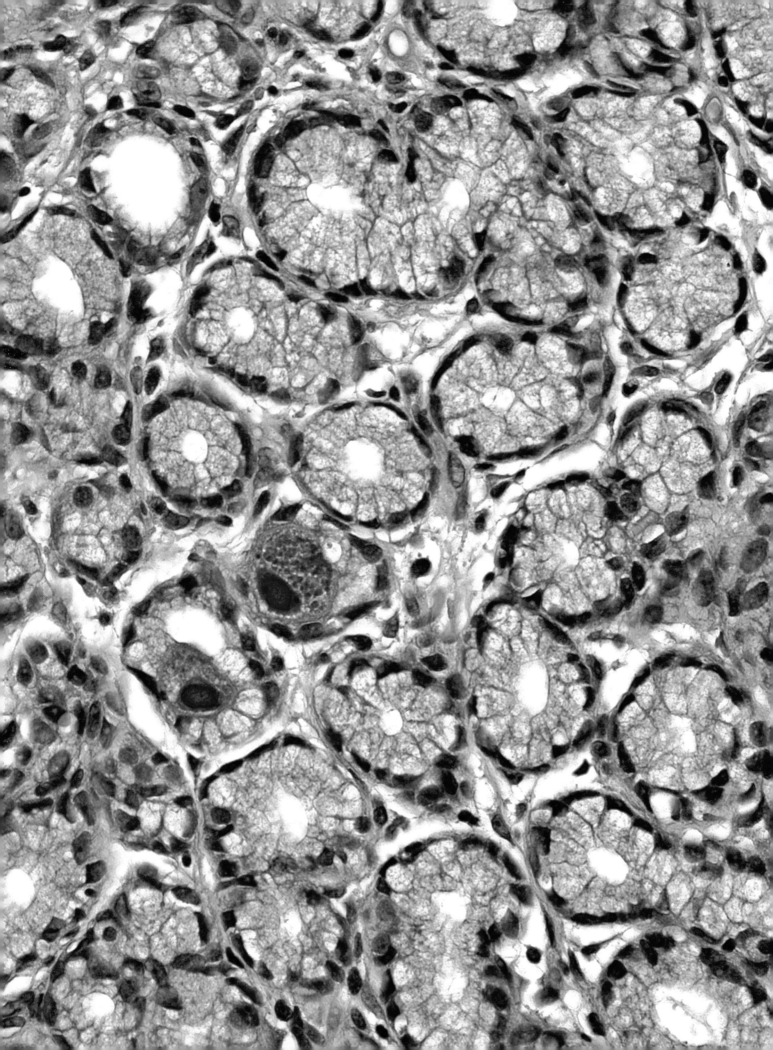

Cytomegalovirus, CMV

Cytomegalovirus (CMV), named from the Greek words *cyto* for "cell" and *megalo* for "large," is a member of the herpes family of viruses. Most individuals in the general population have been exposed to CMV. However, the initial infection causes no symptoms because the immune system easily keeps the virus under control. The virus thus remains alive but dormant within the body. However, in some patients with a weakened immune system, for example due to acquired immunodeficiency syndrome, an organ transplant or cancer, the virus may reactivate and cause fever, pneumonia, inflammation of the eyes or gastrointestinal bleeding. The image at right is from the esophagus in an individual with acquired immunodeficiency syndrome (AIDS) due to human immunodeficiency virus (HIV). This patient presented with chest pain, and a biopsy of the esophagus revealed the presence of viral particles within the cells of a small gland within the esophageal lining. The viral particles are seen as large, bright magenta inclusions in the cells of the gland, in keeping with the Greek derivation of its name. *x600*

Penicillium

Penicillium, like its cousin *Aspergillus*, is a fungus which normally lives in the environment as a decomposer. The many species of *Penicillium* vary widely in color and texture. Cases of human infection caused by *Penicillium sp.* are rare, but can occur in individuals with depressed immune systems due to chemotherapy, organ transplant, or HIV/AIDS. Was it serendipity, or just sloppy lab work, that led to the discovery of one of the greatest compounds in medical history—the antibiotic named for this fungus? Dr. Alexander Fleming, a Scottish bacteriologist, is generally credited with the initial discovery of penicillin. In his laboratory at St. Mary's Hospital in London in 1928, he grew cultures of the bacteria *Staphylococcus aureus*. These cultures were ignored for several weeks while he went on vacation. When he returned, he noticed that the culture plates were contaminated with a fuzzy green fungus; where the fungus was growing, the bacteria were inhibited. What substance was the fungus, later identified as *Pencillium notatum*, producing that kept the bacteria from growing? He isolated an extract and reported these findings in 1929 in the British Journal of Experimental Pathology. Together with Dr. Fleming, Dr. Howard Florey and Dr. Ernst Chain were awarded the Nobel Prize in Medicine in 1945 for their ground-breaking work in the isolation and development of penicillin as an antibiotic. The development and subsequent distribution of penicillin revolutionized the treatment of many bacterial infections, including strep and staph infections, gonorrhea, syphilis and diphtheria. Millions of lives were saved in the 1930s and 1940s, including a large number of soldiers during World War II.

Unfortunately, many bacteria have since developed resistance to penicillin; thus, penicillin is not as widely used today as it was in its earliest years. Dr. Fleming actually predicted that this would happen. The process of bacterial resistance to antibiotics occurs continuously and relentlessly, resulting in the ongoing need to develop new antibiotics. The *Penicllium* mold in the illustration is growing contentedly beside a mucoid yellow bacteria that seems not at all inhibited by any substance that this fungus may be producing. *x4*

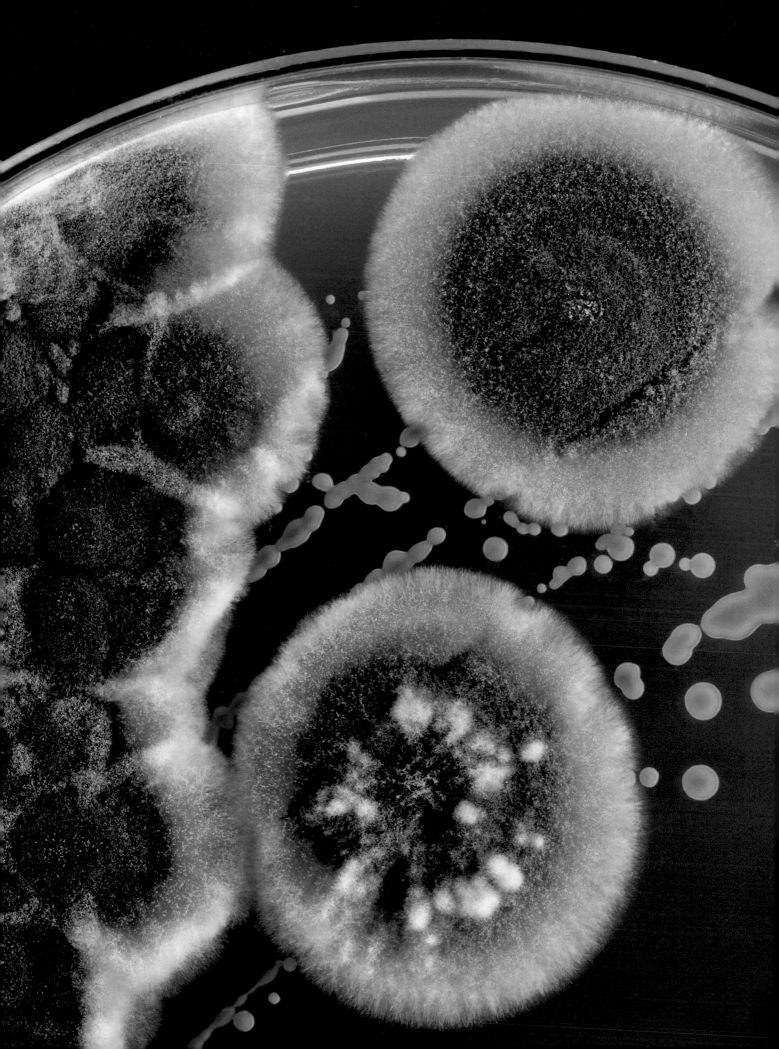

Malaria's cycle of misery and death has ravaged humans for thousands of years. According to UNICEF, malaria affects 350–500 million people every year and kills more than 1 million in Africa alone, most of which are young children. Around the world about 20 different species of the mosquito genus *Anopheles* is responsible for the transmission of malaria to humans. The disease is caused by a group of *Plasmodium* parasites, the most deadly of which is *Plasmodium falciparum*. About half of the human population is at risk for malaria, which occurs, at present, in about 108 countries in Asia, Latin America, sub-Saharan Africa and parts of the Middle East and Europe. In addition, the *Plasmodium* is developing increasing resistance to traditional antimalarial prophylactic drugs. Over the past few decades malaria has spread to previously unaffected highland areas and larger centers of population. The cause of the spread is not only climate change, but also human migration and international travel, the so-called airport malaria. Here we see an adult female *Anopheles* mosquito having a human blood meal. The abdomen is engorged with blood and bodily fluids are being expelled from the abdomen to allow for the consumption of a maximum amount of blood. The disease is spread via the mosquito's salivary glands. In humans, the parasites (*called sporozoites*) migrate to the liver where they mature and release another form, the merozoites. These enter the bloodstream and infect the red blood cells.

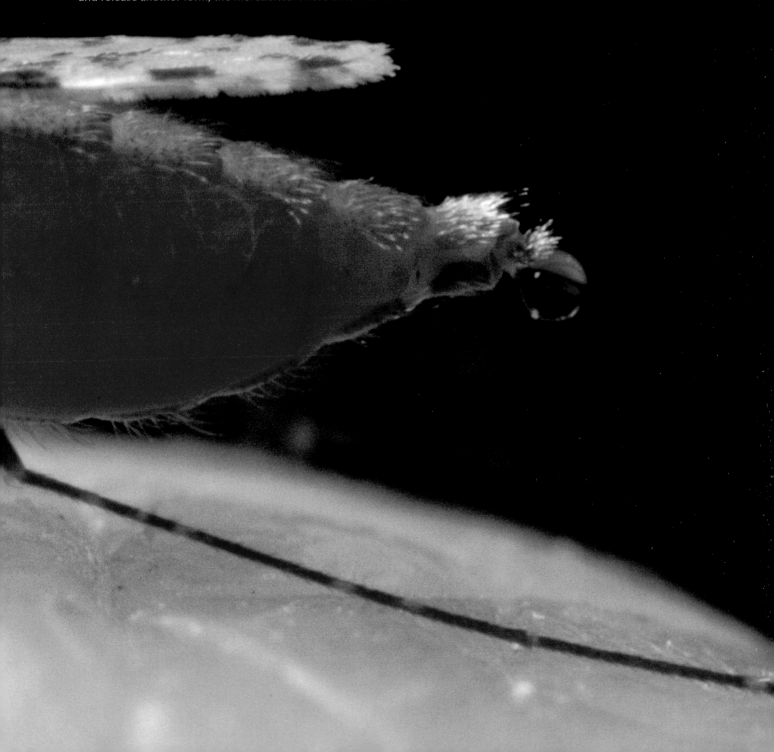

Hepatitis B virus (HBV)

There are eight known genotypes of Hepatitis virus, categorized as Hepatitis A through Hepatitis H virus. These genotypes differ from each other by at least 8% of their DNA sequences and have distinct geographical distributions. For example, Hepatitis A is commonly found in Europe, Africa and Southeast Asia, whereas Hepatitis B and C viruses are pervasive in Asia. The significance of Hepatitis viruses is that they can cause chronic hepatitis that can lead to cirrhosis (*scarring of the liver*) and liver cancer (*called hepatoma*). The greatest risk of developing chronic hepatitis comes specifically from Hepatitis B and C viruses. These viruses are transmitted through contact with the blood or other body fluids of an infected person and are up to 50 times more infectious than the HIV virus. It can be spread by infected blood, through blood transfusions, tattooing, acupuncture and needle sharing by intravenous drug abusers. Worldwide, approximately 2 billion people have been infected with Hepatitis B virus and 350 million live with chronic infection. As many as 300 million individuals worldwide are infected with Hepatitis C virus. Moreover, an estimated 600,000 individuals die each year due to the acute or chronic consequences of Hepatitis viral infections. Vaccinations against Hepatitis B virus represent a major effort to prevent infection and the development of cirrhosis and hepatoma. By contrast, no vaccines are available for Hepatitis C virus due to its ability to constantly mutate its DNA during replication. SEM *x39,760*

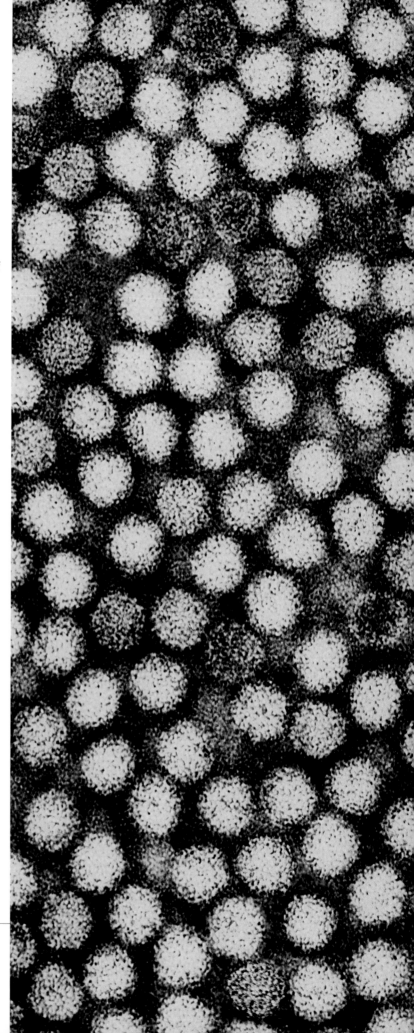

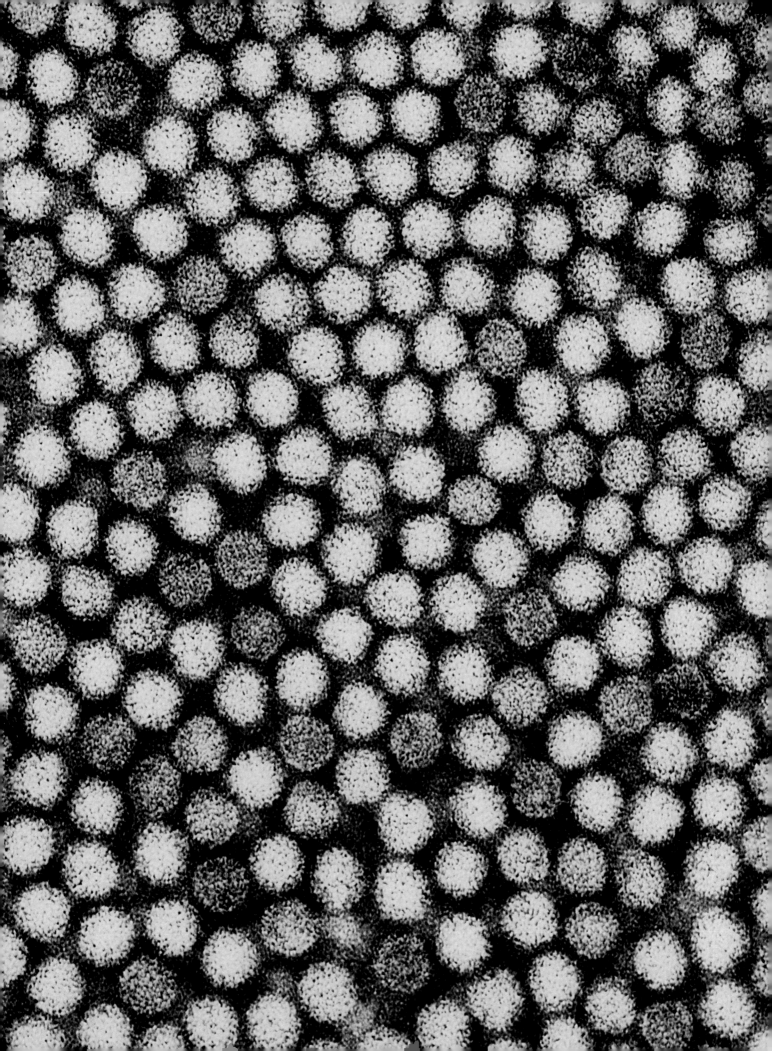

Research

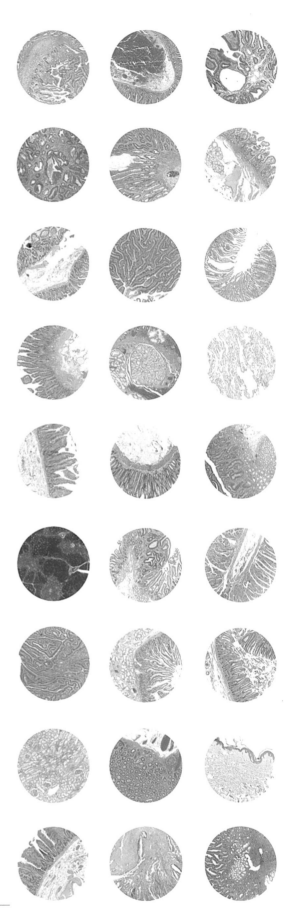

Tissue microarray

Medical researchers are frequently identifying protein molecules, or biomarkers, they believe may play a role in disease. To validate these findings, it is important to determine if these proteins are produced in the diseased tissues and if their presence correlates with the patient's prognosis or their response to treatment.

A rapid and efficient manner to answer these questions is with the use of a tissue microarray, also known as a TMA. Prior to the development of TMAs, the molecular analysis of tissues was tedious, limited by available resources and often led to highly variable results that were difficult to interpret. With TMAs, cores of diseased tissue from many patients can be uniformly embedded (*arrayed*) in paraffin, with paper thin sections cut from the wax and placed onto glass slides for microscopic analysis and evaluation of the presence of biomarkers of interest. A simple TMA is shown at right in which 99 different samples of normal tissue or colon cancer tissue are present within the size of a postage stamp. While a pathologist used this section for histologic analysis, other sections of this same TMA can be used in the laboratory to rapidly determine if a newly discovered biomarker is specifically produced in the colon cancers. *x8*

Co-culture of spinal cord with peripheral nerve

Peripheral nerve is a cable of wire like filaments called axons that convey the command for motion from motor neurons in the spinal cord to muscles in the limbs. A primary goal of researchers is to enhance the regeneration of these axons when they are injured. We designed this model to test the effects of possible treatments on axon regeneration without the need for long-term animal experiments. The spinal cord is removed from mice that have been genetically engineered to produce green fluorescent protein in their nerve cells. The cord tissue is kept alive in tissue culture and joined with segments of peripheral nerve so that motor neurons (*the large green dots in the spinal cord on the left*) regenerate their axons (*the thin green lines on the right*) through the peripheral nerve. Regeneration can then be monitored over hours or days with a fluorescent microscope, and the effects of various treatments can be viewed directly. This technique provides, in effect, color movies of events that were previously known only through black-and-white snapshots. *x30*

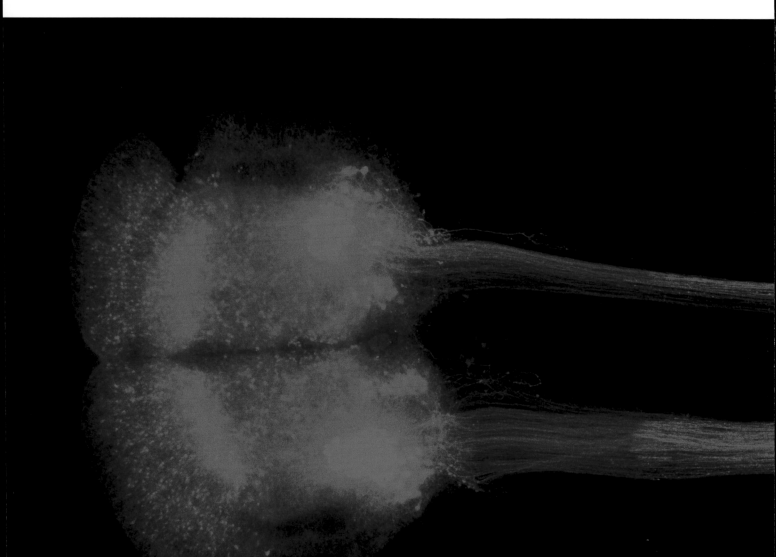

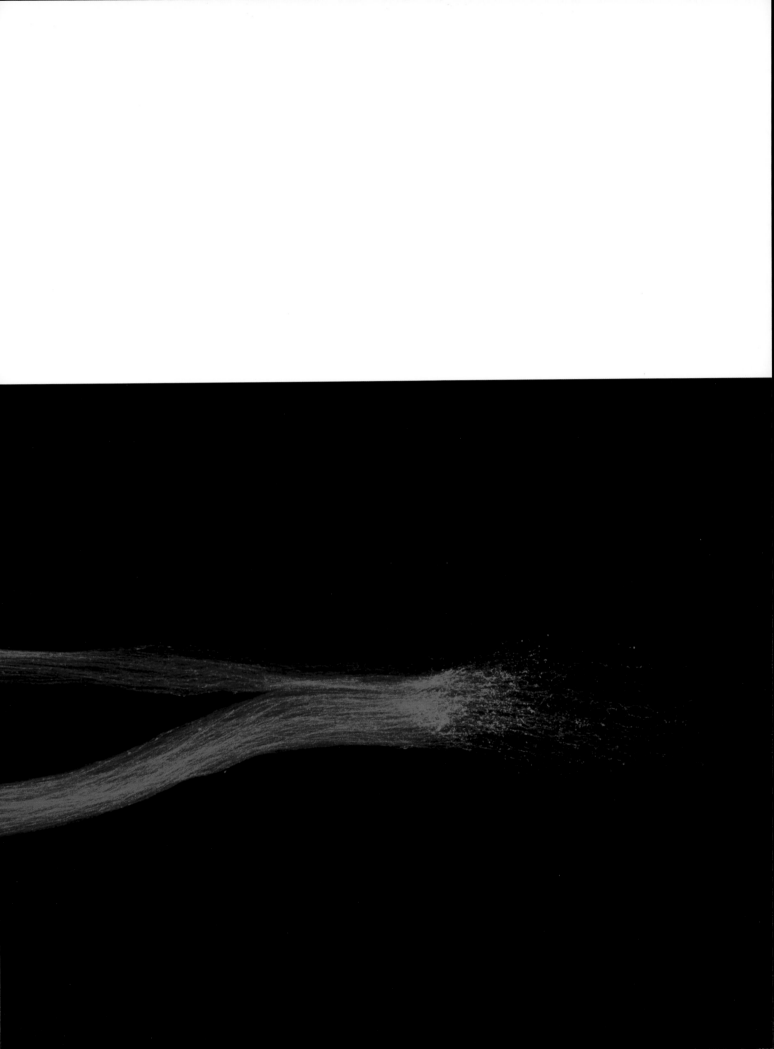

Computers in medicine

Computers have become such an essential part of our everyday lives that many cannot imagine their daily routine without them. This is no less true within a hospital or university setting. Most hospitals rely on computers for organizing their administration, budgets, personnel, financial information and patient information. Doctors, nurses and other medical professions rely on computers to both input and retrieve information about their patients, and medical researchers are reliant on computers to analyze large amounts of complex data. Many of the most current technologies used in medicine are themselves large computers. Radiologists use computers to take X-rays, modern surgeries are now performed through the tiniest of incisions using cameras hooked up to computers and even medical education now takes place using computers. In essence, not only do computers manage everything we know of in medicine, they have vastly improved our ability to understand the process of disease than was possible before their invention. *x40*

The research bench *(overleaf)*

A research bench is the place in a laboratory where a medical researcher performs their experiments and where, ultimately, scientific discoveries are made. At first glance, it seems to contain a chaotic mix of test tubes, jars of chemicals, various colored biological buffers, equipment and an assortment of paperwork and books. However, to the individual who works here, everything you may see has a place and value; it is a bustling environment of intense learning, discovery, frustration and fun. A research bench within a medical laboratory is best compared to a kitchen in a busy restaurant. Laboratory notebooks contain the recipes for how to perform an experiment and the notes for how those experiments may have worked or not. Chemicals and biological buffers are the ingredients for those experiments, and the equipment at the bench is what is used to spin and heat those ingredients according to the experimental "recipe."

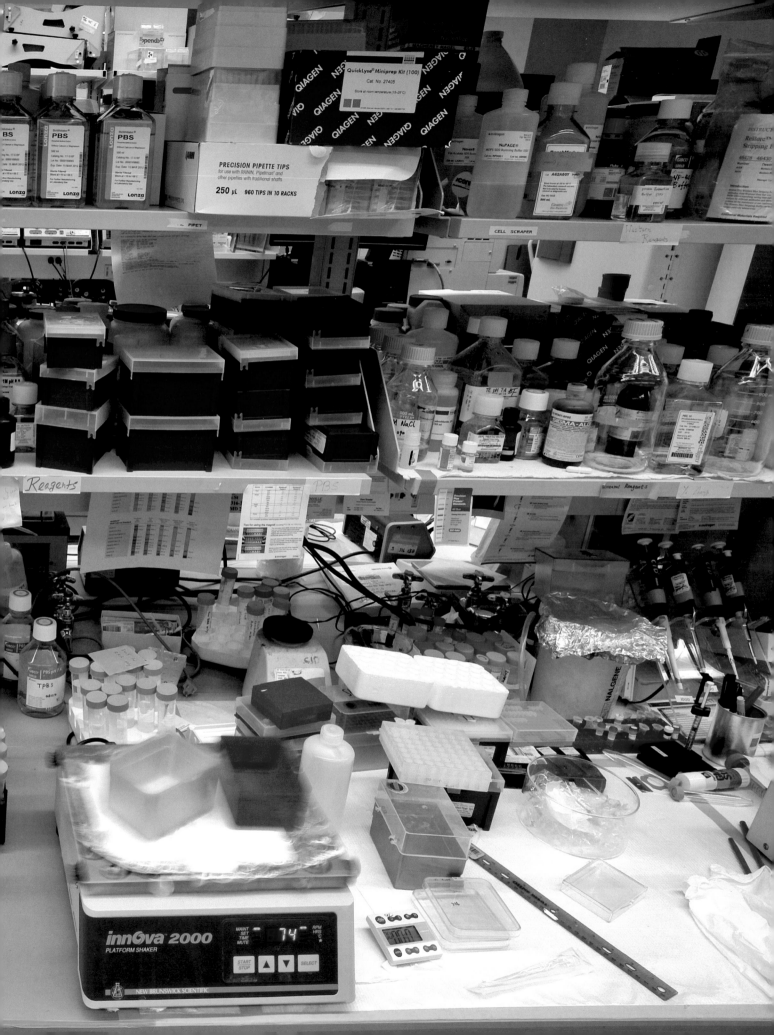

Epithelial-mesenchymal transition

Epithelial-Mesenchymal Transition, or EMT, is a process by which cells that are typically adherent to each other (*i.e., epithelial cells that line the surfaces of different organs*) detach from each other and take on features of non-adherent cells (*mesenchymal cells that comprise connective tissues of the body*). EMT is a normal phenomenon of developing tissues during fetal development. However, cancerous cells may undergo EMT as well, thereby allowing the cancer cells to separate from the original tumor and travel throughout the body to distant sites (*metastasis*). The features of EMT are shown in the accompanying image. Cancer cells with features of epithelial cells are labeled with red fluorescent protein (RFP), and cancer cells that have undergone EMT to mesenchymal-type cells are labeled with green fluorescent protein (GFP). Despite being derived from the same carcinoma, the green labeled cells are more motile, a feature believed to account for why cells that undergo EMT have a greater ability to form metastases. *x400*

Comparative medicine

Discoveries about human diseases are made by studying similar
conditions in animals. This usually is accomplished by veterinarians
sharing their unique training and knowledge with physicians
and other biomedical researchers in the examination of naturally
occurring and experimental diseases in animals. In the field of
comparative medicine, many important discoveries have been
made by these unique collaborative relationships. For example, the
skulls on this page illustrate how study of the human skull may be
facilitated by similar studies in other primates. While they are all
essentially similar, their differences provide important clues as to
how humans have evolved over time.

From L–R: human, chimpanzee, pig-tailed macaque,
rhesus macaque, lion-tailed macaque

Gene expression microarray

If DNA (*deoxyribonucleic acid*) is the genetic code of our cells, then RNA (*ribonucleic acid*) represents the messages produced from that code. More than 30,000 different RNA molecules can be translated from the master DNA code, yet only a fraction of these are actually produced in a cell at any time. The subset of RNA molecules that are produced in a given cell is a major basis for why that cell may develop into a keratinocyte (*a cell of the skin*) versus into a hepatocyte (*a major cell type of the liver*). Changes in the types and abundance of RNA molecules are a frequent occurrence in diseased cells compared to their normal counterparts. Researchers are therefore interested in understanding the changes in the types and abundance of RNA molecules in diseased tissues to identify novel ways to diagnose or treat disease. An efficient method to understand RNA molecules in diseased tissues is to use a technology known as a gene expression microarray. Rather than investigating each gene one by one for any changes in RNA produced from that gene, they can evaluate all RNAs produced by all genes in a cell at the same time using a microarray chip. The image at right, magnified from a region one-fourth the size of a postage stamp, shows the amounts of RNA present in a malignant melanoma sample. Each spot represents a different type of RNA molecule, and the intensity of the color indicates how much RNA is present. Red spots are those in which the amounts of RNA are highest and blue spots are those in which the amounts of RNA are lowest.

Zebrafish models

Animal models are an important tool in a medical researcher's arsenal to study disease. One such animal model relies on the species *Danio rerio*, a popular aquarium fish that is better known as zebrafish. Zebrafish models are particularly useful for studying embryologic development because the embryos are translucent, permitting the visualization of organ development. In this example, researchers have applied cloning methods to incorporate genes that express fluorescent proteins into the zebrafish genome. Red fluorescent proteins are produced in all cells of the zebrafish embryo, whereas green fluorescent proteins are produced only in the cells that develop into the eye, brain and pancreas. *x20*

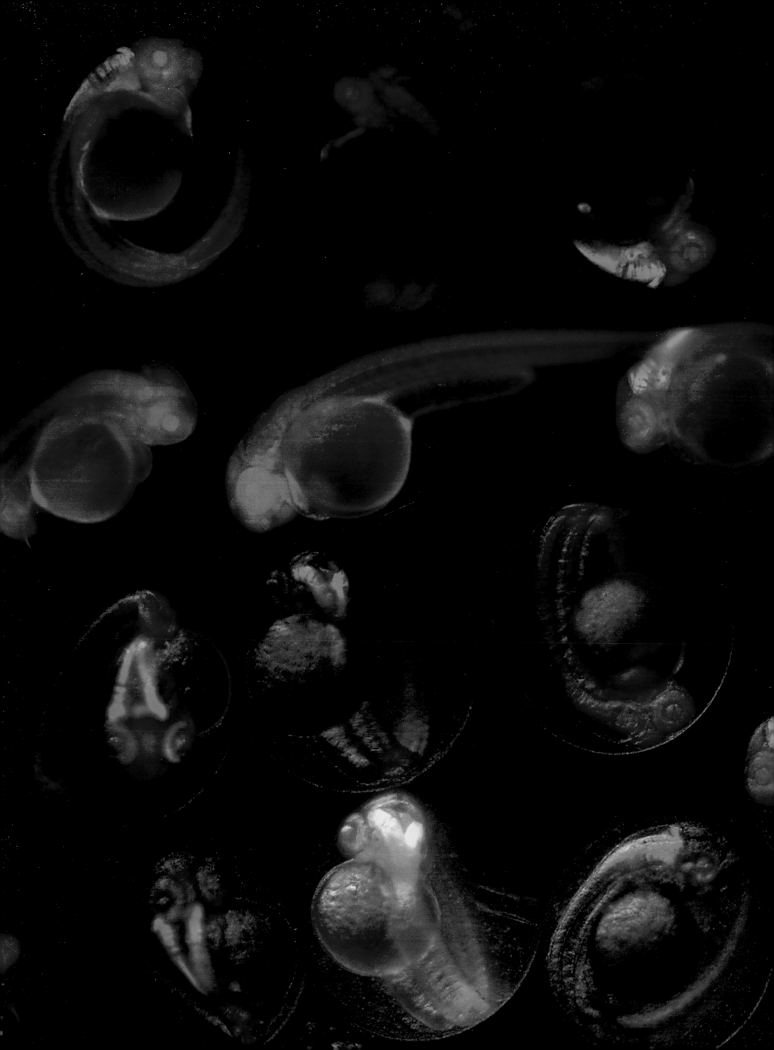

Mouse brain, MRI

Even after so many years of investigation of the mammalian central nervous system, its architecture, especially the way different regions of the brain are connected, is still largely unknown. Diffusion tensor imaging, a new technology based on magnetic resonance imaging, can visualize this complex brain architecture with unprecedented detail. In this figure, the architecture of the axons, which corresponds to the cables in computers, is delineated by three principal colors: red, green and blue represent axons running along the right-left, front-back and nose-neck orientations. Oblique orientations can also be appreciated by the mixture of the three colors. By applying this technique to various mouse models, it provides exciting opportunities to investigate how the brain and neural connections are established during development and how they are controlled by genes.

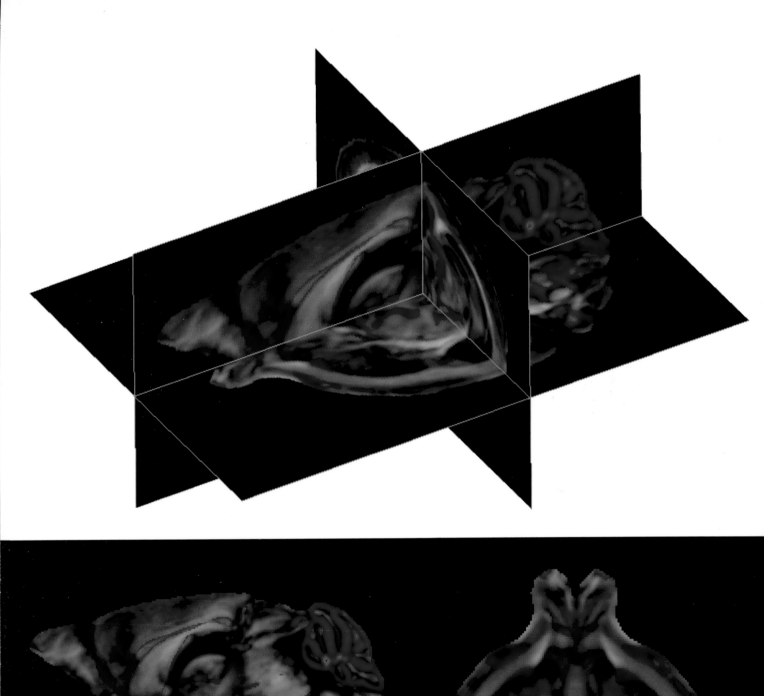
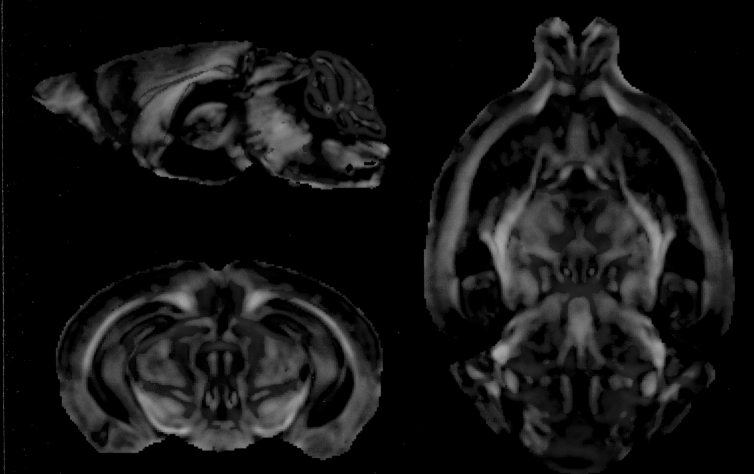

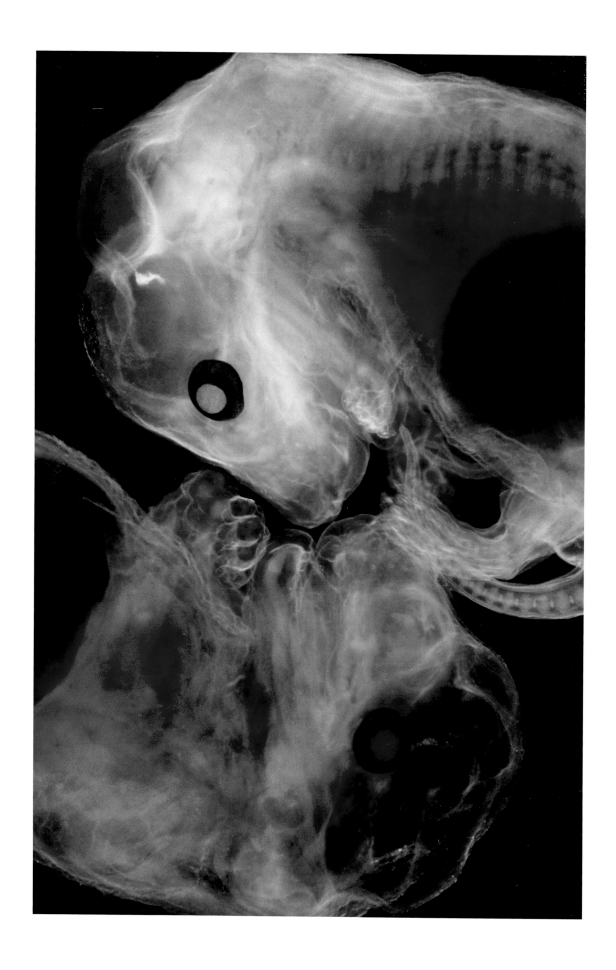

Alzheimer's research

The extracellular accumulation of amyloid plaques in the brain is a central pathological hallmark of Alzheimer's disease, the most common form of dementia of the elderly. Amyloid-b peptide, the major protein component of amyloid plaques, is derived from the proteolytic processing of the amyloid precursor protein (APP) by two enzymes called BACE1 and g-secretase. The molecular basis of Alzheimer's disease is thought to be the abnormal accumulation of amyloid-b peptides, which damage synapses of nerve cells involved in cognition. Presenilin, one of four proteins that constitute g-secretase, is the catalytic subunit of this enzyme and mutations in genes encoding presenilins cause familial Alzheimer's disease that occurs in younger individuals. Apart from APP, other substrates of g-secretase, including the notch receptor that is critical for embryonic development, have been identified. The discovery of the essential role of presenilins/g-secretase in mammalian embryonic development first came from presenilin gene knockout experiments documenting defects that resemble those of notch gene knockouts (an example of one such knockout mouse is shown at left). Because g-secretase is required for the generation of amyloid-b peptides, this enzyme has long been recognized as a therapeutic target for Alzheimer's disease. However, since g-secretase also impacts other important pathways, caution is necessary to ensure the development of a safe and effective anti-g-secretase therapy for the treatment of this devastating disease. *x20*

DNA sequencing

All genes encoded within our DNA are done so with only four
molecules, represented by a four letter alphabet known as
A, C, G and T. With these four "letters," approximately 20,000
different unique genes are encoded. In most forms of cancer,
the genes encoded within DNA also become abnormal within
a cancer cell. In some instances the genes may be deleted from
the chromosome, or, more commonly, the letters within the
gene become rearranged so that the gene no longer functions
normally. Recently, powerful methods have been developed that
allow cancer geneticists to sequence all genes in the genome
simultaneously. Thus, by reading the sequence of the four letters
in cancer cells and comparing them to normal cells, they can
discover the genes that are mutated in cancer cells. The image
at right illustrates unique molecules of DNA moving from top to
bottom through thin fibers that are analyzed with a laser. The four
different molecules (*A, C, G and T*) have been color coded red,
yellow, blue and green to facilitate "reading" of the sequence.

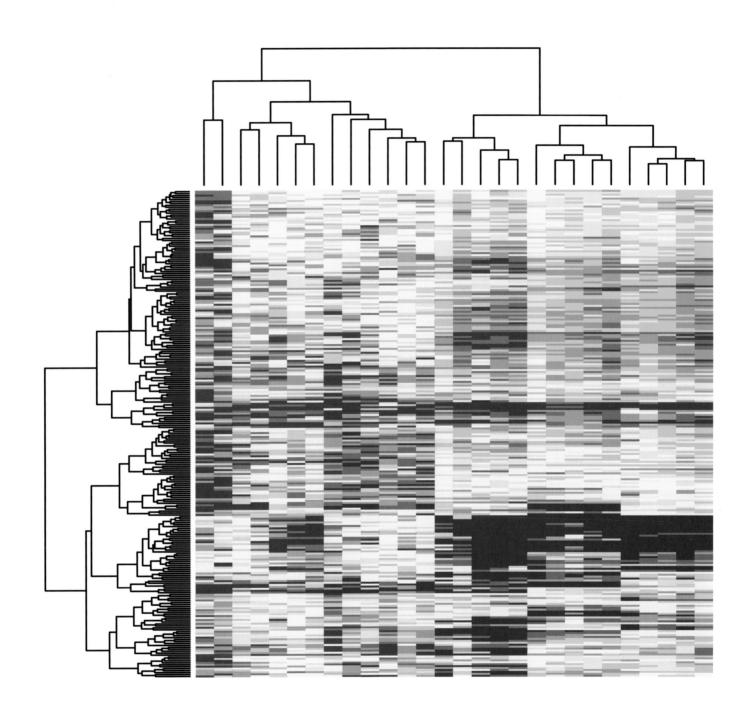

Hierarchical cluster analysis

In medical research, the generation of large amounts of data has required the need to organize that data to find meaningful patterns. As a result, the field of bioinformatics has blossomed to meet this need. Using complex computer algorithms, researchers are able to organize these complex datasets into visual maps. Thus, rather than study each datapoint separately, all data is clustered together based on their similarity to each other so that the most obvious patterns can be visualized with ease, a method known as hierarchical cluster analysis. Shown at left is an example of a complex dataset from an experiment to analyze levels of epigenetic regulation in normal tissues and in colon cancer. Each column represents a different tissue, and each row represents the levels of regulation of a different gene. Data has been clustered on both the vertical and horizontal axes, and the more related specific data columns or rows are to others causes them to be more closely aligned on the trees (*"dendrograms"*) at the top and left of the figure.

Mouse model

Laboratory mice are a strain of the common house mouse (*Mus musculus*) and are among the most important model organisms in medical research. Mice are highly similar to humans at the genetic level, thus the ability to understand disease processes in mice has enormous value in understanding these same diseases in humans. Laboratory mice come in a variety of coat colors including agouti, black and albino. Shown at right is one example of a mouse commonly used in the research setting, known as a "nude" mouse. Naturally hairless as a result of a genetic mutation in the FOXN1 gene, nude mice have an inhibited immune system due to a greatly reduced number of immune cells. Nude mice are thus invaluable to research because they do not mount a rejection response to tumor grafts from humans. These xenografts are commonly used in research to test new methods of imaging and treating tumors. *x2*

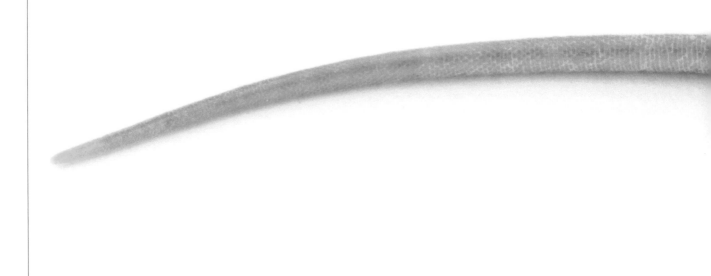

Telomeres

DNA, the genetic code of the cell, is packaged into 23 pairs of chromosomes. Telomeres are specialized regions of DNA, analogous to the protective plastic edges of shoelaces, which are located at the ends of the chromosomes. If cells divided without telomeres, they would lose the ends of their chromosomes, and the important information contained within the DNA. Thus, telomeres are disposable buffers blocking the ends of the chromosomes that are consumed during cell division and then replenished by an enzyme, the telomerase reverse transcriptase. The image at right illustrates the location of specific telomere sequences on different images taken of one representative human chromosome. *x1000*

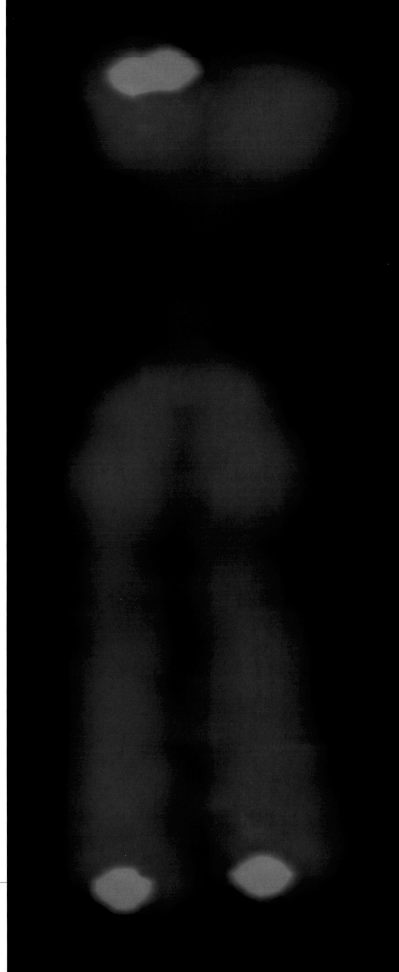

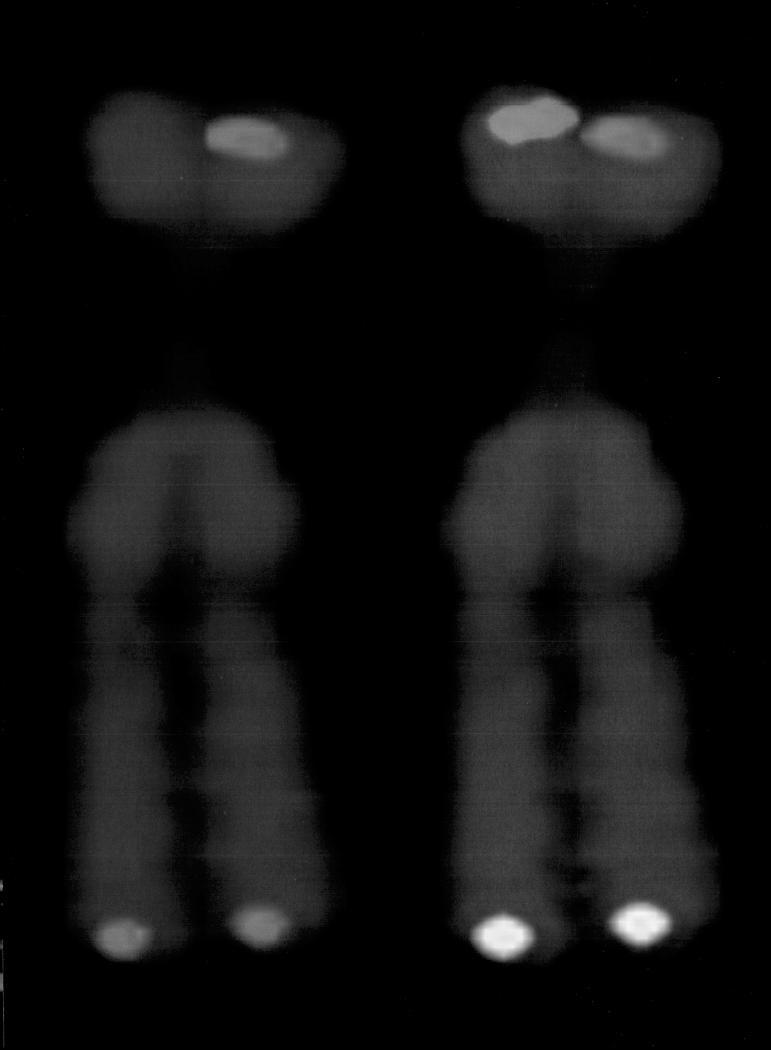

Enzyme linked immunosorbent assay (ELISA)

ELISA is a biochemical technique used to measure the amount of a specific molecule in a sample. ELISA is used as the initial screening test for detecting infection with the Human Immunodeficiency Virus (HIV), the cause of Acquired Immunodeficiency Syndrome (AIDS), but is also commonly used in medical research. This image demonstrates a sandwich ELISA, one of several variations of this assay, that was used to detect the amounts of a protein called Dickkopf1 that were secreted from pancreatic cancer cells. To perform an ELISA, an antibody that will bind Dickkopf1 has been attached to the bottom of each well, and fluid samples taken from these cancer cells were added to each well to allow it to bind the immobilized antibody. A second antibody, also specific for Dickkopf1, was then added to each well to create an antibody-Dickkopf1-antibody sandwich. The second antibody added is linked to an enzyme, and in the final step a substance was added that converted the enzyme to a colored signal, in this example from blue to yellow. Thus, the more intense the yellow color, the more Dickkopf1 protein that was present in the original sample.

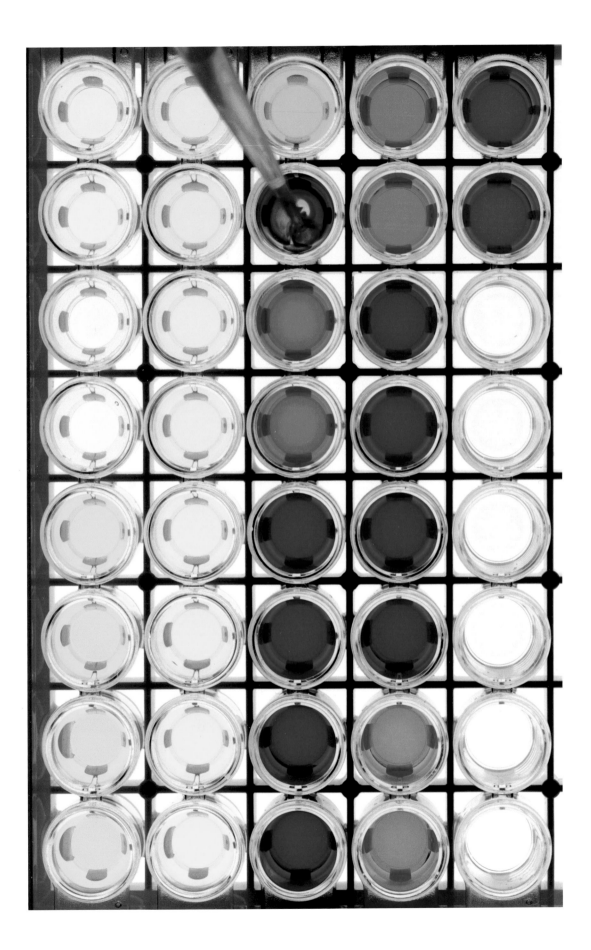

Nanotechnology

The science of controlling matter at the level of an individual molecule or atom is known as nanotechnology. To provide a perspective at which nanotechnology functions, the head of a pin is 1 million nanometers in diameter and thus can hold up to a million nanoparticles. Nanotechnology has many potential applications, including medicine, in which scientists are attempting to use these molecules to better deliver drugs to diseased cells and tissues, or to diagnose disease. This image demonstrates that the colors produced from quantum dots (*nanoparticles*) change as they are progressively produced at smaller and smaller diameters.

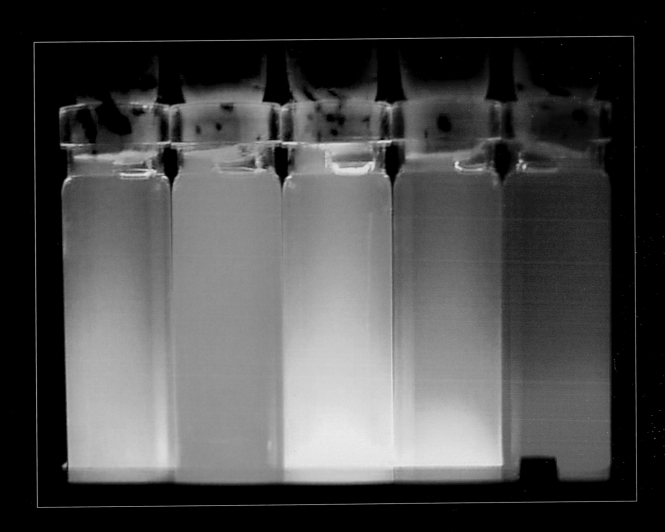

Spectral karyotyping of cancer cell

Deoxyribonucleic acid (DNA) is the set of genetic instructions needed for the development of all known living organisms and to make all components of a living cell. Within the nucleus of each cell, DNA is packaged into structures called chromosomes, and each chromosome contains thousands of genes. Each nucleus contains 22 pairs of chromosomes (one from each parent) and two sex chromosomes. Many types of cancer in humans, and pancreatic cancer in particular, arise in part when these chromosomes break apart and fuse with each other, a process called chromosome instability. Spectral karyotyping, or SKY, is a powerful method to study chromosome instability and determine the chromosomes most often targeted for breakages and fusions. In this method, a fluorescent label that is specific for each chromosome is applied and the chromosomes are then visualized under a high power microscope. Although some chromosomes are labeled with a single color, many others contain two or more colors, illustrating the complexity of the pancreatic cancer genome. *x2000*

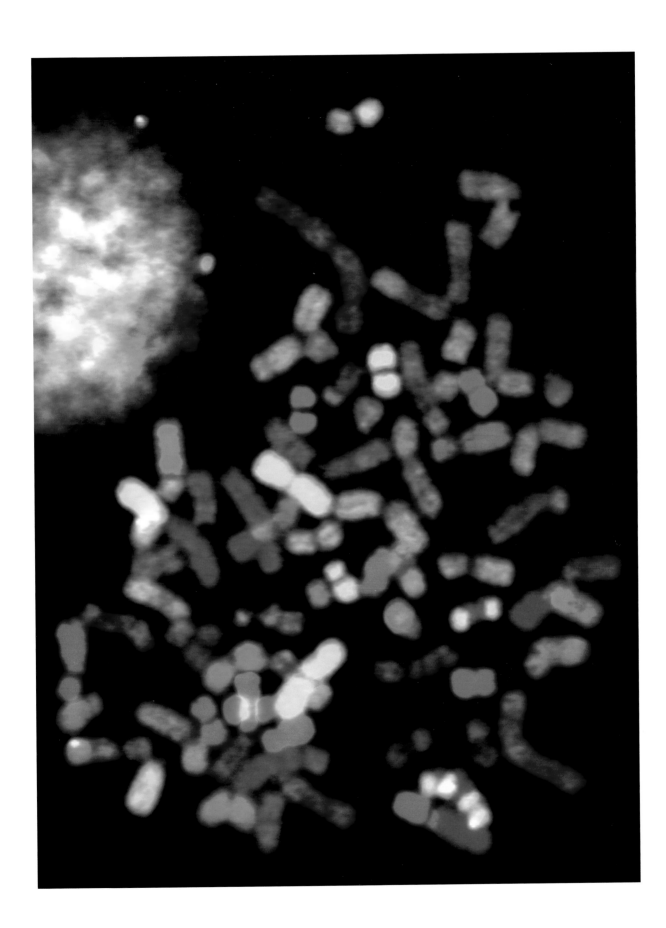

Suggested Reading

Aguilera-Hellweg, Max. *The Sacred Heart: An Atlas of the Body Seen Through Invasive Surgery*, Bullfinch Press, Boston, 1997

Amato, Ivan. *Super Vision: A New View of Nature*, Harry N. Abrams Publisher, New York, 2003

Broll, Brandon, ed. *Microcosmos: Discovering the World Through Microscopic Images from 20x to Over 22 Million x Magnification*, Firefly Books, London, UK, 2007

Burgess, Jeremy, Michael Marten & Rosemary Taylor. *MicroCosmos*, Cambridge University Press, Cambridge, UK, 1987

Gould, Steven Jay & Rosamond Purcell. *Crossing Over: Where Art and Science Meet*, Three Rivers Press, New York, 2000

Ford, Brian. *Single Lens, The Story of the Simple Microscope*, Harper & Row Publishers, New York, 1985

Foresta, Merry. *At First Sight: Photography and the Smithsonian*, Smithsonian Books, Washington, DC, 2003

Frankel, Felice. *Envisioning Science: The Design and Craft of the Science Image*, MIT Press, Cambridge, MA, 2002

Frankel, Felice & George Whitesides. *On the Surface of Things: Images of the Extraordinary in Science*, Harvard University Press, Cambridge, MA, 2007

Frankel, Felice & George Whitesides. *No Small Matter: Science on The Nanoscale*, The Belknap Press of Harvard University Press, Cambridge, MA, 2009

Foster, Giraud & Norman Barker. *Ancient Microworlds*, Custom & Limited Editions, San Francisco, CA, 2000

Goro, Fritz. *On The Nature of Things, The Scientific Photography of Fritz Goro*, Aperture, New York, 1993

Keller, Corey, ed. *Brought to Light: Photography and the Invisible 1840–1900*, San Francisco Museum of Modern Art, Yale University Press, New Haven, CT, 2003

Kemp, Martin. *Visualizations: The Nature Book of Art and Science*, University of California Press, Berkeley, CA, 2001

Kemp, Martin. *The Science of Art: Optical Themes in Western Art from Brunelleschi to Seurat*, Yale University Press, New Haven, CT, 1992

Kemp, Martin. *Seen/Unseen: Art, Science, and Intuition from Leonardo to the Hubble Telescope*, Oxford University Press, London, UK, 2006

Jones, Richard. *Nano Nature: Nature's Spectacular Hidden World*, Metro Books, New York, 2008

Lee, Jennifer & Miriam Mandelbaum. *Seeing is Believing: Seven Hundred Years of Scientific and Medical Illustration*, New York Public Library, New York, 1999

Lindgren, Laura, ed. *Mütter Museum, Historical Medical Photographs*, The College of Physicians of Philadelphia, Blast Books, Philadelphia, PA, 2007

Livingstone, Margaret. *Vision and Art, The Biology of Seeing*, Harry N. Abrams Publisher, New York, 2002

Marmor, Michael & James Ravin. *The Eye of The Artist*, Mosby, St. Louis, MO, 1997

Nilsson, Lennart. *Life*, Harry N. Abrams Publisher, New York, 2006

Petherbridge, Deanna & Ludmilla Jordanova. *The Quick and the Dead, Artists and Anatomy*, University of California Press, Berkeley, CA, 1997

Peres, Michael & Andrew Davidhazy. *Images from Science 1 & 2: An Exhibition of Scientific Photography*, RIT Cart Graphic Arts Press, Rochester, NY, 2008

Rohen, Johannes, Chihiro Yokochi & Elke Lütjen-Drecoll. *Color Atlas of Anatomy: A Photographic Study of the Human Body*, 4th ed., William & Wilkins, Baltimore, MD, 1998

Robin, Harry. *The Scientific Image: From Cave to Computer*, Harry N. Abrams Publisher, New York, 1992

Scharf, David. *Magnifications, Photography with the Scanning Electron Microscope*, Schocken Books, New York, 1977

Stafford, Barbara. *Artful Science: Enlightenment Entertainment and the Eclipse of Visual Education*, MIT Press, Cambridge, MA, 1994

Strosberg, Eliane. *Art and Science*, Abbeville Press Publishers, New York, 2001

Tallak, Peter, ed. *The Science Book*, Weidenfeld & Nicolson, UK, 2003

Thomas, Ann, ed. *Beauty of Another Order: Photography and Science*, National Gallery of Canada, Ottawa, 1997

Vesna, Victoria. *Database Aesthetics: Art in the Age of Information Overflow*, University of Minnesota Press, Minneapolis, MN, 2007

von Hagens, Gunter. *BodyWorlds, The Anatomical Exhibition of Real Human Bodies*, Arts & Sciences, Heidelberg, Germany, 2005

Wilson, Stephen. *Information Arts: Intersection of Art, Science, and Technology*, MIT Press, Cambridge, MA, 2002

Wilson, Stephen. *Art + Science: How Scientific Research and Technological Innovation are Becoming Key to 21st-century Aesthetics*, Thames & Hudson, New York, 2010

Witkin, Joel-Peter, ed. *Masterpieces of Medical Photography, Selections from the Burns Archive*, Twelvetrees Press, Pasadena, CA, 1987

Wagner, Catherine. *Cross Sections*, Twin Palms Publishers, Santa Fe, NM, 2001